My Brother Jason

To my brother, Jason,

Impressions of you remain everywhere in our lives. I will always miss you.

My Brother Jason

The untold story of Jason Corbett's life and
brutal murder by Tom and Molly Martens

Tracey Corbett-Lynch

with

Ralph Riegel

Gill Books

Gill Books
Hume Avenue
Park West
Dublin 12
www.gillbooks.ie

Gill Books is an imprint of M.H. Gill & Co.

978 07171 8128 5

Print origination by O'K Graphic Design, Dublin
Copy-edited by Emma Dunne
Proofread by Jane Rogers
Printed by CPI Group (UK) Ltd, Croydon CRO 4YY

This book is typeset in 11.5/17 pt Adobe Garamond with chapter headings in Frutiger Light.

The paper used in this book comes from the wood pulp of managed forests. For every tree felled, at least one tree is planted, thereby renewing natural resources.

5 4 3

Tracey Corbett-Lynch is Jason Corbett's sister and led the fight for justice for her brother. She successfully fought for custody of his two children, Jack and Sarah, after his death. She lives in Limerick with her husband, David, and their now four children, Dean, Adam, Jack and Sarah.

Ralph Riegel is the southern correspondent for *The Irish Independent* and a regular contributor to RTÉ, BBC, Newstalk and TV3. Previous books include *Afraid of the Dark*, *Hidden Soldier* and *Commando*. He lives in Cork with his wife, Mary, and three children.

Acknowledgements

Tracey:

I would like to thank my husband, David, my companion, very best friend and most decent human being for standing beside me every step throughout the fight for 'Justice for Jason' and the writing of this book, despite losing his own brother to cancer in 2016 (RIP Kevin Lynch). You are the most selfless and giving man.

To my mam and dad, Marilyn, Wayne and other family members who are always there for me. I am in awe of your determination to see the best in the world.

Special thanks to Jason's dear friends, especially to Lynn Shanahan and Karen Gorey, who hopped on a plane to North Carolina without a whim. To Paul Dillon, who travelled almost every time to the US to support Dave and me. To Brendan and Michelle O'Callaghan, Sharon Bowes, Tim Shanahan and Damian McCormack, as well as everyone who came to support us in August of 2017.

To Ralph, who listened for hours as I reminisced, went off on tangents and remained patient when I chopped and changed our chapters while feeding us those lovely cakes from that wonderful Cork bakery! You helped put the feelings in my heart and mind into words to convey the truth. I am so very grateful. Jason would have liked you very much.

To everyone at Gill Books for having such faith in this project and for being so sensitive with the manuscript. Also to Terry, Barry and Aileen at the Communications Clinic who provided such valuable advice.

To Richard Lynch, Mary Fitzpatrick and Simone Dillon for doing so, so much to raise awareness of the case since 2015, much of which I have

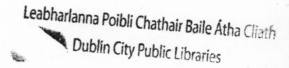

no idea about but I am for ever in your debt. For organising the Limerick vigil, thank you.

To Nuala Galvin for her tireless work on the Bring Justice for Jason social media page – I remain inspired by your posts.

Thanks also to everyone at MPS Limerick and Lexington for their determination to see Jason's memory honoured – he would be very proud of you all. Thanks to the Meadowlands residents who opened their homes, fridges and hearts to us.

To my own neighbours who were so supportive and protective of all our children, I am forever grateful.

Special mention also to my friends, especially to Lisa and Vivienne, who have put up with me being the worst friend over the past three years and someone who never returned calls. I will spend the next years making it up to you all.

I would also like to express my deepest gratitude to you, the many people who saw me through this most difficult time in my life; to all those who provided support, fundraised, talked things over, read, wrote and offered comments, supported the Bring Justice for Jason Facebook page, attended the Limerick vigil, the Mass at St John's Cathedral and all the other events. For all those who allowed me to quote their remarks in this book, I wholeheartedly appreciate your participation.

Special mention also to the Fitzpatrick and Lynch families for their unwavering support.

I am so proud to call Limerick my home and the support of the people of my home county was unquestioned throughout this entire ordeal.

Heartfelt thanks also to Davidson County Sheriff's Department, especially Sherriff David Grice and his team of Lieutenant Detective Wanda Thompson, Lieutenant Detective Young, Detective Michael Hurd and Detective Brandon Smith, Corporal Dagenhart, and all their colleagues who worked so diligently. To the first responders who tried so valiantly to save Jason in such awful circumstances. I am humbled by your work ethic.

Also to Davidson County District Attorney's Office under the guidance of DA Garry Frank: Ina Stanton, Alan Martin and Greg Brown, Karen Coe and all their support staff. To Clerk of Davidson County Superior Court Brian Shipwash – during a time of the most intense pain and grief, you treated us with compassion and fairness. To Shannon Airport management and staff. We will be for ever grateful.

Special mention to Bring Justice for Jason Supporters, Chief Superintendent David Sheahan and the Limerick Gardaí, Senator Kieran O'Donnell, Minister Charlie Flanagan, former Metropolitan Mayor Councillor Jerry O'Dea, Fr Pat Hogan, everyone who fundraised, the Benson family, the Lynch family, Leeann Kennedy Purcell, Greta O'Shea, Tait House Community Enterprise board of directors and staff, Charlie Sherling, Tony and Fíona Hoban, Ciaran O'Callaghan, Young Munster RFC, The Boro Club and Janesboro residents, David Scott and Scott Solicitors, Travis Rose, Melanie Michaels Crook, Tom and Jerusha Maddock, David and Michele Fritzsche, Chip and Beth McDonell, the Viers family, the Oliver family, Tony Turner, the Department of Foreign Affairs, Consuls John Young and Shane Stephen and their colleagues in Washington and New York who guided us all safely home in August 2015. And to attorney David Piskho and Kim Bonuomo of Allman Spry – the most tenacious, hard-working attorney with a tough exterior and a heart of solid gold.

To the ordinary people of North Carolina and Ireland, thank you all for your kindness, compassion and determination to see justice done for Jason. God bless you all.

To my four wonderful children, Dean, Adam, Jack and Sarah, who have blended together so seamlessly. Your resilience, strength, courage and determination are inspiring. I love you all dearly.

Last, I would like to thank my brother, Jason. For all the memories, the experiences and laughter you brought to my life, your can-do, glass-half-full attitude. I was so lucky that you were my brother. It is a gift I will treasure for ever, along with your children.

I would like to dedicate this book to all those families who have been left bereaved by violent crime. May time ease the pain of your loss.

Ralph:

I would like to offer a heartfelt thanks to Tracey and Dave Lynch for entrusting me with this project. Getting to know them as well as Jason's family and their children, Jack, Sarah, Adam and Dean, during the work on this book was a tremendous honour.

Thanks also to Sarah Liddy, Teresa Daly, Catherine Gough, Emma Dunne and all at Gill Books for their unstinting support of this project. The expert legal advice of Kieran Kelly and Zoe Mollaghan was also greatly appreciated. Special thanks to Zoe, who suffered through every single line of copy I filed from North Carolina for almost four weeks.

I owe a debt of gratitude to all at Independent News & Media not only for their assistance during the writing process but also during the Davidson County Superior Court murder trial in July and August 2017. Special thanks to Fionnan Sheahan, Jane Last and Gareth Morgan. Thanks also to Claire Murphy, Rory Tevlin, Kirsty Blake Knox, Paul Sheridan, Eimear Rabbitte, Jerome Reilly, Jason O'Brien and Denise Calnan for all their help while I was reporting on the trial.

Conor Feehan, Mark Condren and Wayne O'Connor offered invaluable help and advice before I travelled to North Carolina – and great tips about the quality of coffee offered by Jeff in The Black Chicken Cafe in Lexington.

While in North Carolina I couldn't have asked for better colleagues or travel companions than Catherine Fegan and Michael Chester of *The Irish Daily Mail*. Their company was greatly appreciated as was all their help and kindness. Thanks also to all the US reporters and photographers, who showed such forbearance to their Irish colleagues during the trial, including Tamara Weitzman, Michael Hewlett, Cat Rakowski, Mallory Lane, Daniel Kennedy, Bob Costner, Ben Coley, Mason Scherer, Scott Muthersbaugh, Lynn Keller, Donnie Roberts and Nelson Kepley.

Thanks to Limerick photographer Brendan Gleeson for the front cover image of this book.

On a personal note, thanks to my wife, Mary, and my children, Rachel, Rebecca and Ralph, as well as my mother, Nora, for their forbearance during the writing process and invaluable advice on key parts of the manuscript.

During the North Carolina trial, my sister, Rorey Ann, her husband, Craig, and their children undertook a gruelling drive from New Jersey to Richmond, Virginia, for a weekend reunion, which offered some much-needed R&R. They even handled my Civil War history obsession with good grace.

Finally, a heartfelt thank you to everyone who assisted with this manuscript, whether it was through agreeing to an interview, supplying information, offering photographs or checking documentation, dates and facts. All help, no matter how small, was greatly appreciated and, I hope, is reflected in the book you now hold in your hands.

It was a very strange sensation standing by the graveside of Jason and Mags at Castlemungret in Limerick – two people I had gotten to know so well through this book yet never had the privilege of meeting during their lifetimes. The truly remarkable people they must have been is borne out by the family, friends and children they left behind. It is my sincere wish that this book does honour to their memory.

Contents

PROLOGUE: WHY I WROTE THIS BOOK   1

1. My Vow to Jason   5

2. A Lost Soulmate   21

3. Cruel Twist of Fate   38

4. A Bleak Marriage   55

5. Protecting the Children   80

6. Character Assassination   101

7. Molly and Tom Charged   127

8. The Trial Opens   140

9. Shocking Evidence   152

10. Left to Die   164

11. A Tribute to Jason   177

12. A Turning Point   189

13. Justice for Jason   208

14. Emotionally Exhausted   223

15. Back in Mags's Arms   236

25 December 2006

Jason's first Christmas card written to Mags after her death on 21 November:

To my Mag Mag – Heaven is a better place for having you. I've found it hard to believe there is a God after what has happened to my baby girl. I feel so sorry that you won't get to see our kids grow up but please don't be sad because they will make you so proud of them and will make your short life so worthwhile. They miss you so much. I hope there is a God and he only knows why he took you from us. He must have had a very good reason. If you are looking down you will see how loved and missed you are and how you touched everyone with your personality.

You know how much I miss you and how sorry I am that I couldn't save you. I'd swap places with you in a heartbeat. I'll look after the kids but I'm just passing time until we meet again. I told you I loved you 10 times a day – I'm sorry it wasn't 100. But most of all I'm sorry for not holding you so tight that God couldn't even take you from us.

You are the girl of my dreams and will always be the love of my life.

Always and forever,
Jason.

Prologue: Why I Wrote This Book

My reason for writing this book is simple. I wanted to validate the truth – to oppose the lies of Tom and Molly Martens. Jason's life had been laid bare. He had been stripped of his dignity. He had no one to speak out on his behalf – until now. Molly and Tom Martens didn't just murder my brother. They didn't just crush his skull and then cruelly wait for him to die before ringing for help. They also tried to destroy his reputation. To manipulate the truth of who Jason really was and how much he was loved, simply to try to evade justice for their crime, they callously, insidiously and maliciously painted a gentle, kind-hearted and romantic husband and father as some kind of alcohol-fuelled brute and thug.

They played to the old stereotype of the drunken Irishman. Jason could not challenge their vile words. Worse still, my family were unable to challenge their lies publicly until the criminal trial had ended. Their campaign was relentless and caused so much compounded pain and heartache, especially for his children, Jack and Sarah, and my elderly parents.

In these pages, you will read about the real Jason Corbett – a man who continued living life for his children after his heart was broken. A man who was a typically devoted Irish son, brother, husband, friend and neighbour. A man who always tried to leave the lives of others better for having crossed paths with him.

So how do I explain what Jason was really like? He was the polar opposite to what Molly and her family had claimed in the bitter build-up to the court case. He was loving, upbeat, ambitious, smart, loyal and generous. Molly's happiness was a priority for him, along with the children. He was generous and did thoughtful things, like paying to fly Molly and her mother to New York for a weekend break. He funded holidays and cruises to the Bahamas with her family. He always insisted on doing his own share around the house and loved to cook dinner, especially when Molly wasn't feeling well.

When Molly objected to Jason coming home to Ireland for a surprise visit at Christmas in 2014, he booked a cruise for her from Florida so she could attend her cousin's wedding. Everything was OK then for his visit home to Limerick. She had her own credit cards and Jason paid all the bills. He listened to what she had to say and took an interest in her views and opinions. He tried to learn what she liked so he could make her life happier. When it came time for birthdays or anniversaries, she received only the best of jewellery from firms like De Beers. On one occasion, I teased Jason because he had organised an art class for Molly and her girlfriends because that is what she wanted.

That he was proud of his clever wife was an understatement. Jason was always talking about Molly's interests, views and achievements. She was interesting, well-travelled, articulate and well-educated. Jason fell in love with Molly and his love was loyal and true. In North Carolina, he went above and beyond to make his relationship with Molly work.

Jason wasn't just generous with Molly – it was his nature, especially with those he loved. He even arranged for Mags's parents, Michael and Marian, to fly to North Carolina to see their grandchildren. On another occasion he shared the cost with me of flying our father out to North Carolina for a visit. It turned out to be one of our treasured memories – all of us sitting outside a cabin in the Smoky Mountains with my father happily racing his grandchildren around the full deck that encircled it. I remember Jason's keenness to bring us to the Smoky Mountains national park. It was a beautiful day and the park was amazing. Dad was able to get near to bears in the wild. It was such a brilliant experience and a happy day.

My brother was nothing like the person described in the vile accusations levelled by Tom, Molly and their supporters. To me, it was like they took all of their own personality traits and mirrored them on to Jason. We were powerless and it was horrendous. He could not respond or defend himself – they had taken his life and now they were taking his good name. The Martens family's betrayal of him and all that he stood for was a blatant attempt to sway public opinion and help Molly and Tom evade justice. Their actions changed my perspective on the world for ever.

In Limerick, an annual football tournament is hosted by Jason's former Multi Packaging Solution (MPS) colleagues in his memory.

His workmates in Lexington erected a special memorial plaque and tree to their late boss as a mark of respect. His office was changed to the Jason Corbett Conference Room. A photograph of him taken by one of his colleagues at the Cliffs of Moher while on a business trip to Ireland now sits on a side table.

His European colleagues now play a golf tournament each year in his name. Jason loved golf and it meant so much to us to have the tournament named after him.

The city where he grew up had a book of condolence for him – the first time that Limerick ever had such a book online. A reception was held by the Metropolitan Mayor of Limerick, Councillor Jerry O'Dea, in his honour.

Mayor O'Dea and Senator Kieran O'Donnell were among the first Irish politicians to offer their support. To have people come and do that for us, just when we needed it most, and God knows we needed every bit of help we could get at that stage, made all the difference in the world. We were flooded with testimonials to his character. His family, his children and his friends cherish his memory. The only people who contradict those memories are Tom and Molly.

Jason's old Facebook profile reads: 'I have two great kids – Jack is six and my little princess Sarah is four and my beautiful wife Molly.'

But I still struggle to read the prophetic words that Jason chose as his favourite quote for his profile. To this day, I think he was writing with Mags in mind but the quote would ultimately prove to be tragically true for himself. It read: 'Don't complain about growing old as some people don't get the chance.'

That quote gives me the strength on the most difficult of days to appreciate life and find the will to cope with the most painful of challenges. We have faced battles we could never have envisaged in a million years: guardianship, custody, adoption, civil cases over Jason's estate – not to mention the fight in the criminal courts to get justice for my brother. But we found the strength to persevere and prevail. In spite of all that we have endured, I believe we have to live life for those who have left us until our paths meet again, please God. In my heart I believe I will meet Jason again, look him straight in the eye and tell him I did everything I could to put things right because I loved him and never forgot him. To this day, every decision we make has Jason and his children at its heart.

1

My Vow to Jason

I stared at the body in the polished mahogany coffin and was shocked by the realisation that I didn't immediately recognise my own brother.

It certainly resembled my baby brother, Jason Corbett (39), yet somehow it just didn't seem to be him. The facial features were different, somehow subtly altered. Jason was always so proud of his appearance – he had been a handsome man with a distinctive, strong face that seemed to light up when he smiled. For a brief second, I recalled that there was a time when Jason had smiled a lot.

That smile could illuminate an entire room.

But the body in the coffin, dressed neatly in a smart navy suit, shirt and tie, seemed to have slightly different features – the face seemed almost altered or blurred, the line of the nose not like that of the Jason I remembered from growing up together in Janesboro in Limerick.

Of course, at that point I didn't know about the horrific injuries that Jason had suffered. It would be a year later, when the post mortem report was finally released, that I discovered my brother's skull had been smashed with a brick and a metal baseball bat. Similarly, it was several days before I understood the enormous skill the mortuary staff at Cumby's in North Carolina had displayed to hide Jason's terrible wounds from his family. They had had to reconstruct my brother's skull and use special cosmetics and fillers in a bid to mask the damage to his face. Without the work of Cumby's staff, Jason could not have been viewed by us in an open casket or by his mother in Cross's funeral home in Limerick, where Jason's body was eventually repatriated.

I was so grateful for the support of the people standing with me in Cumby's that stifling August evening in North Carolina, including my husband, Dave, my sister, Marilyn, and Jason's best friend, Paul Dillon. I simply don't know how I could have endured the events of the previous six days without their incredible support.

Together, we had pleaded, fought, worked and negotiated for an entire week just to make sure we were able to stand there and view our beloved Jason's body. Jason's second wife, Molly Martens (31), had wanted his remains cremated before we could make arrangements to reach North Carolina from Ireland, having been informed of his death the previous Sunday. It had been a race against time that, mercifully, we had won.

Molly had initially engaged J.C. Green's funeral home in North Carolina but when she became aware that I had located the first crematorium, she changed it to Cumby's in a bid to keep us from seeing the body.

I had pleaded with the crematorium staff to ignore her urgent attempts to arrange a cremation, which had started less than 24 hours after Jason's death. Yet now I wished I was anywhere else but there on Eastchester Drive in High Point. The furnishings in Cumby's were plush and luxurious, the reception rooms were tastefully decorated and the staff couldn't have been more sympathetic. But a small group of Irish people were standing there with red-rimmed eyes and hearts breaking, all of us consumed by one simple question – what had happened to Jason?

Through the exhaustion, pain and shock I struggled to comprehend how the course of all of our lives had changed so dramatically just six days earlier. On Sunday, the Corbett family had been whole, happy and united. We were a typical Irish family, all caught up in each other's busy lives. This Friday evening in August 2015 we were struggling to cope with every family's worst nightmare. Our world had just collapsed around us.

Six days earlier, I was on holidays in St Jean de Monts in France with Dave and our children. It was a break we had really been looking forward to – a chance to recharge the batteries after what had been a busy and challenging year, in part due to the problems my brother, Jason, had been having with his second wife in the US. I was very close to Jason. In fact, with the exception of my husband, Dave, I was probably closer to Jason than anyone else on the planet. We shared the same interests, had the same sense of humour, liked the same music and could almost finish sentences for each other. He had an infectious laugh that would brighten your entire day.

We drew particularly close after the tragic death of Jason's first wife, Margaret 'Mags' Fitzpatrick in 2006. Mags was just 30 when she died from a sudden asthma attack. She left behind Jason, who adored her, and their two children: Jack, aged 2, and Sarah, who was just 12 weeks old. Jason was absolutely broken by her death. He was never quite the same carefree, happy soul he had been when he was with Mags. That spark was gone from his eyes. In the dark days after her death, Jason spent a lot of time in our home as Dave and myself tried to help him cope with the pain of her loss and also to care for his two children.

Even when he had moved in 2011 to North Carolina with his new wife, Molly Martens, we had remained close. As a family, we tried to visit with Jason, Jack and Sarah in the US every year even though, given the distance and the flights involved, the costs could often prove prohibitive. He would also pay return visits to our home at Raheen in Limerick and we were in regular phone and email contact.

I had known for some time that Jason was deeply unhappy in the US. I knew he wanted to move back to Limerick with his children, who were now ten and eight. Privately, we were delighted because we missed them all so much, but no one in our family was in any doubt that this move was something his second wife, Molly Martens, was going to be deeply unhappy about, as it would signal the end of their relationship and her contact with the children.

Afterwards, I would bitterly regret opting to holiday in France instead of North Carolina that summer of 2015. It had been six months since I'd seen Jason and I had a gut instinct that things weren't good in North

Carolina. But there were other factors at play – the cost was multiples of a break in France and we are just an ordinary working family. Plus it wasn't just Dave and myself – we would also have the children with us, as well as my niece Kate. I recall leaving Jason a voicemail just a few weeks before his murder telling him how much we missed him, that I loved him and that it was now time for him to come home.

Somehow, deep down, I knew I should have gone to visit Jason, who lived at Panther Creek Court, midway between Lexington and Winston-Salem in North Carolina, instead of France. Maybe nothing would have changed the course of what happened on 2 August, but I will never know if there was more I could have done. It doesn't matter when people say, 'You did everything you could.' There is always more that could have been done, no matter how small. If I had gone, I would have realised how bad it had gotten in North Carolina. Jason would have opened up much more in a face-to-face conversation. Maybe it would have helped? Maybe it would have saved his life? But I will never know that now.

My brother Wayne, who was Jason's twin, was walking back to the family home in Limerick on that Sunday afternoon, 2 August, which was a bank holiday weekend in Ireland, when he got a call from the US. He answered, probably expecting it to be Jason. Our father, John, was due to celebrate his 80th birthday so it could have been a call about the party. Wayne recalls:

I was walking home in Janesboro around 6.10 p.m. that Sunday evening. I got a call and, when I looked, I saw that it was from Molly's phone. I answered but it was Sharon Martens, Molly's mother, on the line. She said that Jason and Molly had a fight. Molly pushed Jason. Jason fell and hit his head. She said Jason was dead. I was shocked. I asked her to put Molly on the phone. She said 'No' and then hung up. The call only lasted around 10 to 15 seconds. I went to my parents' house – Dad was upstairs and Mam was downstairs. I told them about the phone call and that Jason was dead – he had been killed in the States. It was the hardest thing I have ever had to do. I had only been with him two weeks before when I was in North Carolina on holidays. I was the last family member to see him.

I rang my sister Marilyn and then I rang Dave who was on holidays in France with Tracey and their family. I asked him to walk away from Tracey because I wanted him to be able to prepare her for the news that Jason was dead.

There then followed a desperate race to contact family members before the awful news reached them via social media. I was in France and several of Jason's best friends were also away on holidays. We were scattered across Europe on one of the busiest holiday weekends of the year.

It's one of those moments that is scorched onto your memory – I was sitting on the decking in glorious French sunshine. The day was settling into evening, we had returned from a day at the beach and we were planning our evening ahead. The children were messing around, giggling and having fun. And then the world as I knew it came to a shuddering halt.

I heard the tone of Dave's voice and knew instantly something was wrong – badly wrong. I felt this awful sickening ripple in my stomach, an expectation of tragedy about to unfold. I walked into the mobile home and began to hum a nursery rhyme my dad had taught us in childhood, 'Three Little Fish': 'One, two, three, four, five, once I caught a fish alive …'

It might sound childish but it was all I had to hang on to. I somehow knew this was going to be awful. From where I was standing, I couldn't hear everything that was being said to Dave. He looked over towards me, anguish etched on his face, and simply said: 'Tracey, it's Jason.'

If I pretended it wasn't happening, then maybe it wasn't? A soaring 'Nooooo' began in the depths of my mind and swept through every fibre of my being. Dave, doing his best to handle an impossible situation, insistently whispered over to me: 'Tracey, listen to me, Jason is dead.' I started screaming – I couldn't breathe. My mind hurt and denied the truth of it – my best friend, the most important person in the whole world to me apart from my husband and kids, my sidekick, my little brother. It was only when I realised that the children were staring in horror at me that I desperately tried to pull it all together for their sake. 'I'm OK, I'm OK,' I assured them. Yet I was anything but OK.

Several members of our family immediately tried ringing the US to find out exactly what had happened to Jason. But, try as we all might, we couldn't get through to Molly or members of her immediate family. Although I suspected my US sister-in-law was capable of many things – lies, self-centred behaviour, fantasies, manipulation and even drugging people without their knowledge, including me and her own father – I had never for a moment thought her capable of attempting to seriously hurt anyone, let alone kill them.

Before I even made contact with anyone in North Carolina, I had a dark, gnawing inner fear that somehow Jason's death had been at Molly's hands. I tried ringing Sharon Martens from France one more time. Incredibly, I managed to get through and pleaded for information about precisely what had happened to my brother. The call confirmed all my worst suspicions. Sharon proceeded to tell me that Jason was very abusive towards Molly.

She claimed – incorrectly, as it transpired – the Davidson County police had been called six times to deal with incidents of threats and abuse that Jason had directed towards her daughter. Sharon then said Jason had been out drinking with his friends for almost 24 hours from that Saturday, 1 August. According to her version of events he had later gotten into a drunken row with Molly and had attacked her but she pushed him away and he fell, striking his head and suffering fatal injuries. That was the story I was told. It was the story they expected me to believe.

I couldn't believe what I was hearing. Sharon was describing someone that I simply didn't know. I knew Jason better than almost anyone and understood he was simply not capable of the things she described. My brother's natural instinct was to protect people, not to hurt them. I also knew Molly was capable of lies, half-truths and outright fantasies. What also made me suspicious was that there was no sympathy, no 'I am so sorry to have to tell you this, Tracey', no softness and no empathy. She sounded cold and, if anything, I thought she was brisk to the point of being annoyed.

My mind was racing and all I could think of asking Sharon was whether Molly had been arrested after Jason's death. I could tell from the tone of her voice as it turned to ice that she didn't like the question, and she insisted that Molly had not been arrested. 'Why not?' I persisted. Sharon reacted instantly. She challenged me as to how I could dare to ask such a question about Molly. I was left listening to a dead line. She had hung up.

I turned to Dave and told him what she had just said. I began a panicked effort to throw things into an overnight bag, I kissed my children goodbye, not knowing it would be so long before I got to see them again, while Dave desperately tried to book me on the first flight back to Ireland. It was so busy because of the August holiday that my only option was to fly from Paris to Dublin. I knew I had to get to Limerick to be with Mam and Dad and comfort them in what they were going through. Thirty minutes later, I was sitting in the family car as Dave drove me the five hours to Paris to catch a flight to Dublin from Charles de Gaulle Airport.

Desperate for news of the children, I sent Molly a text that if she didn't take my call or ring me back, I would start texting every single neighbour and friend of hers in North Carolina for information. My phone rang a short time later. 'Tracey, it's Molly,' a voice sobbed on the other end of the line.

I wasn't going to be swayed by the dramatics I knew Molly was capable of. 'Tell me exactly what happened. Tell me what happened to Jason,' I demanded.

Molly's voice quavered in reply. 'We had a row. He [Jason] had been drinking all day. He tried to strangle me. I hit him. I pushed him and he fell. He fell backwards and hit his head. He's dead.'

I demanded to know what she had hit him with. There was no answer from Molly. At that point I also had no idea of her father's involvement. I didn't believe a single word of what she had just told me. 'Put Jack on the line right now,' I told her, my voice icy.

A few seconds later, Jack's hesitant voice came on the line. 'Hey Jacko. It's Tracey, love. I am so sorry,' I told him. 'I love you both and I will be over soon.'

As soon as I uttered those words, the line went dead. I knew I had to get to North Carolina as quickly as was physically possible. I also knew I had to involve Irish diplomats, as both Jack and Sarah had Irish passports and were Irish citizens – Jason had been scrupulous about the children's Irish passports and I suspected I knew why. We were going to need all the help and support we could get.

Standing outside Charles de Gaulle Airport at 2 a.m., Dave clasped my face and looked me directly in the eyes: 'Go and do what you have to do – I will sort everything here,' he said. He was as good as his word. Dave then had to drive the five hours back to St Jean de Monts, pack up everything with the children and drive north to catch a ferry back to Rosslare in Ireland. He would then drive to Limerick and, within a few hours, be on a flight to North Carolina.

I had six hours to wait in Charles de Gaulle Airport for the first flight back to Ireland. Paris may be a city of magic but for me it was the loneliest place on earth. It was the worst night of my life. My thoughts were dominated by two things – what had happened to Jason and making sure Jack and Sarah were safe. I located the contact information for the Department of Foreign Affairs and this led to the North Carolina honorary Irish consul, John Young. I provided him with the details of what I knew so far, along with the various contacts I had picked up for the Davidson County Sheriff's Department. In the early hours of that Paris morning, Google was the best ally I had.

I also pondered over the fact that, before I'd received Wayne's call, I had been unusually tense that August day. It is not like me to snap at people but I had been off form since I had awoken early that morning with a nightmare about a baby crying. I never had nightmares but this dream was incredibly realistic. It was so disturbing that I'd woken Dave for reassurance. Sitting in a lonely Paris airport, I wondered now if somehow that dream was connected to the precise time of Jason's death. Was it the young Jason I had cared for as a child in Limerick crying to say goodbye?

In Dublin I was met by my eldest son, Dean, who drove me back to Limerick to meet my parents, brothers and sister. The journey was a blur of fears, suspicions and shock. I was desperately trying to make plans and keep my mobile phone charged. On arrival at my parents' home, we had a family meeting about what had happened. I told them I had to go to North Carolina to get answers and to make sure that Jack and Sarah were safe. 'It is what Jason would have wanted,' I told everyone. Jason's best friend, Paul, and Marilyn, my only sister, immediately volunteered to accompany me.

My abiding memory is of my little mother, Rita, sitting side-by-side with Mags's mother, Marian, the two grandmothers supporting each other. My mother told me: 'Bring my baby boy home to me.' The two grandmothers, with linked arms, added: 'Bring those two children home safe to us and where they belong.'

I also kept ringing Molly's phone, although she wasn't answering.

Through John Young, the honorary Irish consul in Charlotte, I managed to make contact with Shelly Lee, social worker, who worked with the Department of Social Services in North Carolina. My one and only concern was to make sure Jack and Sarah were safe. Initially, I was told by the Honorary Consul after his conversation with Ms Lee that the children would be put in my care once I arrived in the US.

Two days after Jason's death, on Tuesday, 4 August, at 9 a.m., Paul, Marilyn and myself flew from Shannon to Newark in New Jersey, where we would catch a connecting flight to Charlotte. I had been operating on adrenalin for the previous 48 hours. I hadn't slept since Saturday night and was on the verge of mental exhaustion from trying to juggle travel plans, dealing with North Carolina police, Irish diplomats, North Carolina child protection services, my family, Jason's friends, the media and, most time-consuming of all, trying to get information about what had happened from Molly's family. They had shut us out completely.

When we arrived in New Jersey, I suddenly realised we faced a new problem. I had luckily managed to make contact with Lieutenant Detective Wanda Thompson of the Davidson County Sheriff's Department. She was going to be the supervisor on the investigation into Jason's death. I felt it was vital to let her know my suspicions that Molly's version of events may not have been exactly what transpired. I felt it was critical that she fully understood the kind of person Molly was and that Jason had been planning to bring his children back to Ireland. Jason wasn't in a happy marriage and Molly wasn't all that she seemed to be. I was determined that the US police should understand this.

The detective listened to what I had to say and, thankfully, her years of experience proved decisive. They didn't accept at face value everything Molly said about the events in Jason's master bedroom that night, and I was told that a full investigation would take place. It was being treated at the time as a domestic violence incident, but forensic tests would be conducted. But the most vital product of our conversation was my discovery that Molly had been pressing for the release of Jason's body. The suggestion was that they wanted to cremate his remains as quickly as possible in North Carolina. I pleaded with Lt Det. Thompson that we needed to see our brother. I simply couldn't bear the thought of not seeing Jason again and not being able to say a proper goodbye. The haste with which Molly seemed to be pushing for a cremation and funeral further fuelled my suspicions about her role in his death.

Securing access to Jason's remains wasn't our only problem. I rang Shelly Lee again, hoping to be able to see Jack and Sarah, only to be told that they had both been left in Molly's care. I couldn't believe it. It felt like being punched in the stomach. The woman I strongly suspected to be responsible for my brother's death now had charge of his two children? I could only fear the worst.

I was right to be worried. A short time later we discovered that Molly hadn't just filed legal papers seeking custody of Jack and Sarah – she had also filed for guardianship of the children and for their formal adoption. She had also obtained an *ex parte* order on the grounds that I was going to kidnap the two children, which gave temporary custody to her and more or less removed the Department of Social Services, as the courts were now involved. It was something I was determined to stop because I knew Jason had specified in his will that Dave and I were to be guardians of his children. Despite a four-year campaign by Molly, firmly supported by her parents, Thomas and Sharon, Jason had steadfastly refused to sign adoption papers giving her equal rights to his children. As it transpired, he had good reason to be so cautious.

The first few hours in North Carolina felt a little like walking into a war zone. We were met off the flight by the consul, then brought to a meeting with Lt Det. Thompson. We discovered that Jason hadn't died in a fall as Molly had initially claimed, and that it was Tom and Molly who had beaten him to death. In a 911 call to Davidson County emergency services in the early hours of 2 August, Tom Martens had said he had intervened when Jason was attempting to strangle Molly during a row. Tom said he'd struck Jason with a baseball bat after being awoken by the sound of a disturbance upstairs – he had been asleep in the guest bedroom in the basement with his wife, Sharon. (Tom and Sharon had arrived at Jason's home unexpectedly for a visit on 1 August.) But there was no mention in the call of Jason being struck with a concrete brick, despite the fact that a heavy paving slab, soaked in Jason's blood, hair and tissue, was found on the bedroom floor.

Then, at around 9 p.m., Paul, Marilyn and I had driven to Jason's home at Panther Creek Court. I had been hoping the children were still there but, needless to say, Jack and Sarah were long gone. A neighbour immediately rang Molly when they spotted us and she telephoned Davidson County Sheriff's Department. We didn't even make it to the front door before the police were in contact with us.

All we wanted was to go and see Jason – to pay our respects and to grieve. We wanted to see our brother one final time. But even that was initially denied to us. His body, when the authorities were ready, would be released to his next of kin – and that was Molly. She had already made it abundantly clear to us, both through Davidson County Sheriff's Department and her lawyers, that she didn't welcome us being in North Carolina and she was adamant she didn't want us involved in any funeral arrangements.

The campaign to blacken the name of Jason and his family had already commenced. Through the North Carolina police, we heard that Molly had claimed our family had threatened her with the Irish Republican Army (IRA). She also used my loving reassurances to Jack to claim, via the US media and social media, that we planned to take the children by force if necessary.

Through the kindness of a nurse at the hospital where the post mortem was performed, we discovered that Molly had changed the funeral home where Jason's remains were to be brought. They were now to be brought to Cumby's just outside Lexington.

Incredibly, we were refused all access to the remains, despite the fact that Marilyn and I were Jason's sisters and Paul was his best friend since childhood. Marilyn eventually managed to speak to Sharon Martens and pleaded for access. But Sharon bluntly told her to talk to their attorneys. We had no option but to hire attorneys of our own in North Carolina. We were lucky to secure Edward Griggs, an attorney in WCSR, a firm of solicitors in Winston-Salem.

Five days after Jason's death the impasse was resolved when, after tortuous negotiations between the two teams of attorneys, a deal was hammered out. Molly would allow us access to Jason's remains and for him to be buried in Ireland but only if I signed a legal guarantee to underwrite all of his funeral costs, both in the US and Ireland. I signed the legal document for access to Jason's remains without a thought as to the cost or consequences. Getting Jason back to Ireland to my parents and his siblings and friends for a proper burial in the county he loved so much was one promise to my brother I was going to fulfil immediately. But protecting his two children was now my main priority.

Molly had arranged a hasty memorial service for Jason at the Church of Mary Immaculate in Lexington on 6th and 8th Streets. Jason's body was not there for the memorial service. Neither were his sisters, brothers, brother-in-law or best friend. Dave had arrived in North Carolina by this time from Ireland. We weren't at the memorial service for a very simple reason – Molly had warned us we were not welcome. To enforce the message, we learned that the Martens family had even arranged for a team of off-duty police officers from a neighbouring county to be present as security just in case we decided to show up.

Just when we were at our lowest ebb, we received a number of unexpected supports. The first was a contact from Colin Bell, who runs the Kevin Bell Repatriation Fund in Ireland. The fund was set up by Colin and Eithne in memory of their son, Kevin, who died in New York. The offer of help was like a gift from heaven. The fund not only offered to help with bringing Jason's body back from North Carolina to Limerick but, crucially, they also helped with the massive amount of paperwork surrounding such a repatriation. It was one less headache to have to worry about. For that, our family will always be in debt to the Bells.

The second boost was when WCSR referred us to Kim Bonuomo, another Winston-Salem attorney, who specialised in divorce and custody matters. Kim would now spearhead our legal fight for custody of Jack and Sarah. Today, if you mention Kim's name to anyone in our family, their reply is: 'Thank God for Kim.' She threw herself into the case on a 24/7 basis and was a fierce advocate for us.

By Friday, the staff at Cumby's were ready for us to view the body in the coffin I had chosen. I had picked one that resembled as closely as possible a traditional Irish casket, dark mahogany with brass handles. Our feet sank into the soft carpet, the music softly piped around us and we were led to the private room where he had been laid out. The coffin was flanked by two displays of flowers that I had chosen. This was as much for Mags as for Jason. Mags had loved flowers and I prayed that two people who had loved each other so dearly in this life were now back in each other's arms in the next life.

I also wanted my brother to have some emblem that reflected his deep love for his two children. I decided upon a framed photograph with three coins inset on the right side – each coin had a simple motif that reflected on life, love and those we care about. In a time of unending heartache, it was a reminder of what my brother had lived his life for. Today, that framed photograph with coins has pride of place on Jack's bedside table in our Limerick home. The photograph has long since been stained with Jack and Sarah's mixed tears of heartache, as they carried it on the day of Jason's funeral.

But the flowers, the emblems, the kindness of Cumby's staff, the elegant surroundings and the soothing music couldn't soften the pain of seeing Jason for the first time in that reception room. It was like suffering a body blow. I just could not believe it was my brother lying there. I was physically and emotionally exhausted by this time. My mind was a blizzard of thoughts, fears and conflicting priorities. I simply don't know what I would have done without the support of Dave, who was as exhausted as I was. What made me all the more weary was the knowledge that, while we may have cleared one hurdle, many more challenging obstacles now lay ahead.

Cumby's had kindly told us we could have as much time with Jason as we liked. For a long time we simply stared at the body in the coffin and wondered whether it really was Jason. We were staring at a man in a casket who looked about 60 years of age. The more we looked, the more his features appeared different: the face we had loved so dearly seemed to have a different outline. I began to comprehend the reference by the mortuary staff to the fact it would take some time to have Jason 'presentable' for viewing. Several of us became very upset at what we now realised was evidence of what he must have gone through in his final moments. Paul, Dave and Marilyn were horrified by what they saw.

Carefully, the men went up and checked Jason, particularly around the face and head where it was clear he had suffered serious injuries. It was Paul who discovered that the entire rear of Jason's skull had been crushed. The damage to his head was horrific. It simply added to the pain of what was a heartbreaking evening for all of us. Eventually, I asked the others if they would mind giving me a little time on my own with Jason. It was something I needed because it would strengthen me for the legal battles that lay ahead. Kindly, everyone slipped out of the reception room and I was on my own for one final time with my baby brother.

I placed my hand on his cold fingers, carefully folded across his chest. I gently stroked his cheek. I placed my hand on his chest, praying for a heartbeat, for a miracle and for someone to tell me this was a nightmare I now had to awake from. Touching my baby brother, where warmth and kindness had once run through every inch of his being, was now like touching a mannequin. It was like a shell of Jason. It was shocking to realise that this was all that was left of a person whose personality would lift your entire day.

I stood before the polished wooden coffin and wept for Jason and for the manner in which his life was taken from him. I wept for how Jack and Sarah had lost first their mother and now their father. It just wasn't fair that life could be this cruel. I cried when I thought about what Jason had suffered in his final moments and wondered whether he had called out in vain for help or mercy. 'What happened, Jason, what happened? What did they do to you?' I kept asking.

Then I softly chatted to Jason about happier times back in Limerick and about Jack and Sarah. Those children were his reason for living after Mags's death. They kept him going through the darkest times. I even gently sang a few songs that we both loved, including 'The Dance' by Garth Brooks. It was Jason's party piece but it was just too sad – I couldn't finish the verses as the tears streamed down my face. I sang 'Maybe', the theme song from *Grizzly Adams*, one of our favourite childhood shows, over and over again. It broke my heart but it also gave me the strength for what I knew I had to do.

We had arranged for a Catholic priest to attend Cumby's. We wanted Jason sent home properly and in accordance with his faith. In truth, it was a comfort to all of us. I said Jason's favourite Gaelic blessing: 'May the road rise up to meet you.' But I also knew – despite the trauma that it would cause all of us – I couldn't allow Jason's Requiem Mass to take place in Limerick until Jack and Sarah were safely back in Ireland.

In that room, alone with Jason, I made several promises before God. I promised my brother I would protect and care for the children who were the centre of his world. Somehow I would find a way to get them back to Ireland where they belonged. I vowed that Jason would be buried beside Mags, the woman he loved so dearly and who was his soulmate.

I had one further promise to make and this promise was made not in sadness but in cold, calculated fury. Standing at the foot of his coffin I promised my brother that I would spare no expense and undertake any sacrifice necessary to see that justice was done for his death. No one could be allowed do this to another human being and then walk away as if nothing had happened. As I stared for one final time at Jason's face, I knew beyond all reasonable doubt that he had been murdered. Worst of all, he had been murdered by the one person he had sworn to love, honour and protect. I knew at that moment, with a clarity that defied my exhaustion and stress, that Molly Martens had murdered my brother.

With my family, I would now move heaven and earth to see she faced the justice she deserved.

2

A Lost Soulmate

Love literally shimmers across the image that I'm staring at. The two young people, so enthralled with each other, seem to glow with an inner happiness as they prepare to take another exciting step on life's journey together. If ever an image defined the meaning of happiness and love this was surely it.

Mags and Jason are standing on the cliff overlooking the wild Atlantic as the waves crash onto the rocky Clare beach below. They are all smiles, eyes meeting constantly. Mags fiddles with Jason's cravat.

Their laughter is caught on the breeze as the members of the wedding party, myself included, stand across the path sipping champagne as the photographer carefully places them for a picture.

That photographer never had an easier job. Jason and Mags were so photogenic. They were easygoing and had totally embraced their whole wedding day. Most of all, every image of them glowed with the love they shared. You know those kinds of days where all the pieces of life fit perfectly – friends, family and atmosphere all coming together on a lovely sunny day.

It is an image I have treasured because it keeps reminding me of who my brother Jason really was, a time when life was 'normal'. But every single time I stare at the photo, it brings tears to my eyes because it belongs to a different era – a time of such innocence, happiness and hope. A time when murder was something I'd only read about in crime books and lurid newspaper headlines. A time when the cruelty of life was a total stranger to our family and we had no inkling of the depths of betrayal and insidious manipulation that some people were capable of.

At home I have the scrapbook Mags and Jason put together of images of their fledgling new life together from 2003 and 2004. Gorgeous images of their wedding, their honeymoon and the building of their 'dream home'. In one photograph, Jason is posing with a beaming Mags as they inspect the site at Ballyneety, just outside Limerick city, that they had chosen for their bungalow. The drawings are beautiful – the house is traditional old Irish stone and the property is located just across the road from the Swan pub, which was listed as one of the top ten places in Ireland to have a pint by a cosy log fire. I can see the immense pride on Jason's young face over the construction project – and the sheer joy on Mags's beautiful features.

I close my eyes and I can still remember that day. Both insisting on showing myself and Dave where their furniture would go, chatting to each other about what colours the walls would be and how they planned to landscape the bungalow to maximise the impact of its sweeping driveway.

This home was his gift to Mags and their children. I can't help but smile because, at that stage, the 'dream home' was literally a pile of dirt excavated by a JCB and trenches filled with poured concrete as foundations. But to Jason and Mags it was the stuff of magic. They were always a glass-half-full type of couple.

It did become their dream home. It was a house I always associated with such joy and happiness – until that awful day in 2006 when, without warning, Mags left us and Jason was never quite the same afterwards. The property left our family in 2010 when Jason sold it because Molly kept complaining about living there under what she called 'the shadow of Mags'.

There were eight children in our family, six boys and two girls, Marilyn and myself. The youngest children were twin boys born in February 1976, Jason and Wayne. I was just a couple of years older.

Our parents, John and Rita, both hailed from the Prospect area of Limerick – in fact, their two families were next-door neighbours. My father had attended the same Leamy's school as Frank McCourt, the author of *Angela's Ashes*. I recall Dad relaying stories of the school he shared with Frank McCourt who, of course, went on to win the Pulitzer Prize for the story of his difficult Limerick childhood.

We were born and raised in Janesboro in Limerick. It may now be considered a suburb of Limerick city, but when it was built back in the 1960s, it was a suburb surrounded by orchards. When we were growing up, Connery's and Murphy's were our local shops; we had ready access to open fields, horse chestnut trees bent double with conkers across Toppins' fields for schoolyard games, streams rich with frogs and tadpoles, ditches that seemed to explode with blackberries late every summer and even an ancient fairy fort that seemed our own magical playground.

My father and mother would both attend local Leamy's school reunions and a picture of them proudly smiling into the camera has sat in our kitchen for as long as I can remember. Unlike Frank McCourt, who would head back to New York, my father never contemplated emigration. He had spent a few years in England and it was enough for him to determine to raise his family locally and stick close to the things he loved.

Foremost among those things was my mother. She worked in a local firm and, many times, my father would cycle to meet her after work and carry her home on the bar of his bicycle. After they married, they had a flat on Lord Edward Street, then a council house on Lenihan Avenue, but, as with the McCourt family, dampness in poor-quality local housing was a problem at that time. My eldest brother suffered from asthma and the damp made his condition very troublesome. My parents fought to secure better accommodation and eventually our growing family was allocated a dry, healthy new home at Colbert Park in Janesboro. It is our family home to this day.

My father got a job as a truck driver with Shell. Having married in 1960, my mother had no option but to quit her job – such was Ireland 58 years ago – and focus on raising her family. If Nobel Prizes were awarded for running a warm, happy home, my mother would be a multiple award-winner. My abiding memory is the smell of cooking wafting through the house – we had hot porridge every morning before school and dinner was on the table when we got home.

My mother was the typical 'Irish mammy'. She was the centre around which all our lives revolved. Our home was always warm, safe, happy and with something cooking on the hob or in the oven. Mam became sick when I was in my teens and had to stay in hospital for a while. It was only then we realised just how much she gave of herself to organise our lives and make sure we wanted for nothing.

My earliest memory of Jason is of him and me teaching Wayne to walk. Jason had learned first because Wayne had become ill after his birth. We were both kneeling in the hallway holding out our hands while Wayne practised walking. Back and forth he went – Wayne would walk and tumble into the safe hands of Jason and myself.

All of us started our schooling at Our Lady Queen of Peace primary school. The friends you made at four and five years of age in the junior infants class generally became your friends and classmates for the next 14 years. Jason made one friendship in school that would prove critical for him in later life. On his first days in the Queen of Peace, complete with short pants, high socks and leather satchel schoolbag, he became firm friends with Lynn Shanahan. They remained friends right up until the day of his death. Little did any of us realise back then that Lynn would go on to introduce Jason to Margaret 'Mags' Fitzpatrick, the love of his life.

Jason also made friends with Paul Dillon, a neighbour, Brendan 'Blondie' O'Callaghan and Damian McCormack in his first year of secondary school at St Enda's – wonderful men who would continue to be his bosom buddies for the next 30 years. You can gauge the measure of Jason's friends by the fact that they all came to North Carolina to support us during the 2017 murder trial. For two years they helped us through some of the most tremendously difficult times and never once complained about the expense involved.

The other reason I remember Jason starting school was the fact that he was a twin and, with Wayne, was one of four pairs of twins starting school in Our Lady Queen of Peace that day back in 1980. It was such an unusual event that the *Limerick Leader* sent a photographer out to record the occasion.

Ours was a childhood packed with happy memories, fun and laughter. We never considered ourselves poor; though, in hindsight, I now realise that there wasn't much money and my parents worked miracles making it go as far as they did. But we were the same as lots of Irish families of the era.

In the late 1980s, my father lost his job with Shell and things became a little tougher. We always had food on the table but careful budgeting became that bit more important. Jason took a part-time security job in his school sports centre and swimming pool for pocket money. He had a few other jobs before he got a position with Field Boxmore, the firm that would, after several mutations, turn into MPS. Jason began working for Field Boxmore, as it was known then, around 1994/95 as a general operator.

By this time, Jason had moved in to live with Dave and myself. It was an arrangement that suited everyone. Dave was initially seen as the slightly older, wiser figure in the house before, typically of Jason, he adopted Dave as one of his best friends. Jason relied on Dave for friendship, advice and support from his teens. There was incredible respect and admiration between them. Jason trusted Dave like few others, as evidenced by the fact that he made Dave, along with Lynn, executor of his will and effectively entrusted Jack and Sarah to him. They shared a strong bond until the day Jason died.

We still laugh when we recall Jason and his friends taking our son Dean, who had gorgeous blond hair as a child, to the beach because they were convinced girls would be impressed by young men willing to share their day with a child. Of course they never considered the fact that each of them was better looking than the next.

My brother took on his new job with a zeal that impressed everyone. He volunteered for extra work, loved the opportunities it created and was promoted. In 1996, he became the union representative for MPS and served until 1998. In the same period, Jason sat on the European Works Council, representing employees from all sites in Europe to the most senior management. He received another promotion, to shift supervisor, in 1997 – his colleague and friend Morgan Fogarty, who would replace him later when he moved to the US, was on the opposite shift.

He also accessed further education opportunities, mostly through attending night courses. Jason was appointed Operations Director in 2005. The role came complete with a new company car – he was so excited and I was so proud of him. He had worked hard and it had paid off for him. After Jason moved to take the position of Plant Manager for MPS in Lexington NC, he returned to Europe on many occasions to share some of the best-practice projects he was working on. Over the four years he worked in the US, he doubled the turnover at his MPS site and secured a $5 million investment for a new press for the plant.

In our childhood, Spanish Point on the Clare coast became a special place for us. It was where we would spend two glorious weeks in a small mobile home and we believed the wild Atlantic coastline was a better holiday bet than anywhere else in the world. It was under the Bell Bridge, not far from the current Armada Hotel, that my father taught Jason, Wayne and me the nursery rhyme 'Three Little Fish'. He promised us that, in times of crisis, reciting its verses would help you cope with whatever life would throw at you. They proved prophetic words.

The Clare coast became our home away from home in the summer. We would play by the beach, swim in the coastal lagoons, build sandcastles and have card games by candlelight. When we got older, a major treat was being brought to a *céilí* or traditional Irish dance in Miltown Malbay.

It wasn't long before Jason was walking out with some beautiful girlfriends. In fact, one was later a bridesmaid at my wedding. Typically of Jason, even when the romances ended, they remained on really good terms. The young women stopped being girlfriends and became pals. This is something to remember given the awful claims later levelled against him by Tom and Molly. Tragically, one former girlfriend would also die young, just like Mags, contracting cancer and losing a heroic battle for health in April 2009. Both Jason and I attended her funeral.

It was February 1997 when fate intervened in all our lives. Jason's friend Lynn was working at the Kiddies Campus Crèche on O'Connell Street in Limerick. They had lost touch for a while but Lynn and a friend had gatecrashed Jason and Wayne's 21st birthday party in The Sally Port, a popular Limerick club. Their friendship resumed immediately. Later that year, they were both going to a birthday party and Jason approached Lynn to ask about her beautiful work colleague, Margaret 'Mags' Fitzpatrick. Mags was a gorgeous person in every sense of the word – she was strikingly beautiful, had the most unique hazel eyes, was always elegant with her clothing and make-up but was also one of the nicest, kindest, most warm-hearted people you could ever hope to meet.

Needless to say, Jason was smitten. I'd known since his younger years that my brother was a true romantic and now he began to prove it. Mags was showered with flowers, cards and invitations to meals and the cinema. Jason would collect her if she ever needed to go anywhere. Lynn recognised it was love at first sight:

I think it was after the party where they had met, everyone went back to a house for a few drinks and a sing-song. People fell asleep in chairs, sofas and even on the floor. The following morning, Mags was up and cooking an Irish fry-up for everyone – that was Mags. She needed some ingredients and had to go down to the shop. Jason immediately volunteered to go with her. As they walked down the road, they were holding hands. From that moment, there was no one else in the world for them bar each other.

Jason later admitted he fell head over heels in love with Mags on that brief walk to Sean's shop on 31 August 1997.

Brendan recalled the night of their first date, when Jason lost his heart to Mags:

It was an easy date to remember – it was the day of Princess Diana's funeral. Jason borrowed my pride and joy (my peach shirt) as he wanted to impress Mags. He came home from his date and kept me up all night talking about Mags and this continued night after night. Mags and my now wife Michelle became very good friends as well and we were always in each other's company.

Mags also became a fixture within our Corbett–Lynch family social circle. I first met Mags in the Bellbridge House Hotel, where she instantly loved the turf fire and friendly staff. She was a hit with our son Dean, who was five at the time, when she began colouring with him. Dean was besotted.

'The Dance' eventually became Jason's musical tribute to Mags. On an evening in the pub, he would do his best Garth Brooks impression. I would watch and realise that Jason was singing it directly to Mags. I would look over at her and see her beam with combined embarrassment and pride.

When Jason and Mags moved in together in a rented apartment on the Dock Road it was like old times because Dave and myself were renting the apartment directly underneath theirs as we waited to buy our own home. They were glorious times – we would all often socialise together and some of my fondest photographic mementoes are from trips with Mags on 'girly' weekends or as couples to Westport, Clare,

Dublin, London and across Europe for rugby matches – one of the most memorable being the 2006 European Cup semi-final in Biarritz with our beloved Munster team. Often, Jason and Mags would babysit Dean so Dave and I could have a night out on our own. When Dave and I went to the Admiralty Lodge near Spanish Point to celebrate an anniversary, it was Jason and Mags who again looked after our boys. When we arrived, a bottle of champagne was waiting in the bedroom. I knew instantly it had been organised by Mags – that's the kind of person she was, incredibly organised and always thinking of others.

Jason and Mags were on holidays in Barcelona in Spain in 2002 when he proposed. He picked the famous magic fountain at Montjuic to ask Mags to marry him. It wasn't a surprise to any of us who knew them because they were already true soulmates – there was no other word for it. Our family loved Mags like a sister and daughter.

Their wedding in 2003 was like something from a fairy tale. Jason and Mags had chosen Clare for the wedding. The service was held in the Star of the Sea church looking out onto the Atlantic and, needless to say, it was hosted in the Bellbridge House Hotel, the location of so many of our golden childhood memories. Mags's maid of honour was her sister Catherine, who became close to the couple. The wedding brought Jason's romantic instincts to new heights. Because of all the wedding demands, Jason and Mags had agreed not to meet up for the three days beforehand. But, on the first day, Mags realised that Jason had left a note for her. In fact, he had left a note for each of the three days that they wouldn't see each other before they walked down the aisle to exchange vows. He had given them to Catherine with the instruction to give Mags one to read on each of the three days before the wedding. He had also bought her a beautiful watch as a wedding gift. Inspired by a romantic TV advert Mags had seen, Jason had left the notes to outline how much he loved Mags, what he wanted for their life together and the dreams that they would share. I can't read those notes today without crying because of the tragedy that lay just ahead for those two beautiful young people.

Catherine remembers:

When Mags read each of the notes, she started crying. After the third note on the day before the wedding, she went into the bathroom and was crying so loudly everyone in the family heard her. My father thought she wanted to call the wedding off and that's why she was upset. But she was crying out of sheer emotion and happiness – I think she was just overcome by having found someone who she realised was her soulmate.

If you look at any of the wedding photographs, all you can see is two young people staring at each other in total, blissful happiness, the kind you hope never ends. Dave and myself were in the bridal party, as groomsman and bridesmaid, as were our children. It was such a joyful day with not a sign of the dark clouds of fate that were only three years away.

In September 2004, Mags gave birth to Jack and I thought Jason's chest would burst with pride. Here was his little 'Mini-Me'. I remember Jason holding Jack cradled in his arms with a look of complete love.

As soon as Mags got home from hospital, they both took a baby cardiopulmonary resuscitation (CPR) class to make sure they were fully equipped as new parents. Jack's name was put on the school list at just six months old and Jason was already planning on being rugby coach for Jack's future team which, given our family allegiance, had to be Young Munster. Jason all too briefly got to fulfil that role.

In September 2006, Mags gave birth to Sarah and Jason was again beside himself with pride, happiness and contentment. Sarah was beautiful and such a placid little thing. They had their little prince and princess. By now, they had moved into their dream home and Jason had been promoted at work. Life, it seemed, couldn't get any better for my young brother and his beautiful wife.

Then, at the height of their happiness, just three months after Sarah was born, tragedy struck. It was 21 November 2006, a night I will never forget. Jason and I had been chatting earlier that evening. Dave and I had gone to bed and were woken by the phone ringing. It was a doctor saying we need to get to the emergency unit at University Hospital Limerick (UHL) immediately.

Everything had seemed so normal earlier in the evening and, at one point, Mags had even scolded Jason and her sister, Catherine, over the fact that the dishwasher wasn't emptied. She had been feeding Sarah at midnight while she and Jason chatted and laughed, falling back to sleep after Sarah was settled.

In the early hours Mags woke Jason to say she was having an asthma attack and decided to take her nebuliser. Soon, she realised it was not giving her relief – she knew these chest pains were somehow different. Jason called an ambulance and went to wake Catherine, who was living with them at the time while she waited for her new house to be ready. Mags told Catherine how scared she was. Instead of waiting for the paramedics, Jason stayed on the phone with them as he drove Mags towards the city to meet the ambulance en route. Catherine later said she knew something was badly wrong when Mags, who was so image proud, got into the family car in her pyjamas. 'Mags kept saying in the kitchen: "I'm going to die, I'm going to die." But it was when she got into the car in her pyjamas that I got really worried because that just wasn't like Mags,' Catherine said. 'Even when Mags went into labour with her children, she insisted on getting changed into nice clothing for the trip to the maternity hospital.'

Jason pulled in at the agreed meeting point and was told the ambulance was almost there. Mags suddenly slumped forward onto the dashboard. Jason pulled her from the car and immediately began CPR. My brother got Mags breathing again and the paramedics, who arrived minutes later, then took over resuscitation work. Jason was instructed to follow the ambulance as it raced Mags to UHL. Seconds after he parked his car,

Jason was taken into a private room by a doctor and informed that the paramedics had done everything they could but Mags had died in the ambulance. Jason was taken straight to Mags's side while doctors rang Dave and the Fitzpatrick family.

On the phone, the doctor would tell us nothing other than Jason and Mags needed someone to attend UHL immediately. I knew Mags had asthma and had been treated for attacks before in hospital, but they were managed and nothing that you could describe as severe. UHL is only a kilometre from our front door and we were there within minutes.

I will never forget the sight that greeted us. Mags was surrounded by life-saving equipment. She was dressed in a beautiful blue and white pyjama set and looked so delicate lying there with her eyes closed. She looked as if she was simply asleep. Jason was pacing up and down, holding his head in his hands. The sheer scale of the loss my brother had suffered made the scene appear primal. He was begging Mags not to leave him, pleading with her to stay. Dave and I stood there and struggled to cope with the heart-rending agony of watching someone so beautiful, so full of life, so loved and so needed leave us all behind. It was the worst day of my life. Little did I realise that we would go through it all again less than nine years later.

Poor Catherine was one of the last to make it to the hospital. She had stayed at the Ballyneety house looking after Jack and Sarah, while sitting in the hallway by the phone waiting for news of her sister.

Jason rang to tell her the awful news:

He rang and just said: 'She is gone.' I then rang Lynn and Tim to tell them. I just couldn't believe it. Jason and Mags were so good to me. When Jason gave Mags a present at Valentine's Day of a pampering day voucher, he would also give her one for me so that she wouldn't be alone for the day. They were inseparable and were so good to each other. We used to call Mags 'MacGyver' because she would try to fix anything – a broken electrical socket, a leaking water tap or even a flat tyre. We just couldn't believe she was gone.

Jason's best friends arrived at UHL that 21 November night to discover him inconsolable with grief. Brendan described the scene as the most heartbreaking he had witnessed. 'When we arrived we saw Jason outside with his head in his hands – I parked on the footpath and the four of us embraced for what seemed like an hour. We went to see Mags with Jason and it was then we knew his whole life had just crumbled in that one night.'

Lynn was also incredible. She met the coroner with Jason and went through the post mortem examination report. Mags had suffered an asthma attack and her heart had simply stopped. The pathologist had described her heart as a ticking time bomb – her fatal attack could have happened when she was 13 or 93. But Mags had only made it to 31.

Her funeral was simply heart-rending. Jason had written a special farewell to Mags but knew he would be too upset to deliver it so he asked Dave to read it out on his behalf. There wasn't a dry eye in the church when Dave finished.

The letter read:

To my soul mate and beautiful wife, Mag Mag. You've just heard how much I loved you before we got married and it has been a million times better than I could ever have dreamed. I could talk about how great, funny and crazy you were all night. Words cannot express the depths of despair, anger and hurt I am feeling at the moment. That you have been taken from me, your little monster Jack and little baby Sarah at just the beginning of our life journey. I know we crammed in so much in the little time we had together but it was only a fraction of the life we had planned together. I am taking some solace in the 10 years we spent together and, in particular, the last three years. I had the chance to share my life with someone special and you made me the person I am today.

Don't worry about the babies – all of us here today, family and friends, will make sure that they always remember how great their mommy was. I promise I will stay strong for our wonderful kids. The love and warmth and offers of support we have received from everyone makes me so proud of the person you are.

You always said that I was lucky to have you – you were the girl of my dreams and then became the love of my life. Now you are the girl of my dreams again. My Mag Mag – I'll love you all of my life. Please look in on us from time to time. Love you always and forever – Jason.

Sarah was just 12 weeks old. The months before had been spent having a wonderful party at their house for Jack's second birthday with all their family and friends, and then, a couple of weeks later, they gathered again for Sarah's christening. Mags was elated with her little princess and none of us could have guessed at those two celebrations that, such a short time later, we would attend the funeral of this wonderfully vivacious young mother. Mags had carefully boxed away Sarah's first set of clothes and shoes, both of which I'd gifted her, for future keepsakes. Jason left these, along with two suitcases full of mementoes for the children, with me to store when he first moved to North Carolina.

Jason was 30 and a widower. It was devastating for everyone. I thought none of us would ever endure 24 hours like it again. But how wrong I was. Over the next few days we did everything we possibly could. Mags was like a sister to us and we were all broken-hearted. But it was nothing compared to the level of grief that was now engulfing my brother.

His friend and MPS colleague Morgan Fogarty spoke eloquently of the courage shown by my brother in those dark days.

Jason was a gentleman all the way through, in the time that I have known Jason, I have witnessed him going through the highest and lowest points of his life. The highs being the marriage to his lovely wife Margaret who he dotingly referred to as 'Mags' and the birth of their two children Jack and Sarah who he was so proud of. The low being the tragic and sudden loss of his dear wife in her prime, leaving

Jason to look after his new born daughter and very young son. I have never been so proud of anyone as I was of Jason and how he managed to keep going through this extremely difficult time, never leaving the kids from his side. Every ounce of energy Jason had went into making sure Jack and Sarah were well provided for, surrounded by those who loved them and brought up the way Mags would have wanted.

Jason kept a wedding photograph of Mags in work right up until the day he cleared his desk in May 2011 to head for a new life in North Carolina.

What astonished me most about Jason was his ability to be empathetic even through his toughest times and how he was able to spare a thought for others – he wanted to help people wherever possible, whether it be financial or emotional support that he could offer. Jason was one of a kind.

In the tributes to Jason since 2015, they all list his date of death as 2 August. But, truth be told, a large part of Jason's heart vanished that awful 21 November evening in 2006. All his hopes, dreams and ambitions were shared with Mags. She was his everything. It was as if a huge chunk of his soul had been ripped out. In the Celtic tradition, an anam cara is someone whose unique connection with another binds their souls together eternally. Mags was Jason's anam cara. It was like a part of him was now missing and he knew it was never going to be replaced. Mags was his home.

They were very dark days. When Jason lost Mags he thought the world had done its worst to him. It was if fate had conspired against him. I was proud of how he faced up to the devastating loss and decided to fundraise for the Irish Asthma Society (IAS) in Mags's memory. By 2008 he had raised €34,145. Part of the money from the Mags Corbett Trust was used to fund the IAS 'Asthma in Pregnancy' booklet.

After the funeral, we started caring for Jack and Sarah alongside our own two children, Dean and Adam, sometimes, to give Jason a break as he struggled to balance his work commitments with home life. Catherine stayed for a few months to help him with the children before she moved out, as her own house in Limerick city was ready. She still played a very supportive role for Jason in caring for both Jack and Sarah. In fact, he had lots of us supporting him.

There were tears, there were silences, there was a rawness to his loss that was hard to witness and there were moments when I knew he was struggling to find the will to continue. Every day he would visit Mags's grave and he continued to do this until he moved to North Carolina. If you drove past Castlemungret Cemetery at any lunchtime, he would be propped against the headstone with his lunch, reading Mags the paper or telling her the news of his day. It was gut-wrenching. He would drive to Spanish Point with Jack and Sarah for some solace but I sometimes think he was searching for something that he could never find again – a faint, shadowy remnant of a happier time. From the day of her death, he never forgot Mags's birthday, their wedding anniversary, Christmas or Valentine's Day. Jason would buy the most beautiful cards, carefully inscribe them with a handwritten tribute and then bring them to Mags's grave so he could read them out to her. All those letters and cards were carefully stored but I still cannot read them without dissolving into tears.

What kept Jason going, what gave him a reason to put one foot in front of the other, were his two beautiful children. Jack and Sarah were Jason's life now, his reason for existence, and my brother would do everything he could for them. It also dawned on Jason, as it did on all of us, that the children were a living link with Mags. She would never really be gone while we had them. Someone gave him a gift of a photo session with the children, which I encouraged him to go to. The portrait from that session now hangs in our sitting room alongside the other family pictures.

By mid-2007, I thought we were slowly adjusting to workable arrangements. My family had rallied around Jason to a remarkable degree. His friends were incredible. It was the same with the Fitzpatrick family, who had also done everything possible to support him. Whatever

Jason needed, there was always someone on hand to help. If anything, he was fending off offers of help with the children. I suspect now that maybe it was his determination not to be any kind of burden that led him to take a fateful step. He decided that, to minimise disruption to the lives of his family and Mags's family, he would look for outside help with the children. He hoped that it would help ease the day-to-day duties of washing, cleaning and cooking around the house.

Jason decided to advertise for an au pair. Over a six- to nine-month period he had a Spanish girl and a Czech girl work as live-in nannies. Jason's friend Karen recalled that the decision to hire an au pair was seen as a positive step. 'I think we all looked at it as Jason getting back to being Jason – trying to take control of his life and do what was best for himself and Jack and Sarah. It was as if he had taken our help but now needed to do things on his own. But there were problems over language and the fact the girls weren't planning on any medium or long-term stays in Ireland. I think Jason also felt the constant changing of nannies wasn't good for Jack and Sarah.'

Just when he was getting his life in order and setting a routine for the children, everything was suddenly thrown out of kilter again – his latest au pair had only been with them for a short few weeks when she had to return home after her brother was injured in a car accident. When the nanny said her goodbyes and flew home to care for her injured brother, Jason informed us he had decided to advertise for an English-speaking au pair to help care for Jack and Sarah.

That was how Molly Martens entered our lives.

3

Cruel Twist of Fate

In 2008, Molly Martens was 25 years old. She was the only daughter of Thomas 'Tom' Martens and his wife, Sharon Martens *née* Earnest. The couple also had three sons, Bobby, Stewart and Connor. Molly was second eldest. The family lived in Knoxville in Tennessee in the southern part of the United States. Their home on Comblaine Road was a reflection of the American dream and quite impressive. It had a swimming pool, six bedrooms, expansive lawns and a split-level deck, as well as stunning landscaping and interior decoration.

Sharon was a maths graduate and a housewife. Tom Martens was a graduate of Emory University and had retired after serving for more than 30 years in the Federal Bureau of Investigation (FBI). He was a qualified lawyer and, after retiring from the FBI, went to work in the counter-intelligence section of the US Department of Energy facility at Oakridge in Tennessee. Bobby, Stewart and Connor had all excelled at both school and sports, going on to attend college.

Molly arrived in Ireland for the first time on 10 March 2008 with her all-American good looks, denim cowgirl outfit, bouncing blonde curls, beaming smile and a career resumé that made it seem Jason was the luckiest man on earth to have secured her nannying services. She stepped off the plane and into our lives with a heady mix of accomplishments, qualifications, stunning looks and magnetic personality that threatened to dazzle everyone she met. What none of us realised that miserable rainy day was that Molly had been carefully scrutinising au pair websites and job opportunities until she found exactly what she was looking for – a young, lonely widower with very young children.

She had first emailed Jason in early February 2008 and expressed an interest in the job he was advertising. Molly claimed she was a qualified Montessori teacher. She was also a graduate of the prestigious Clemson University and had been on the fringes of the US Olympic swimming team. She was even vetted as a foster parent. It was only years later we realised that all of these claims were lies.

She had never graduated from Clemson and had held a succession of relatively low-paid jobs, including working at a beauty parlour called Visage. One of her first serious relationships was with a young man called Jeremiah Taylor who, like herself, hailed from Knoxville and was working at the same beauty parlour. The relationship lasted for around 18 months from 2004 to 2005. It became serious enough for Jeremiah to be asked as Molly's date to her brother's wedding in Puerto Rico.

Molly then became involved in a second, more serious relationship while again working odd jobs, including minding children whose photographs I discovered she had kept over the years in her family picture box. Molly apparently used the photos of these children in a bid to make Jack and Sarah jealous. This relationship was with Keith Maginn, who was originally from Ohio. The duo struck up a strong bond and quickly moved in together at an apartment owned by Molly's parents. We didn't know it in 2008 but they were still engaged when she suddenly flew to Ireland to begin a new life. Keith was totally in the dark about Molly's plans.

Jason, who was now desperate for English-speaking help with Jack and Sarah, thought Molly's reply to his advert was a godsend. He was without an au pair and taking time off work to fill the position. Within a short exchange of emails, it was agreed that Molly would fly to Ireland.

It was not that straightforward, though – Irish immigration services at Shannon Airport had taken one look at her one-way ticket and total lack of documentation and ordered her on the first plane back to the United

States. It was as if fate had decided to take pity on us. But, if fate was sending us a sign, none of us was wise enough to read it and take action. In truth, none of us knew just how systematically, cunningly and subtly we were about to be manipulated and deceived.

By happenstance, Lynn was in Shannon Airport that morning, about to fly out on holidays with her husband, Tim. Jason realised she was there and, having received a panicked call from Molly, rang Lynn for help with the situation while he figured out what to do. Lynn agreed to find the young American woman and offer her some company while Jason rang Dave for advice. He immediately advised Jason to buy the cheapest one-way ticket to anywhere he could, which would allow him access to the departures area.

Lynn recalled that day:

> I walked over to the area where he said she was standing and immediately found her. I took one look at her blonde curls, fur-lined jacket and cowboy boots and thought to myself that she was precisely what Jason did not need. I also immediately thought it was very unusual for a woman of her age to be paying so much to fly to Ireland for a job that, let's be honest, isn't exactly the highest paying.

Lynn stayed with Molly until Jason arrived in the departures area with his one-way ticket. He chatted with Molly but nothing could be done to resolve her immigration impasse – she had arrived in Ireland with a one-way ticket and immigration officials were not happy with her employment status and credentials. She was put on a flight back to Boston. Molly was in contact again with Jason the following day and stepped on another flight to Ireland, this time via Dublin and with a return ticket. She waltzed through Dublin Airport with no difficulty.

In the beginning, it seemed to be working out fine for Jason. Molly had taken to Jack and Sarah instantly and the house began to operate better than it had under any of the previous au pairs. Jason was very conscious that she was a long way from home and introduced her to his family and friends, trying to help her settle. On her days off, he encouraged her to tour Ireland and make friends.

I first met Molly in late March 2008. I had been on a short break in Lanzarote with Dave and the children for the St Patrick's Day holidays so I wasn't in Ireland when she first arrived. I met her at my parents' house a few weeks later and, if the truth be told, I liked her. She was dressed in a very simple cardigan outfit, almost like something Julie Andrews wore in *The Sound of Music*, and had her long blonde hair tied back. She was quiet, reserved but friendly.

Over the following months, I noticed that Jason seemed to be happier. There was no questioning how devoted Molly appeared to be to the children, though her attention to them could be a little intense at times. Molly was happiest when she was spending time with Jack and Sarah. I knew she was far from home so I tried to help her settle in. I discovered we shared a love of literature so I would swap books with her and we would discuss our favourite authors. I invited her to join me at a Zumba fitness class I was taking, and we got on well at various family events and social outings. We would go for walks when the family met up at Spanish Point in Clare and do simple things like going to the cinema or out for a meal. At the time I found Molly to be good company and I liked the way she had helped Jason to smile again.

Looking back, I wish I could point to something specific and say I should have recognised the danger signs of what lay ahead. But Molly initially came across as a very nice person, kind and considerate.

There was nothing to hint at anything suspicious. Most of all, her arrival into our lives seemed to transform Jason. He was cheerful for the first time since he lost Mags.

With the blessing of hindsight, I now understand that Molly was on her full medications at the time. We learned, much later, that she had had a stay in an Emory University Hospital in Atlanta, Georgia in February 2008, which had obviously stabilised her mental health. She had been diagnosed, according to a psychiatric report done at the time, with potential bipolar disorder during her adolescence. Yet this was something she later denied during the guardianship hearing.

According to the psychiatric report, she had been on a combination of several antidepressants and other medications – at one stage up to 16 daily. These included lithium, Focalin, Lunesta, Seroquel, Provigil and Tramadol. The report also referred to a paternal family history of depression and reportable bipolar disorders.

Of course none of us had any inkling in 2008 of Molly's troubled mental health history or medications. She came across as a pleasant, polite young woman who seemed to enjoy being around children. As far as I was concerned, Jason, Jack and Sarah seemed happy, so that was that.

By May, I had the first suspicions that there was more to Jason and Molly than an employer–employee relationship. On one outing to Clare, I noticed that they seemed to prefer to be on their own. We would all go for a walk and both Jason and Molly would lag behind, content in each other's company. I also noticed that Jason had taken to calling her 'Molls', his own pet name for her. It suggested a growing intimacy. I took the view that Jason was happy and appeared to have escaped the dark cloud of pain and grief that seemed to stalk him every day since Mags had died. Jason was also almost 33 years old – he wasn't going to take lectures from his sister about affairs of the heart.

I was relieved for Jason and hoped Molly felt happy too. My only concern was that Jason and Molly seemed to have a burgeoning relationship while she was living in his house and looking after his children, which I considered to be a potential complicating factor. But I assumed it was a short-term thing and that she provided some comfort for Jason.

There were times I struggled to make an assessment of Molly. She could dazzle you with her cheeriness and her attention. If the mood took her, she could make you feel like the most important person on the planet. I explained away a lot of odd things on the basis that she was American and not Irish, that she was brought up to be super-confident and not shy about telling you her qualifications and achievements. At the time, I guessed she was simply trying to impress us. I do recall questioning her when I realised on occasions that she had contradicted herself about something. But she would brush off such queries with great skill.

There were other times when I got the sense she was very guarded around us – as if there was a barrier about personal details we were not allowed to cross. She never discussed her friends. She could be quiet, only responding to questions put to her, and, over time, I realised she was sharing very little about her previous life in the US. It was as if her life was carefully compartmentalised. When she did share stories, they very often conflicted with things she had already told us.

All of Jason's friends were very kind to her. Years later, when chatting about the situation, we agreed that in all the time we spent with Molly in Ireland we never really got to know her. I suspect we were never allowed to. Put bluntly, the Molly I met in Tennessee in the run-up to her 2011 wedding to Jason was a totally different person from the quiet, friendly Molly we had known in Limerick three years earlier. It was if the disguise had finally been discarded with abandon. We were now surplus to her needs.

I also noted, within a few months, that Molly had taken a strong dislike to Jason's best friend, Paul. It slowly dawned on me that Molly didn't like Paul being around the house and, over the years, would subtly do everything possible to ease him out of Jason's life. I didn't realise at the time but Molly was trying to do precisely the same thing to me. In the end, I think she despised Paul because he simply ignored her and focused solely on Jason. Paul, God bless him, wouldn't allow Molly to drive him out of Jason's life. She seemed more tolerant of Jason's other friends, Brendan 'Blondie' O'Callaghan and Damian McCormack, though Damian readily admitted he was very wary of her from the very first time they met.

Paul explained his dilemma.

I met Molly the day after she arrived in Ireland. I tried to be friendly but, over time, I found that when I'd strike up a conversation the answers would be either 'yes' or 'no'. I found it was a bit like trying to pull teeth, Molly didn't seem to particularly want to talk to me. So I just chatted to Jason. I was also probably one of the first to know that there was a relationship developing between them but, at the time, I took the view that it really wasn't any of my business. As time went by, I saw a different side to Molly. Once, Jason and myself went to play golf in Ballybunion. You don't take your phone on the golf course and, if you do, you make sure it is turned off. When we finished our round and Jason checked his phone, there were about 16 missed calls from Molly. That's the kind of relationship it was – she seemed to want him all to herself.

Molly was also very wary around Lynn and Karen. They were very protective of Jason and the children. They are both strong-minded, independent ladies and not shy about calling you out on something if needed. It is what Jason always liked and admired about them. Lynn recalled an incident from the crèche she had founded with Mags.

One day, Sarah came over to me and called me 'Mammy'. It was a perfectly normal thing for her to do because other children were doing the same to their mothers and she was clearly confused about her own situation. It was perfectly understandable. But I felt it was important to mention this to Jason because I didn't want him getting upset about it. Molly was there and overheard us. The next thing there were three or four books on a table in the house with titles like 'Mommy Goes to Town' or 'Mommy Goes Shopping'. Molly had bought them and was reading them every day to Sarah.

Sarah didn't attend the crèche the day following the overheard conversation with a supposed cold. Sarah didn't return to the crèche until the following week. The next thing I heard was that Sarah was calling Molly 'Mom' or 'Mommy'. I remember wondering about it at the time because I thought it was very strange.

Molly also seemed to have bizarre stories to explain any questions raised about her life in the US. She told Lynn she was once engaged and her mother had planned a great white wedding but her boyfriend turned out to be gay and that's why she ran away. Whenever we had social events or gatherings, I noticed that she wanted Jason to be giving her his undivided attention. Anything less and you could see she was very unhappy and would act up. Jason dreaded her creating a scene.

Once, at an outing in Clare, the boys were preparing to go off golfing. Lynn told everyone to go and get ready and leave her alone with Molly, as she wanted to hear all about her life in the US. Molly was visibly horrified and everyone struggled to contain their laughter at the pained look on her face. Over time, I began to suspect that a lot of the stuff Molly was telling us was either exaggerated or simply made up. But I explained it away as someone trying to perhaps impress us or justify why, at her age and with her claimed education, she was working as a nanny for an Irish widower. We were all leading our busy daily lives. At the time, none of us saw any harm in her wild stories or exaggerations.

One bizarre incident followed a family holiday in the US where Dave and Dean, to celebrate their 40th and 18th birthdays respectively, went on a skydiving trip. Dean was enthused about the experience and told everyone who would listen about what it was like. Molly, on hearing about it, excitedly agreed and related for 20 minutes in astonishing detail her own skydiving jump in the US from years before.

When we relayed that story to her family during a subsequent US visit, her brothers laughed and told us Molly had never gone skydiving. Molly just sat there mute. I was extremely uncomfortable as I recalled the incredible level of detail she had gone into with her skydiving story. It was as if telling lies was second nature to her.

Catherine, Jack and Sarah's auntie, also noted peculiarities with Molly. 'Everyone tried to make her feel welcome and get her involved in things. But it was as if she didn't want to. Molly didn't seem to want to get involved in anything outside of Jack and Sarah,' Catherine said. 'I also realised she was telling lies about things. I have a brother who is a referee and Molly claimed that she too was a ref. But it quickly became clear she wasn't and was simply making things up.

'She could also be very odd about small things – if Sarah held my hand during a day out, Molly would immediately seem to take exception to it. I also found it very strange that we never met any of her friends even when I visited the US in 2012 with Colm [Catherine's partner].'

We all realised, as we got to know her, that Molly craved being the centre of attention – even if it meant telling outrageous lies or creating a drama. From 2008 to 2014, each Christmas Day when we all met up she would insist on having all her presents opened last – so she was the focus of all the festive attention, even in front of the children. Molly's first present was only opened after every other person there, including the children, had opened all their gifts.

My first major problem with Molly involved her taking my son Adam to a Limerick swimming pool. Due to a security incident involving a relative's child in the US, I had specifically asked Molly not to leave Adam, who was seven, alone in the changing rooms and to make sure he was OK at all times. Molly dropped Adam home that evening and he seemed a bit upset. I learned from him that Molly had told him to go into the men's changing rooms on his own and, when he emerged, there was no sign of Molly. He had to wait for her for what seemed ages in the reception area of the pool complex before she reappeared. I was not happy. I told Molly so and she never looked after our children again.

In May 2008, Lynn was flying to Lanzarote for a holiday and Jason told her that he was now involved in a relationship with Molly. He seemed almost guilty about it, as if moving on with his life was somehow a reflection on his relationship with Mags. We were all worried because I think everyone felt he was still emotionally vulnerable, very lonely and not in the best place to make clear decisions about his personal life. He was still grieving for Mags and we all understood that. I was by now increasingly apprehensive because things with Molly seemed to be moving very fast. Yet it was a very awkward situation because it was Jason's life and, if it made him happy, we were all loath to intervene.

It was clear that Jason was also conflicted over the speed with which things were progressing. In June 2008, he suggested that Molly went home to visit her family in the US. He wanted space to think and to slow things down with the relationship. Talking to Jason, I realised he somehow wanted to separate the relationship with Molly from that with his children. It was one thing to be dating her – it was entirely another thing to be dating her and have her living in the house looking after his children. It was a move Dave and myself fully supported.

Molly went home but clearly wasn't happy. Jason was then bombarded with emails and phone calls from Tennessee. He told none of us at the time what was happening. I was able to access copies of all Jason's email traffic after his death and they made for heartbreaking reading. For instance, on 8 August 2008, Molly wrote that it hurt to have someone she loved so dearly doubt her.

'I wish you wouldn't think of me as such a weapon for the kids. Shut up … it feels horrible and even if I was with you it would be eating me up and tearing me to pieces knowing you weren't sure you wanted me. Sorry, I sent more than I meant,' she wrote.

'I just want to be loved – not even as much as I love you. I just want to be loved back. What I am saying is that neither one of us should live life with so much doubt. It hurts to carry doubt and it hurts more to know that someone you love doubts you. Are you still there?'

Jason wrote to her explaining that things were moving too fast, that he was concerned for the children and that he wasn't sure about marrying

47

again after the devastation of Mags's death. 'I'm not made of stone,' he explained. 'I'm sick of fighting. I feel bad because I am as upset as you are. It hurts me too, you know. I just want a normal boy–girl relationship.

'You are right that (this) does put pressure on us to sink or swim. That is pressure that after five months we should not be under. We should be having fun getting to know one another. Going on dates – not husband and wife.'

Molly replied on 8 August: 'You want to stay together even though you know you won't want to marry me?' Another email warned Jason that: 'I know you don't want to lose me but I'm not sure you want to keep me either. I wish you were as sure about me as I am you. I'll be missing and mourning you and the kids for a long time to come.'

Other emails from Molly were short and succinct. 'Did I say I love you? I do.' Another warned Jason: 'I love you so much and won't understand if you want to throw away what we were lucky enough to get.'

A further email told Jason: 'I'm not one to really be OK with just sitting around while someone else makes up their mind – especially if what they have to make up their mind about is me. I obviously cannot persuade you into thinking you shouldn't throw us away.'

Throughout the emails, Jason is constantly pleading for understanding and, above all, for time to think. On occasions he asked Molly not to be cruel with some of her comments. In other emails, he challenges her on her claims that he is only hiding behind 'a sob story'. Jason, in an email on 5 August, bares his soul to Molly and reveals his inner fears about another relationship so soon after Mags's death.

He wrote:

I hate putting this on email but it is hard to talk properly. Please know that I miss you and love you so much. But I am scared, scared to let go in case I lose someone again or the kids lose someone again. I couldn't live through it. I really want to work through this Molly – it may take time but I want to try. Lot of love and please don't cry. You are the closest person to me and the last person on this Earth I want to hurt.

The young widower added that his primary fear was for his two children.

My concern is for Jack and Sarah – they have had enough tragedy in their short lives and while I know that they are resilient, I am nervous about putting them through anything further. I'm really scared Molly … I don't want to lose you but more so I don't want to risk Jack and Sarah losing another mother if we don't work out.

My poor brother must have been at his wits' end. I can imagine him wrestling with the fear that, if he ended the romance with Molly, maybe he was throwing away a second chance at happiness that life had offered him after Mags's death. Molly was also demanding that she be given a proper chance to say goodbye to the children if he ended their relationship. Even at the time, this struck me as very unusual. She had only known Jack and Sarah for a matter of weeks. Jason finally relented and said she could come back to Ireland but only if she got another job that somehow separated their romance from his life with the children.

In August 2008, Molly flew back to Ireland. She never got the job she had promised to find and the blurring of the lines in her relationship with Jason and with the children continued. In desperation, Jason asked Lynn if she could do part-time work at her crèche. Lynn agreed as a favour to her friend and Molly arrived for work on the first day dressed in an outfit straight out of a designer shop window. Molly had a hot cup of coffee in her hand, something never allowed near toddlers. When Lynn asked for her Montessori qualification papers, Molly blithely said they wouldn't transfer to Ireland. She also suggested that, if anything, she was overqualified.

Lynn doesn't stand on ceremony and warned her that, without proper credentials, Molly wasn't working at the crèche.

From August 2008, Molly effectively tried to install herself as the second mother to Jack and Sarah. I noticed that Jason was now concerned about Molly's reaction to social events. If Molly wasn't happy, the four of them would invariably leave early. She became the emotional fulcrum of all their lives. None of us knew it at the time but the emails also revealed that Jason and Molly had developed a roller-coaster relationship. Molly would single out something she was unhappy with and Jason would be bombarded with complaints about the issue until it was tackled to Molly's satisfaction.

Molly was by now also constantly complaining that she was living under Mags's shadow in the Ballyneety house. She told Jason that, to give their relationship a proper chance, they had to find a new home for a fresh beginning. This might seem a perfectly natural thing for any person to do when their partner had been in a previous relationship. But it was the manner in which Molly went about it that made us all very uneasy. Jason finally agreed to sell the house – I knew he was very undecided about it – and the final papers for the deal came to him for signature on 21 November 2009, the third anniversary of Mags's death. 'This is a sign I made a mistake,' a dispirited Jason told me at the time. Selling that house was the final step in letting go of his old dreams and previous happy life. It was a huge wrench for him.

Molly clearly didn't like the idea of living in a rented house in Raheen, so close to Dave, myself and our children. I also realised that she was now constantly complaining to Jason that she was homesick and hated life in Ireland, particularly the weather. Jason confided in me that she believed a move to the US would offer them all a new start – and much better opportunities later in life for Jack and Sarah. Having secured the sale of Jason and Mags's old home, Molly had now set her heart on a move back to the US.

My brother loved the US. His own life was an Irish version of the American dream – success delivered by hard work, personality and courage. Jason and Mags had spent their honeymoon in the US, visiting

Boston, Cape Cod and finally New York. They adored the holiday and never stopped talking about it.

Jason's employers, MPS, had been incredibly supportive after Mags's death and it just so happened that there was a vacancy for a plant manager at their North Carolina facility outside Lexington. Jason knew that if he applied for the transfer he had a very good chance of getting it. From Molly's point of view, it was a golden opportunity – Lexington is just five hours' drive from her hometown of Knoxville.

I didn't like the idea for very selfish reasons – I didn't want my brother on the other side of the Atlantic, and I most certainly didn't want to lose almost daily contact with Jack and Sarah. I tried to explain that as gently as I could to Jason. I also knew that he would miss Limerick and his family more than he perhaps understood. Other members of my family also didn't like the idea of Jason moving to the US. But I could appreciate his reasoning – God knows he had suffered enough since 2006. He had by now fallen hopelessly in love with Molly and judged that a move to the US might be critical to giving that love a chance to blossom and grow. Yet I felt a sliver of doubt about whether it was the right thing for him to do.

My response was to book him into three sessions with an Irish counsellor who had previously provided expert assistance to a local rugby hero, Alan Quinlan. I knew that would convince Jason to attend. Dave and I wanted Jason to get good advice – an outside perspective, if you like, on his life and where it was going. He deserved happiness and I did not want my love for him and the children to get in the way of what was best for them all. I paid for the sessions knowing that this would ensure Jason attended – he was so loyal he couldn't bear the thought of me being out of pocket for something done for him. He did attend and, ultimately, decided that he should follow his heart. Jason explained to me that Molly wouldn't stay in Ireland and had given him an ultimatum – if he didn't follow her to the US, as she demanded, he risked losing her.

Critically, Jason was also thinking not just of himself but of the children. 'I can't take another mother away from the children,' he bluntly told me as he came to the decision to move from Limerick to the US.

By this stage, I had come to the conclusion that Molly was definitely not normal, at least not our definition of normal. I had discovered that she was using different spelling variations of her name. I remember wondering why anyone would bother to do that. I also realised that, in all her time here, no friends had ever visited her from the US, which struck me as really strange, particularly for someone who seemed to be making a big issue about being homesick.

She had been visited by her parents, Tom and Sharon, while in Ireland. We tried to be as hospitable as we could and do honour to the old Irish adage of *céad míle fáilte* or one hundred thousand welcomes. We organised outings to famous tourist sights around Limerick and the mid-west for them, such as Adare and the Cliffs of Moher. The visit made Molly happy, which now seemed increasingly important to Jason.

Lynn later told me that she thought Molly was 'normal crazy', certainly not the type of crazy that was capable of inflicting the horror that was to unfold. It was the same for Karen, who felt there was something strange about the girl, as if she was dealing with all of us via a mask or disguise. Damian echoed that opinion. Tragically, none of this information was pooled between us at the time. Karen, Lynn and I were each Jason's confidantes. But we didn't really know each other that well then. We met up at the odd social occasion or children's parties. But we weren't sufficiently friendly to talk openly about Jason and Molly between 2008 and 2011. If we had, and if we had shared everything we all separately knew about Molly, every single one of us would have taken a much tougher line about Jason's proposed move to the US.

We put a lot of it down to oddness. Molly would often totally transform her look from one week to the next – going from a denim cowgirl look to wearing businesswoman power-suits. There always seemed to be a 'new'

Molly about to be unveiled, often in response to a character in a book she had read or a film she had seen.

Jason proposed to Molly in Freddy's Bistro in Limerick on Valentine's Day 2010 – he even got down on one knee to ask her to marry him. They immediately came to tell his family and friends. We did our best to look happy and delighted for them but we were all pretty shocked, Lynn recalled.

What should have been a happy evening for Jason also turned sour because Molly was clearly totally underwhelmed by the manner in which he announced their engagement to his family and friends. Maybe she had expected a grander gesture or a public declaration of undying adoration. Whatever happened certainly didn't meet Molly's standards and she clearly made her feelings known to Jason because they left early that night. But what she never once gave Jason credit for was how gut-wrenchingly hard it must have been for him to tell Mags's oldest friends to their faces that he was now going to marry someone else. I wore my happy face but inside I was a storm of emotions, from worry to alarm. My biggest fear was what was going to happen next.

When Jason broke the engagement news to me and Dave, we hugged, congratulated them and shared a glass of Champagne. Their wedding was planned for June 2011, the same month that Jason and Mags had got married. I noticed that Molly was slowly eradicating all tangible memories and reminders of Mags. She even seemed intent on assuming ownership of the various anniversaries shared by Mags and Jason. Bit by bit, she was trying to erase all traces of Mags from the world the children inhabited.

In hindsight, I believe Jason thought selling the house might slow the pace of the relationship. Then I suspect he thought the engagement would ease things and offer Molly the 'public verification' she sought in terms of their romance. It would, he thought, allow the relationship to be tested by time and provide him with the space he needed to find himself again. But things were moving to Molly's pace and her plan, not Jason's timetable. My brother just couldn't understand that. Then again, none of us did back in 2010/11. Jason's friend Karen explained it best when, after 2015, we were trying to piece together precisely how the murder had unfolded and whether we could have spotted the signs of impending tragedy. Karen said it was clear that Jason was being subjected to a form of 'gaslighting' or manipulation. He was being shrewdly made to question his own judgement, doubt his own instincts and even distance himself, without knowing it, from the people who 'had his back'. He was also slowly having his confidence eroded through barbed comments from Molly about his weight, his diet, his clothes and even his education. He was being made to feel that he was very lucky such a glamorous young woman was in his life and that, no matter what, he couldn't afford to lose her.

The galling thing is that none of us understood this at the time, otherwise we would have immediately intervened.

Molly was playing her own subtle, careful game and she was now about to savour her most significant victory by persuading Jason his future lay in the US and not in Ireland. Critically, Molly would have Jason to herself in North Carolina – he wouldn't have his family or friends there for support or advice.

4

A Bleak Marriage

Bleak House was stunningly beautiful and bathed in searing Tennessee heat that June day in 2011. It would have been impossible to select a more magical venue for a wedding. The wedding was being held outdoors and the staff had even arranged for special lanterns to be hung from the trees and shrubs, which meant guests savoured an atmosphere that seemed straight from a Hollywood epic by nightfall. Fairy lights were sprinkled throughout the greenery under the covered walkway that descended from each tier of the garden and twinkled in the dusk. Soft music played in the background. The food was delicious, the service was impeccable and the staff couldn't do more to help guests enjoy their day. Dinner was served on a terrace with Bleak House as the backdrop and it was jaw-droppingly impressive. The house was chosen by Molly and, in particular, by her father, Tom. Bleak House had long associations with the Confederacy and, for a time, had been the headquarters of the famous Confederate General James Longstreet during the battles of the Tennessee campaign. It was also the base of the local chapter of the Daughters of the Confederacy. The ceremony was hugely expensive – yet it was specifically what Molly had wanted. She had wanted the full Disney-princess wedding. Almost 100 guests were invited. Jason had given €45,000 ($49,000) to Tom Martens towards the cost of the wedding, something he never told us about at the time. Tom readily accepted the cash – and certainly portrayed to everyone that he had carried the full cost. It was turning out to be a lovely day until the high-pitched screeching alerted us to the fact that something was badly wrong.

Molly was screaming and crying, creating an escalating scene and becoming the focus of every eye at the wedding. My panicked brain realised that Dave and myself were somehow involved in the awful soap opera unfolding in front of us even though we hadn't a clue what was happening. Adam, my son, wandered by sipping from a McDonald's soft-drink cup, blissfully ignoring the commotion. I cringed when I realised that most of the guests gathered on the lawn of Bleak House in this stunning Tennessee setting were now gazing over at Molly screaming at Dave, wondering what on earth was going on. Dave looked stunned. Molly screamed at my husband as he sat beside her brother Bobby and his wife, Ellie.

My son Dean told me later that Dave looked dumbfounded as Molly launched into a tirade against him, shouting, 'Do you realise what you have done? Do you realise what you have done – you have ruined my wedding. Do you not know how much this cost?' Dean said that Dave looked as if he wanted the earth to open up and swallow him as every eye in the wedding turned quizzically to stare at him. Dave is a quiet, reserved man who prefers to shun the limelight. But my husband is not someone to be trifled with. The instant Molly raised the issue of money, Dave turned in his seat and stared at her. 'Two people got married here today, not just one. You paid for nothing.' Molly stormed off from Dave and stomped over to Jason, who was dancing with Sarah. My brother refused to get involved in the drama. Molly then turned and dramatically ran up the stairs and back inside the house. She vanished in a flood of tears, her gorgeous princess-style wedding gown sweeping along behind her as she ascended the steps to Bleak House. If I hadn't been so mortified at what was happening, I would have laughed at how the drama resembled a Scarlett O'Hara scene from *Gone with the Wind*. Molly was quickly followed by her mother, Sharon. Her brothers seemed oblivious. I had begun to realise that they were used to this type of behaviour from Molly.

On the steps in front of me, one of Molly's bridesmaids, Suzannah 'Susie' West Vincent, was looking ashen-faced, her own family rushing to support and comfort her. Dean watched as Tom Martens stalked directly over to Dave. 'Dad was sitting down and Tom was standing directly behind him, staring at the back of his head. He wasn't moving away. Bobby intervened and ushered his father away before the scene became any worse. I just didn't know what was going on. It was off-the-wall kind of stuff,' Dean recalled. Bobby later offered Dave an apology. But my husband insisted none was necessary. 'I told him you have nothing to apologise for. You and your wife have been nothing but gracious and pleasant to us all day. You are not responsible for your sister,' Dave said. What I hadn't realised initially was that, seconds before she had screamed at my husband, Molly had also verbally lashed out at Susie. A short time later, Susie, who was maid of honour, and her family quietly left the wedding. She was one of Molly's oldest friends but was apparently dismissed without a thought because of an incident most people would laugh at. I was staring in horror at Dave who was equally shell-shocked over what was going on. Molly seemed to have become even more irritated because Jason was staying out of the drama and hadn't come over to berate Dave.

Susie, a kind-hearted and bubbly person whom we had instantly liked, had been checking on the children's table at the wedding and realised that Adam looked crestfallen. She asked him what was wrong and he explained that he was allergic to eggs so he couldn't eat the meal and was hungry. Susie took him by the hand and brought him inside the house to see if the kitchen could organise something special for him. Unfortunately, the kitchen was closed by that stage and the bridesmaid, remembering a fast-food outlet from her drive to the wedding venue, decided to get him a Happy Meal and sort the problem. Adam was delighted. But when Molly spotted him walking across the lawn with the McDonald's cup she totally lost it. She started shouting at her bridesmaid, claiming she had gone to enormous lengths to organise a special meal and now her entire day had been ruined. Somehow, probably because Adam was our son, the blame was equally apportioned between the bridesmaid, Dave and myself.

Jason gazed at us with a look of bewilderment and embarrassment on his face. After a short time, he slowly walked back into Bleak House to try and console his distraught new bride. One of the bridesmaids later told us they had seen Molly in the bridal changing room lying on a sofa, kicking and punching the pillows like a child having a tantrum.

Sharon Martens made it perfectly clear she blamed us when she privately took Dave to task minutes later. I didn't get a chance to chat to Jason on our own for the rest of the wedding day. The incident created an unspoken rift that was only resolved when Jason and myself had a long clear-the-air conversation when he flew home three months later. That three-month period was the only time in our lives there was any difficulty or coolness between us. But I was willing to put up with Molly's manipulations if it meant the difference between seeing Jason, Jack and Sarah or not.

I also made a point of contacting Susie the following day to say how sorry I was to see her leave the wedding. By then, I knew Molly had been spreading stories about us and I wanted to thank Susie for her kindness, especially to Adam. In a series of texts, she told me she was actually glad to leave the wedding early because 'the whole day had been so uptight and tense'. But for the fact that it was so serious, I felt like laughing at Susie's reference to Molly as 'Bridezilla'. Susie also commented on what she noted was the 'mean spiritedness all week. I don't know why people have to create hurtful drama especially to those that care most about them.' She then told me she felt sorry for Jason. She said that, in her opinion, the behaviour of Molly and some of her family members had been 'nutz' that day. 'I am appalled at how rude some people are – I am done. It was nice meeting you and I truly think you and the rest of your family are nice despite the negativity I had heard.' I acknowledged to Susie that I was aware of and upset about the misconception some people had about our family because of the lies and stories being told about us by Molly. One text I sent Susie was prophetic in terms of its observation. 'We have been nothing but nice and helpful to Molly while she was in Ireland – she has changed dramatically in the number of weeks since she left,' I wrote. Privately, I was relieved that my elderly parents had not attended the wedding to witness Molly's behaviour. It was an ominous incident on a day that was supposed to be a fairy tale for all involved. The stunning bride, in her expensive princess dress, marrying the young, handsome Irish widower, with his two children deeply involved in the wedding ceremony as page boy and flower girl. It was supposed to be the most potent of symbols of a fresh start and a new, hopeful beginning. The stuff that romance is truly made of. Sadly, it was anything but.

While Molly insisted on the best venue, flowers, food and drinks for her special day, not to mention two lavish wedding cakes, she opposed other spending. My son Dean had been involved in the bridal party when Jason married Mags. There were only 13 years between Jason and Dean and there were times when Jason was more like an older brother to him than an uncle. Jason wanted Dean at the Knoxville wedding but Dean demurred because he was in the middle of his apprenticeship and didn't have the money to attend. Jason wanted to pay for his airfare but Molly vehemently opposed it. In the end, Jason paid for Dean's ticket but was discreet about the fact. Jason also invited Catherine and members of the Fitzpatrick family. But they felt it best not to attend the wedding. He also hosted Catherine and her partner, Colm, when they travelled to the US. Jason never visited Ireland without making a point of going to visit the Fitzpatrick home in Pallaskenry.

Some time before the wedding, Jason was at home in Ireland and met Dean at our house. Dean found some issues easier to talk over with Jason than either Dave or me, particularly when it came to relationships. He was involved in a romance that was ending and he wanted advice from Jason about how to end it without causing unnecessary hurt. Jason immediately took Dean out for a walk to chat it over. 'He said to me: "Sometimes, Dean, in life people just need to settle for things in relationships." But

Jason didn't look at me when he said this. He looked at the ground. There was an awkward silence and I felt he was a bit embarrassed. I never forgot it though – and I wondered if it was advice to me or a half comment on his own circumstances,' Dean said.

On the wedding day, after Molly vanished into Bleak House in tears, all I wanted was for it to be finished and for us to get out of Tennessee. My family were shell-shocked over what had just happened and felt deeply embarrassed. We were all mortified because, even though we had done nothing to cause the scene, no one wants to be seen to contribute in any way to spoiling such a special day. The rest of the wedding vanished in a blur of hushed conversations and furtive looks to see if the bride would reappear. I was weary of the mind games, the emotional roller-coaster and all the drama. During the wedding ceremony rehearsal, Molly had dramatically fainted. The heat in Tennessee had soared to 38 degrees Celsius (almost 101 degrees Fahrenheit) so if anyone should have fainted it should have been the frazzled Irish contingent who almost had steam coming from under their collars. In a rock-strewn piece of ground, Molly gently collapsed onto the only available stretch of grass. I saw members of her family rolling their eyes and walking away.

It was at that point we also discovered that Molly's uncle, Michael Earnest, would serve as the 'Reverend' for the marriage ceremony itself. Michael, who worked for a US federal agency called the Special Inspector General for Afghanistan Reconstruction (SIGAR), had, so we were told, done an Internet course to allow him use the title 'Reverend'. The centrepiece of the ceremony was the lighting of a special 'unity' candle by Sharon and myself as supervised by 'Reverend Earnest'. We all found it somewhat bizarre, given that we were used to the more traditional form of wedding ceremony with a properly ordained cleric. But we thought it best not to say anything lest we offend Molly and her family.

The week leading up to the wedding had also been challenging. We had flown over for the ceremony a week early and, during our US stay, had decided to briefly link up with Dave's sister, Linda, who at that time was living in Atlanta, Georgia. Not wanting to impose too much on the wedding build-up, we rented a cabin in the Smoky Mountains on the Tennessee–North Carolina border, which was every bit as beautiful as it sounds. Molly and Jason met us at the cabin and Molly then invited me to attend her bridal shower or hen party the following evening. It was being held in Knoxville, which was almost a four-hour round trip away. I would have loved to attend but it would have ruined a full day for Dave, who would not only have had to drive to Knoxville but then wait around to drive us back to the cabin again. I politely apologised to Molly for not being able to attend but I got the impression she was offended by my non-attendance even though she had waited until just the day before to tell me about the party. It was as if she was deliberately creating specific situations where I appeared to be uncooperative to Jason. It was the beginning of years of trying to undermine our relationship.

I later heard there was consternation at the bridal shower because Molly had, with typical drama, waited until the end of the evening to confirm who was maid of honour. Several of her friends had been led to believe they would get the honour and there was obvious disappointment when they didn't. Molly took umbrage at their disappointment and the evening apparently ended in rows, tears and disappearances, or so we were told. I was told later that some party-goers were driving around Knoxville city centre for hours into the early morning looking for guests who had stalked off in a huff.

Jason had suggested that Marilyn's daughter, Kate, who was 14, might serve as one of Molly's bridesmaids. Molly had agreed and all Kate's sizes were sent from Ireland to the US weeks before the wedding. We arrived to find that Molly had selected deep-pink-hued dresses for the bridesmaids – and Kate's was at least two sizes too big. Kate was lost in the folds of the dress. Sharon Martens brusquely dismissed her concerns and said the dress could be pinned up and would be fine on the day. Kate was so upset that Marilyn went to Sharon and asked whether the dress would be properly altered by a seamstress. Marilyn politely said that, if it wasn't, Kate wouldn't be walking down the aisle as a bridesmaid. Sharon took great offence and it appeared to be yet another example of the Irish contingent causing problems. There was an also an issue with wedding-party suits, which had originally been fitted in Limerick with a plan to bring them to the States. Molly was unhappy with this and changed the arrangements so that they were supplied in Knoxville. The lads arrived for the fitting to discover the suits provided were either too big or too small. 'It was very embarrassing,' Brendan recalled.

Tom and Sharon had kindly agreed to host a pre-wedding party for all the Irish 'in-laws' who had travelled over. We were told the party would be from 6 p.m. to 9 p.m. and would be a barbecue in the garden of their stunning home. I like to bring flowers to such events to thank the host but couldn't find a local florist so a bottle of wine from a local off-licence had to suffice. They didn't have coolers so the wine was at room temperature. When I gave the bottle to Sharon and thanked her for going to such trouble for us she simply replied: 'Thank you for the bottle of warm wine.' I didn't think it was a good start to the evening.

Tom, who we knew was very house-proud, had placed a sand bucket at the corner of his home where smokers could dispose of their cigarettes. Paul smoked at the time but was so conscious of the Martens that he decided to walk entirely off their property and smoke while standing almost on the street. It was only later I discovered that Tom and Sharon never once spoke to Paul during the entire barbecue. Somehow, he had become *persona non grata* with the Martens.

I noticed there was no sign of Molly and was told she wasn't feeling well and was in bed with a headache. When I went up to see her, she was curled up in a ball on the bed and weeping. To be honest, I was shocked. I tried to comfort her and suggested that maybe she would feel better if she came outside into the sunshine and joined the children by the swimming pool in the back garden. She seemed pitifully sad in the bed and I couldn't help but think that this wasn't how a bride was supposed to be just days before her wedding. I gently gave her the special gift I had brought, a beautiful necklace, which I intended as a token of welcome to the Corbett family. I then left the room. But Molly remained deeply upset and never appeared in the garden to greet the guests.

When I went back outside, I tried my best to be sociable. Tom told me he had arranged a white-water rafting expedition for everyone at 8 a.m. the following day. I was stunned. It was the first I had heard of it and, given that we had only 48 hours to the wedding, I wasn't sure it was the best idea. I politely explained that we already had plans for the following day and couldn't avail of his kind offer. But I stressed how appreciative we were of his efforts. Privately, I thought an expedition like that needed to be flagged well in advance, particularly so close to the wedding day. But it was clear that Tom didn't take kindly to our decision to decline his invitation. He seemed very taken aback. From then on, I found him downright rude to us. I was so concerned by his attitude that I even offered to pay any costs that he might be out of pocket for from the rafting expedition.

If I'm honest, I found it impossible to fully relax at the party. There was a sense, commented on by all of us afterwards, that the atmosphere was one of barely concealed condescension. It was almost as if we were being gauged and judged, our behaviour and every comment being remarked upon. I put the atmosphere down to the fact that Tom, who can come across as quite arrogant, was simply being overly protective of his only daughter and maybe excessively careful towards his new Irish in-laws. But when that pre-wedding party was being discussed at Tom and Molly's 2017 murder trial, as you will read later, it was clear that something much deeper was involved. Tom had already taken an intense dislike to Jason. While all of us accepted just one drink at the barbecue and tried our best to be sociable and appreciative of their hospitality, Tom from that point on also extended his dislike to our entire family. Yet, to this day, I can't point to any one specific reason.

The tragedy is that none of us understood just how troubled the relationship between Jason and Molly was, right up to the point of their wedding. I only discovered it when I went back over Jason's emails in the build-up to the murder trial. It was horrifying to discover that, in 2009 and 2010, Jason found himself at the centre of a succession of emotionally charged rows over the fact that Molly wanted to get married and wanted to move to the US. Every time he pleaded for time to consider their next move, he was met with outbursts about him not caring for Molly and using his children as an excuse not to move to the US. One email from 23 October 2009 illustrates the point. Molly wrote: 'I am not going to wait around forever while you change your mind back and forth. It really, really hurts. I am not strong enough to handle it … sorry for everything, as usual, I am sure I caused it all.' Jason replied: 'I am very sure I want to spend the rest of my life with you and I want to move to the US.' Just over three months before their wedding, Molly had packed up, left Jason and the children and travelled to the US to supervise arrangements. On 14 March 2011 she sent a storming email to Jason about their move to North Carolina and what she claimed were the sacrifices she was making for them. Molly even blamed Jason for her having to postpone foot surgery in Knoxville. 'I am in a great deal of pain at least one week out of four and I will more than likely be unable to have a child without undergoing the operation. This is all seemingly unimportant to you.'

I believed you when you told me we should try for a child after marrying. I believed this was exciting for you. I feel so, so, so, so, so stupid, ridiculous, ashamed and humiliated for believing in you and I will look like an idiot to everyone. I know, I know – who cares what other people think? I care that I look (I am) an absolute fool who believed you loved me and every other sentiment that came out of your mouth.

Jason reacted and asked Molly why she was threatening him and said he couldn't understand the reasons for her anger. He also cited emails where Molly had reacted to such issues as their new house in the US, furniture, cars and even a pair of earrings. On 17 April 2011, literally just weeks before their wedding, Jason wrote:

> It is really not fair Molly and not very nice. We can't even talk on the phone. You don't have to go on about 'who cares if I don't have earrings?' It is so unnecessary Molly and, as usual, over the top. There are, I am sure, people who can live without an extra pair of earrings. Of course you do not need to be one of them. I just bought you a car for $22,000. It is not as if I don't get you things but if I mention that money is tight or something is expensive, then you go on autopilot.

Eleven days later, after another emotional email from Molly, Jason again found himself appealing for calm. On 28 April he wrote to Molly:

> I won't be able to make a go of it in the States under this emotional pressure you are placing on me. You just accuse me of things off the cuff when you have no valid reason for doing so. Please think about what I actually said in conversation and point out what I did wrong? [But] you bang the phone down – you sound like an emotional wreck … I am moving to your country to be with you. I need YOU to be strong for us and not constantly crying, accusing me of things, banging down phones. You are supposedly getting what you want and yet you sound more sad now than ever. You even told me you hate talking to me because you end up curling up in a ball?

Jason once again reaffirmed his love for Molly and pleaded for calm in their relationship. 'I am truly sorry for your latest health setback and I am sorry for your pain. I do love you but you sound like the phrase "be careful what you wish for as you might get it". I do think you are doing great with all the jobs.'

Molly instantly fired back an email that claimed Jason was the one emotionally threatening her all the time. In a message typed entirely in capital letters Molly raised everything from sex to her health and from missing the children to the family's US move. 'I am an emotional wreck right now – I have every right to be … I will hang up every time you threaten me. That is not how a relationship works.' She even accused Jason of 'putting on a show' over his relationship with her just for the benefit of his children. A few minutes later, she sent Jason another email warning that, if he truly loved her, he would ring a named estate agent within 20 minutes and give her his banking details in relation to a house that Molly had picked out in North Carolina for them. 'I am sure I have more faults, those seem to be the most significant, so please examine them and decide if I am worth it.'

But one of the most startling passages in all the emails I studied between 2008 and 2015 came next. Molly wrote to my brother:

> I do love you and would live or die for you or either of our children. I am a pretty good mom. I am mildly attractive. I am somewhat intelligent. I am a decent cook. I am generally good in social situations. I am capable and willing to do a lot. I have made you happy in the past and will try my best to be good enough for you always. I think I could be a great wife.

The association of death with a relationship, almost as if to prove commitment to it, struck me as alarming. Why would Molly say something like that? And why would she go to such lengths to reassure Jason about what she brought to the relationship? The wedding had also gone ahead despite Molly revealing to Jason just weeks before the ceremony that she had a history of diagnosed mental health problems. They had known each other for three years and Molly had waited until the ceremony was almost at hand to reveal that she had been treated for manic depression and bipolar disorder. It was devastating for my brother. He was obviously in love with Molly but was being driven to distraction by the bizarre and inexplicable mood swings and emotional confrontations. Now he understood why.

Paul was one of the first that Jason contacted. 'He was very upset about it. He just didn't know what to do,' Paul recalled.

He knew Molly suffered from bouts of depression but not that she had diagnosed psychiatric problems. Shortly before Molly left for North Carolina, I dropped Jason home after a golf outing and, despite the fact it was only around 4 p.m. or 5 p.m., his rented house at Raheen was in darkness and all the blinds were drawn. When we went in, Molly was lying on the sitting room floor after pulling lumps out of her hair. I didn't know what to say or do – it was quite embarrassing, really. Jason just cuddled her, picked her up and helped her upstairs to her bedroom. Then, just as I was leaving, he told me that she had told him she suffered from a bit of depression.

Jason knew that depression and mental illness issues impacted thousands of families across Ireland – a friend of mine was diagnosed as bipolar. With love, support and proper treatment, people can overcome their illnesses and lead full and happy lives. He was determined that his support would help Molly back to health. But I got the sense that rather than be open about her mental health issues, Molly had spent years trying to hide them, with predictable consequences.

She only revealed part of the truth to Jason. She didn't go into the full details of her previous relationships, the fact she had been in an Atlanta psychiatric clinic just weeks before she had travelled to Ireland in 2008 or that she had once been on up to 16 medications daily. Molly's mental health issues dated all the way back to her teenage years but Jason was given the impression they had only been an issue for a relatively short period of time. He was left reeling by the news. But I suspect he felt that Molly could be helped to recover and would return to being the person she was when he first met her in 2008 in the supportive atmosphere of a loving marriage. The decision to proceed with the wedding was typical of the generous, kind-hearted and caring person that Jason was. I believe he never lost faith that love could overcome anything and that he felt he could help her. It was a decision that would ultimately cost him his life.

I have in my possession an 11-page typed essay by Molly with a single page of handwritten inserts, along with a separate diary about her father, his depression and her parents' relationship. The essay was entitled 'Molly's Inferno' and was apparently written as some kind of schoolwork. It is a bizarre, disturbing piece that seems inspired by Dante and involves Molly's own vision of the various circles of hell. But two elements of the story brought an icy chill to my soul. In one image, Molly writes about trying to help two abandoned and abused children through social services. In another, she writes of being surrounded by the 'pure hate of the truly lost'. 'And so, I ran from the spreading virus of the passion to kill and found myself again in the hopeless haze I had awoken to,' she wrote. The final, awful image of the essay is Molly writing of meeting a young woman being punished in hell for leaving two small children to suffocate while strapped into their car seats. I am not a psychiatrist but only a tortured mind could conceive of the grim images in that essay. It was dominated by constructions of pain and death, most alarmingly the death of children, and the punishment of those responsible for the loss of those innocents. Jason was never aware of these documents. Shortly before Molly left Limerick for the US, she gave me a present of a book, *A Reliable Wife*. It was a gesture typical of the sweet-hearted Molly we'd gotten to know in 2008/2009. But when I looked at the book, after she had left, I discovered it was about a woman who planned to murder her husband. A synopsis of the book read: 'In the bitter cold, Ralph Truitt, a successful businessman, stands alone on the train platform waiting for the woman who answered his newspaper advertisement for "a reliable wife". But when Catherine Land steps off the train from Chicago, she is not the "simple, honest woman" that Ralph is expecting. She is both complex and devious, haunted by a terrible past and motivated by greed, Her plan is simple – she will win this man's devotion and then, ever so slowly, she will poison him and leave Wisconsin a wealthy widow.' I found it strange at the time but, years later, I couldn't help but wonder whether it was a deliberate hint to us of things to come.

God only knows what was going through Jason's mind as his wedding day finally drew to a close. The very name of Bleak House probably accurately reflected his private concerns as to what was now going on in his life. It breaks my heart to recall how Jason's wedding to Molly cost multiples of what his marriage to Mags cost – and yet they were worlds apart in terms of the unbridled joy, happiness and hope involved. On what was supposed to be the happiest day of their lives, Jason couldn't seem to escape the emotional soap opera. In the 72 hours before the wedding, Molly wouldn't let Jason out of her sight. Paul had wanted to have a private chat with him at the dress-suit fitting but Molly arrived at the rental store and never left Jason's side. When it was suggested the men might take some time on their own, Molly insisted she had an errand she needed Jason to help her with. I suspect her eagle-eyed focus on Jason was linked to the evening wedding-rehearsal party in Knoxville. It didn't bode well that, while everyone was out dancing, the DJ invited Brendan 'Blondie' O'Callaghan to sing and the song selected for him was the Elvis Presley classic 'Suspicious Minds'. I still have a video clip of it.

Michael Earnest, who was also at the Knoxville pub, was incredibly warm and friendly. It was as if he took it on himself to help make all the Irish guests feel at home. His friendliness was greatly appreciated by all of us on an evening that should have been a relaxing get-together but somehow was nothing less than tense. During the evening, Jenny Walker, a bridesmaid of Molly's, had commented to some of the group how romantic it was that Molly was fulfilling Mags's final wishes. Paul, for one, was gobsmacked. He asked the woman what on earth she was talking about. Rattled, Jenny explained how Molly had been a pen-pal of Mags's and the Irish woman had asked her to look out for her children if anything ever happened to her. Paul immediately informed us but, try as we might, we couldn't get Jason alone in the 24 hours before the wedding to ask him if he was aware of precisely what fiction Molly was now claiming as fact. It was only after the wedding ceremony we learned that Molly had also spun another story to her friend Susie – that she was Jack and Sarah's godmother and that was the reason she had initially gone to Ireland in 2008. She claimed she had travelled to Limerick to take care of Jack and Sarah after Mags died from cancer.

What horrified me was that this woman, who seemed to struggle with truth and lies, was now caring for my niece and nephew. I was also increasingly concerned about what else she had lied about. Marilyn added further to the confusion with the shocking revelation that a guest of Molly's had commented to her at the wedding on how Sarah was the spitting image of her mother. Marilyn asked how the woman had known Mags, presuming she must have seen photos of Jason's wife in an album. The American woman, looking perplexed, said she was referring to Molly, Sarah's mother. The ensuing conversation revealed the woman had been told that Molly was Sarah's biological mother – and had even heard from Molly about how difficult the labour had been.

Paul, despite being a member of the wedding party, found himself seated at the bottom table at the reception at Bleak House, physically as far away from Jason and Molly at the top table as he could be. It was as deliberate an insult as you could imagine. We were embarrassed for him and his wife, Simone. But he never raised a word of complaint. Molly had handled the seating arrangements personally. 'If I was seated any further away, myself and Simone would have been in the river,' Paul had joked. Almost as an afterthought, a member of the Martens family asked him if he wanted to say a few words at the wedding. 'I told them I didn't want to make any speeches because they wouldn't like what I had to say.' But Paul was determined that his friend should know what had been happening around Molly. Try as he might, however, he couldn't get

Jason alone before the ceremony. As Jason and Molly walked up to the area that doubled as a marriage altar at Bleak House, Paul was whispering desperately to his friend's back: 'It's not too late, it's not too late.'

As the wedding concluded, Molly walked to the limousine to be driven away with her new husband. Before Jason could walk from the dancefloor to follow her into the back seat, Paul grabbed his elbow and took him aside for a brief chat. By that point, Molly's eyes were red-rimmed from her earlier tantrum. Paul recalled:

I told him what Molly had said about Mags. I also told him that I'd seen how happy he was on the day he married Mags. But he looked absolutely miserable here. That's not how it should be – it was supposed to be the happiest day of his life. I told him there was something he could do about it. I whispered into his ear: 'You know, you don't have to get into that car – you can just walk away.' But Jason shook his head and explained he couldn't take a second mother away from the children. It was Jack and Sarah he was most concerned about rather than himself.

None of us realised that it was already too late. Jason and Molly had already married in a civil ceremony. The Bleak House ceremony was simply Molly wanting to have a lavish party at which she was the centre of attention.

It was the act of a true friend, courageous and selfless. Paul was willing to risk his friendship with Jason to act in what he perceived as his pal's best long-term interests. None of us knew it at the time but fate hinged on the next few seconds. Jason smiled, gently brushed Paul's hand off and walked up to get into the back of the car to be driven off. Molly now had Jason all to herself.

As the lights of the wedding car receded into the night, I couldn't help but feel that something had shifted for ever. It was an ominous sensation on which to end a wedding.

Molly wanted an exotic honeymoon so Jason took her to Cancun in Mexico. We were flying home the day after the wedding, and Jason and Molly were due to fly to their Mexican resort that evening. But first Jason called to our Knoxville hotel to say goodbye. Molly was with him and it was clear she was only there because Jason had insisted on it.

Molly attempted to apologise for her behaviour but immediately launched into a saga of how someone else was to blame for the entire debacle. With Molly, it was always someone else's fault. Dave wasn't having any of it, as he believed her apology wasn't sincere and was only being offered because Jason had insisted on it. He was also livid over her selfish behaviour. 'You humiliated me in front of a hundred people and I have nothing to say to you,' Dave told her. There was silence and then Molly fled down the hallway in hysterics. The 400-kilometre drive from Knoxville to Charlotte for our flight home was one of the longest journeys I can recall. We were all upset over the awful events of the previous few days. What shocked me most was that Molly was now totally unrecognisable from the person we had met in Limerick in 2008 – it was as if she had mutated into someone else. But the die was cast.

Jason had by now applied for and secured his transfer from Limerick to the MPS plant at Lexington in North Carolina. He enjoyed the new challenge, made firm friends within the plant and got involved in all the MPS social activities in North Carolina, such as sports days and barbecues. The couple settled on a family home at Panther Creek Court in Wallburg, roughly halfway between Lexington and Winston-Salem. It was a gorgeous house in a gated community and Jason paid almost €370,000 ($400,000) for the property. As he had sold his home in Limerick, the Panther Creek Court property was purchased for cash and without a mortgage. Best of all, Jason found himself living beside great neighbours who would become close friends. From 2015, without being asked, neighbours David Fritzsche and Tony Turner mowed the lawn around Jason's old house every time they mowed their own grass. Tony explained: 'We do it to respect Jason's memory. The love we had for him as a true friend wouldn't let us leave his grass overgrown. It was difficult initially, as his parting was too fresh, particularly as some of the residual blood stains remained on the sidewalk. The first time I cut the grass, my eyes were watery but I held a stiff upper lip and continued as did Dave. It was the right thing to do and continues to be.'

In 2011, Jason gave Molly €75,000 ($80,000) to furnish the house to her tastes. The property had a spacious basement bedroom that could be used for guests – mostly Tom and Sharon Martens, who became regular visitors to Panther Creek Court. Molly was also bought a luxury car. Jack and Sarah were enrolled in a local school and preschool. Both made the adjustment to life in the US very well. They made firm friends in the quiet estate community and Jack became a very talented swimmer and got involved in a myriad of local sports. Sarah boasted a wide circle of friends in school, though it quickly emerged that Molly seemed intent on treating her like a human Barbie doll – Sarah arrived in school every day wearing a different dress. While other youngsters had clothing suitable for rough and tumble school play, Sarah arrived looking as though she had stepped out of a Laura Ashley catalogue.

Just four months after the wedding, Molly secretly visited a North Carolina divorce lawyer and asked what her rights were to Jack and Sarah. She was told that, while she was Jason's second wife and had rights to his property and financial assets in the US, she was not the children's natural mother and therefore the children would, in any straightforward divorce, go to the sole custody of their father. Molly then claimed that Jason had promised to sign adoption papers giving her equal rights to Jack and Sarah. It was an issue that Tom Martens would repeatedly raise with my brother. Tom would later claim that Jason had promised to sign the papers as part of his marriage commitments. His failure to do so was portrayed almost as though he was breaking a marriage contract. But, unlike his old Limerick house, the engagement and the move to the US, on this issue there was no budging Jason. I am convinced that Molly's antics in the weeks before the wedding, coupled with his shock at learning about her bizarre claims about being Mags's pen-pal, had convinced Jason there was no way she should be allowed to adopt his children. He even placed Jack and Sarah's passports in safekeeping outside the family home. The adoption was never going to happen because Molly had broken Jason's trust.

On 28 November 2012, Jason sent an email to a law firm in Charlotte, North Carolina, asking for advice about what was being demanded. 'I have been married to Molly for just over a year now and we live in Forsyth County. We have lived here for just over a year. Is it possible to structure this that if I ever get divorced (not planning to) that the right to keep the children is with me over Molly? What would you need from me if we were to proceed?'

But Molly wasn't going to give up easily. Having gotten all she wanted – marriage, the children and the move to North Carolina – she seemed to decide that Jason was now surplus to requirements and that her life would be better off with just Jack and Sarah. But it was clear that in any divorce scenario she would lose the children. So what could she do? One of the things I find hardest to deal with are the signs that I couldn't understand at the time but which, with the awful blessing of hindsight, now make sense.

One incident occurred on a visit to our home in July 2013 when I found Molly's lithium and other medications left lying around in our main bathroom in reach of all our children. On another occasion, during a US holiday on which we visited Jason and Molly, I was sitting on the deck enjoying the summer sunshine when Molly asked me if I wanted one of her special drinks. I accepted but, in the minutes after I finished the cocktail she had offered, I suddenly felt unwell. It was the only drink I had taken that evening, yet I was so overcome that Dave and my sister Marilyn had to physically carry me to the bedroom. I wasn't fully recovered for two days. Looking back, I am convinced Molly drugged me for her own amusement. Later, during a visit the following year, I was dumbfounded when I heard her family laughing about an incident when she had given one of her own powerful sedatives to her father after he had asked for an aspirin for a headache. He had to be almost carried from the baseball game they were attending.

It was only after Jason's death that we learned from neighbours that Molly had also been waging a determined campaign to destroy his reputation. We now know she told several of the wives she was friendly with that Jason was a drunk, that he neglected the children and that he would be violent towards her. These admissions would often be accompanied by tearful scenes and the overt display of bruises. Jack and Sarah would later explain to us that Molly would inflict the bruises on herself. Sarah once walked in on Molly hitting herself with the handle of a hairbrush on her arm to cause bruises that she would tell her friends that Jason had inflicted.

While Molly was spreading lies about Jason behind his back, she was telling *him* a very different story. Jason told me that Molly wanted to move from Panther Creek Court because she said nobody liked her. In a breathtakingly brazen claim, she also complained that people in the community were talking behind her back. But Molly's revelations also came with the realisation among the neighbours that not everything she said or claimed would prove to be true. Molly was emotional and erratic with them as well. As one neighbour said, Molly was known to 'bend the truth on occasions'. She had rows with some neighbours and was particularly cruel in comments towards one. It gave the wiser, more perceptive and astute people in the area pause for thought. Her claims also seemed to run totally contrary to the kind of person that Jason appeared to be. Images can be deceptive but I later learned that several of the husbands in the community felt the claims just didn't ring true with the kind of person they knew Jason to be. On one occasion, which we were only told about after Jason's death, several local men chatted about whether to bring the claims to my brother's attention. Tragically, they decided not to. I can understand their position because it is a nightmare situation – how on earth do you tell someone their own partner is spreading such malicious lies about them? But if Jason had known he might have expedited the plans he had in mind about bringing Jack and Sarah home to Ireland.

He first broached his plans with me in August 2014. I knew he wasn't happy in the US and that, despite all his hopes that the relationship with Molly might settle down, he was close to acknowledging that the marriage hadn't worked. But he was adamant that any move home would have to be handled very carefully. I suspect he was mindful of Molly's state of mental health and the problems he would inevitably have with the Martens family. As you read this, you're probably wondering why he didn't just flee with the children in 2013/2014. If the truth be told, Jason should have – he should have run for his life with Jack and Sarah. But he loved Molly, he hoped that things would work out and, most crucially of all, he didn't know the full facts. He only had one piece of a very complex jigsaw. None of us, including Jason, knew the full, terrible facts about Molly's behaviour.

I firmly believe that Tom and Sharon Martens could have helped the situation by taking responsibility for Molly's mental health issues rather than being ashamed of them. If only they had told Jason the full scale of her troubles and that she had been in a Georgia clinic just weeks before she had travelled to Ireland for the first time. Letters written by Molly in December 2006 underline how fragile her mental health was. 'It should come as no surprise that I am still a distressed mess. What's going on in my life now? Mom's been particularly depressed and in addition to hers and mine, my dad has been added to the list of depressed. I've most recently sabotaged a relationship and a half. And then what? I drug myself awake, I drug myself asleep. I am a continual disappointment to myself and my mother and pretty much the world at large. I want to be in love – I want children.'

In December 2014, Jason told me he was getting involved in a business venture with Lynn. Together, they would pay €60,000 each to buy the crèche premises in Limerick. Jason knew it was a sound investment and, critically, it would give him a source of income if he had to move back to Limerick from the US without a job already secured. It was a key part of his escape plan. But Jason was killed before the deal was finalised. Jason had sent texts and told Paul, Dave and me that he was about to come home with the children. There was no mention of Molly coming. In Jason's emails, I later found a record of his flight researches with Expedia for an August trip, which was conducted 24 hours before he was killed. He even had a reminder to himself to complete his booking. Proof of this came when Wayne visited Jason during a US holiday in July 2015, just two weeks before his death. Jason told his twin he would see him in Ireland in August.

Wayne recalled:

I was the last member of our family to see Jason. I had flown to Charlotte from Ireland on 18 July for a ten day holiday. I stayed with Jason and Molly at Panther Creek Court and then we went up to Washington for a few days. In Washington, we stayed with Michael and Mona Earnest. Jason, Molly and Jack and Sarah travelled up there as well. Sharon Martens was there but Tom Martens stayed back in Tennessee. We did all the tourist sights – Arlington, the White House, Ford's Theatre, the Lincoln Memorial and the Washington Monument. I didn't get any sense of things being badly wrong [between Jason and Molly]. I got no whiff of tension while I was there. The only thing that happened was, while we were having dinner with Michael and Mona Earnest in Washington, Sharon said: 'If Jason would only sign these papers we could look at colleges for Jack.' Jason didn't say anything and I took it that she was talking about adoption papers. I knew that Jason was never going to allow Molly to adopt the children … A few days before I was due to leave, Jason did say to me if I could stay another week? But financially I just couldn't stay. Molly drove me to Charlotte Airport with Jack. Jason had a meeting in Greensboro and Sarah couldn't travel with us. The last time I heard from Jason was during a stopover on my flight home when I got a text from him when I was at John F. Kennedy Airport in New York. Jason sent me a text which read: 'Wayne, it was really good to see you and I appreciate you coming over. We will have a pint in August.' That text was sent at 7.42 p.m. on 27 July. I replied and a second text arrived shortly afterwards which read: 'Cheers Bro – stay safe.' That arrived at 8.27pm.

Jason's Facebook page is a mine of clues as to what he must have been going through in mid-2015. Less than 36 hours before his death, he posted his last message on his Facebook page. To those who didn't know him, it must have seemed like a 'quote of the day'. But, reading it now, after his death, I understand what he was trying to say to those who knew and loved him. His message was posted on social media at 11.15 p.m. on Friday night, 31 July 2015. It read: 'People will question all the good things they hear about you but believe all the bad without a second thought.' Jason wasn't an avid user of Facebook or social media. What always struck me as strange about this Facebook post was that Jason normally never indulged in sharing clever quotes or sayings. And what was he doing posting something like that at 11.15 p.m. on a Friday night? The answer came from a message sent by a neighbour. Jason and Molly had spent that Friday evening at a cornhole party, a North Carolina summer tradition in which a small bag filled with dried maize kernels is tossed at a wooden platform with a target hole. Molly had started passing nasty comments about Jason's weight, humiliating him in front of their friends. One neighbour later wrote to me: 'She was belittling him, calling him a Fat Ass, saying that he must have taken all the nutrition from his twin because he looked like he had eaten for two. Jason actually left the party early and seemed down, not like himself.' My brother was obviously deeply hurt by Molly's vicious remarks. He left the party and walked home alone. The Facebook posting was written a few minutes later. Just 26 hours after that, Molly and Tom Martens savagely murdered my brother Jason and orphaned Jack and Sarah. With treachery that surpassed belief, they would then try to pass off their horrific crime as an act of self-defence.

5

Protecting the Children

I knew beyond a shadow of a doubt that Jason had been murdered. I had no proof, as yet, and the only detailed version of how he died was Molly and Tom's concoction that they had acted in self-defence. Jason couldn't speak the truth of what had happened, so our family became his voice, his demand for justice to be done. It was our job now to fight to shed light on what had really happened in that bedroom. But while we prepared for the long battle for justice, our priority switched to another fight – the struggle to get his children into our custody and back home to Ireland. Jack and Sarah were in Molly's care and I was prepared to move heaven and earth to get them away from the woman I knew was responsible for my brother's death.

We needed allies and help – and we needed them now. Back in Limerick, a support campaign was getting into gear, and I knew we also needed every bit of help possible from the Irish government. Our family rang the politicians we knew in Limerick and, somehow, I managed to secure a contact with then Minister for Foreign Affairs Charlie Flanagan. It was a telephone conversation I will never forget.

There was a shocked silence on the phone. I knew I shouldn't have spoken to a senior government minister in such a blunt manner but I was beyond caring. I was at my wits' end and all I was worried about was making sure Jack and Sarah were safe. A few days earlier, on 3 August 2015, I had sent a desperate appeal for help to Irish diplomatic services headed: 'Suspicious death – support needed urgently.' I'd sent the email as I raced to North Carolina to stop the hasty cremation of my brother. But our attention had now switched from the investigation into what we suspected was Jason's murder to the battle for his children.

I had bluntly told Charlie Flanagan on the phone that I would hold him personally responsible if anything happened to Jason's two children in North Carolina while they were in Molly's care. It certainly wasn't a very diplomatic way to speak to a senior minister. But the previous few days had convinced me beyond all doubt that Molly had murdered Jason. My fear now was what might happen to Jack and Sarah.

I also knew we desperately needed help if we were to get Jack and Sarah home. I was fully aware of the financial resources that the Martens family could call upon if required, not to mention that several members of the family worked in federal jobs that offered an insight into how the US legal system worked. From my time in the US, I knew just how much respect people had for the FBI.

I was worried too about what influence Tom might be able to wield through his current employment. He never spoke about the work he did at the US Department of Energy but I knew it was connected to counter-intelligence matters.

In contrast, we were an ordinary, working Irish family. We didn't have huge financial resources to call upon and were already trying to counter deliberate attempts by Molly and Tom to blacken Jason's name and the reputation of his Irish relatives. We needed the Irish government on our side. After a few seconds of silence, Mr Flanagan responded politely. He reassured me that the full resources of the Irish State would be behind ensuring the safety and well-being of Jack and Sarah, who were both Irish citizens. Furthermore, he promised me that all possible consular services would be provided for the battle by Dave and myself to get the children back home safe to Limerick.

Mr Flanagan was as good as his word. I am not an overly political person. But I believe our family owes a debt of gratitude to the Laois TD and the Department of Foreign Affairs staff for the staunch manner in which they supported us. Better still, once the custody battle shifted to a battle to see justice done for Jason's murder, Irish diplomats were behind us every step of the way.

My first email to Honorary Irish Consul John Young in North Carolina was on 3 August, within hours of getting the news of Jason's death. John immediately swept into action and proved of vital assistance in directing us towards expert legal advice, liaising with Jason's employer and helping with other matters such as dealing with Davidson County Sheriff's Department and the Department of Social Services (DSS). By 7 August, it was dealing with the latter that had become our overriding priority.

Shane Stevens, the poor man, had only been in the role of Irish consul in Atlanta, Georgia for a few weeks when suddenly he found himself dealing with a murder investigation/custody battle that would have taxed the skills of a veteran United Nations diplomat.

By this time, we had successfully prevented Jason's rushed cremation by Molly and had secured the repatriation of his body. After the service at Cumby's Funeral Home I made one of the toughest decisions of my life. I spoke with my siblings and Jason's friends before deciding that we would postpone any funeral in Ireland until we had secured full legal custody of Jack and Sarah. Nothing would happen with the funeral until they were home safe in Limerick.

It was a decision that almost broke my heart because I knew how desperately my parents wanted to view Jason's remains and see that his wishes for a proper Requiem Mass in Limerick were honoured. But I also knew my brother. His priority in life had always been the protection of Jack and Sarah. He wouldn't want anything to come before ensuring their safety, including his own funeral. In death, I would honour his wishes.

Amidst all the grief, tears and mourning, I knew there was urgent work to be done. Outside our hotel, we held an impromptu family conference. I distributed credit cards and everyone was given tasks to do – sort proper medium-term accommodation, arrange transport, secure phones for ringing home to Ireland, as well as organising adequate food and clothing. I had arrived in North Carolina with an overnight bag and just two changes of clothing. We didn't even have a laptop and had to purchase one locally.

We had been flooded with calls from the Irish media and decided we needed to highlight our plight and the battle for justice. Dave was tasked with doing three quick question-and-answer sessions with RTÉ, Newstalk and Today FM from North Carolina so that everyone at home understood the importance of what we were doing. After that, we declined all interview requests so as not to interfere with the work of the Davidson County authorities.

I was determined to focus on the DSS and the legal battle to prevent Molly and the Martens family from securing full custody of Jack and Sarah. We were all furious at the DSS decision to allow Molly to retain custody of the children after 2 August, despite her and her father now being suspects in Jason's death. Ultimately, the deciding factor for the DSS was the lack of charges or the knowledge that charges would definitely be levelled. I felt they did not act in the best interests of Jack and Sarah. By this time, we had learned that Molly had taken the children out of their Panther Creek Court home and gone to stay with her brother Bobby, just outside Charlotte, in the southern part of North Carolina. We were also informed that the children would be told Jason had died in an accident and that nothing of the events of 2 August was to be discussed with them.

Two different social workers were reviewing the status of the children's care. They were assigned on 3 August and the case was marked urgent, with a 72-hour response time. I first spoke with the DSS at 10.42 a.m. on 3 August and stressed to them that Molly had a history of mental illness. I also stressed that I had no knowledge or suspicion of domestic violence in Jason and Molly's relationship. The DSS report filed recorded these concerns: 'Tracey is worried about the children as Molly has not been responsive to family calls/texts. She (Tracey) wants to make sure the children are OK.'

It helped enormously that both Dave and myself had qualified as foster parents and had the Tusla (Irish child protection service) credentials to prove it. That seemed to count for a lot with the DSS. It also helped that we had two children of our own who were aged 14 and 24. I wanted them to understand that Jack and Sarah would be returning to a safe, happy and protective environment. It was also a family environment familiar to them.

My biggest fear was that Molly would take the children to Tennessee which, because of state law in the US, would create yet another legal headache for us. I later learned that this was something the Davidson County Sheriff's Office was also concerned about. Later on 3 August, Molly was formally advised by the DSS not to leave North Carolina until the completion of their investigation report.

Molly was by now referring in all DSS interviews to Jack and Sarah as 'my children'. In one interview, she admitted she had never adopted or obtained legal custody of them. The DSS also noted that both children were Irish citizens and travelled on Irish passports. Molly also astonishingly confirmed that she had first sought legal advice about her rights to the children in any divorce in 2011 – just months after her marriage to Jason. But apparently this didn't strike anyone as strange. She sought advice about her rights to the children from a lawyer in 2013 and again in 2014.

The report added: 'Molly was emotional stating that Jack and Sarah are my children – she has raised them for about eight years. Molly states that she is the only mother the children knows.' The DSS also noted that Molly was determined to secure custody of the children and was prepared to go to an attorney and launch a legal fight for them.

By this time, a North Carolina children's support unit called Dragonfly House was drafted in to assist. Their experts would conduct interviews with both Jack and Sarah, all of which would become key elements in the murder trial to follow. But those interviews would take place after the children had been left in the care of Molly and her family. I felt they had been brainwashed. Later, back in Ireland, the children would be able to tell us they saw Jason's phone and laptop in a Ziploc bag in Molly's possession along with other items.

The children also later told us that on Saturday morning, 1 August, the day before his murder, Jason was sitting on the couch with Jack and Sarah snuggled beside him. They said it looked like he was trying to book tickets on his laptop. Jason also asked them if they wanted to go shopping for clothes, something that was very unusual for him. A short time later, Molly asked Sarah to get a book from a nightstand and, when Sarah picked it up, three passports fell onto the floor. Sarah immediately put them back, but it is almost certain that Molly saw what happened. That night, just before the children went to bed, Jack and Sarah said Molly gave them grape melts or sleep aids. Sarah told us she felt very groggy during the night. I later found those grape melts or sleep aids in the Panther Creek Court house.

Our repeated requests to meet with Jack and Sarah were met by a wall of silence from the Martens. In desperation, I turned to the DSS but they insisted it was not an issue for them. They advised that any such visit would be entirely up to Molly. I made it clear to the DSS that I was not happy with the decision to leave the children with Molly. They responded that there was a 'safety plan' in place for the protection of the children, though I immediately suspected this wasn't worth the paper it was written on if my worst fears were realised.

I found it incredible that, despite the circumstances of Jason's death, and the fact that Molly had mental health issues, the DSS were not willing to petition a court for custody of Jack and Sarah. Molly informed the DSS that her refusal to allow us to see Jack and Sarah was on the grounds of legal advice she had received from her attorneys. I later learned that Molly was claiming I had made threats towards her. A DSS report recorded: 'She (Tracey) plans on taking the children and returning back to Ireland. The kids were very upset when they heard that and they will never see their mother (Molly) again. Molly states that the children have gone through enough.'

Just 30 hours after Jason's death, Molly formally filed for guardianship, custody and the adoption of Jack and Sarah. She also, for the first time, raised questions over the circumstances in which Mags had died in 2006. Molly raised doubts over the asthma attack, despite both of Mags's children having asthma and Sarah even having been hospitalised with an asthma attack in 2013. The battle lines had been drawn and I realised that the coming custody fight was going to be nasty and bitter.

It began with some vile social media posts about Jason from Molly's friend Billie June Jacobs. She posted to one 'Justice for Jason' supporter:

You need to understand that everything that happened that night was a result of Jason being a monster to his wife and children. He was physically violent and verbally and mentally abusive. None of this would be happening now if he had been a good person. I support Molly until the day I die. Everything she has done and will do is in the best interests of her children in an attempt to get them back where they should be – with her! Do not reply to this – we are finished communicating. God be with you.'

Sometime later, Billie June made a grovelling attempt to apologise to us after she had been warned that we were taking legal advice over her outrageous social media comments. It was by then clear that she had believed the lies her friend Molly had told her. While it is understandable, perhaps even admirable, for someone to stand by a friend in trouble, that in no way excuses such shameful, hurtful and false claims against an innocent person who had just been brutally murdered. Billie June finished her social media post with a religious sign-off. It is just a pity she didn't demonstrate such Christian charity in her own views.

Thankfully, we had by now secured the services of Kim Bonuomo who would prove to be one of the best lawyers I had ever dealt with. She was a veteran of the Judge Advocate General's Corp (JAG Corps) in the US military and was now setting up a practice in North Carolina.

Systematically, Kim prepared us for what lay ahead – challenging the guardianship and adoption grounds set out by Molly one by one.

Dave was not only adamant that he didn't want Jack and Sarah in Molly's care, he also objected to the Martens family as temporary guardians. He bluntly told DSS officials that he did not trust the Martens. We made it clear to DSS officials that Molly was relying on very strong medications, including lithium. It was ironic that Molly would attempt to exploit the old caricature of the drunken Irishman through Jason's enjoyment of a few beers on social occasions when we knew that she drank margaritas, wine and mojitos on an almost daily basis.

Finally, a preliminary court hearing was set for Friday, 14 August. By now, the DSS was beginning to have concerns about Molly. Interviews with neighbours verified that she had claimed she was being abused by Jason but the same people admitted they simply didn't know what to believe. They were aware of Molly's capacity for exaggerating matters. They also knew Jason and 'had good things to say about him'.

On 13 August, the day before the court hearing, the Irish Consul General in Atlanta, Shane Stephens, met with DSS officials about the case. The DSS report stressed that the Irish government's priority was the best interests of the children. Mr Stephens pointed out that they would be taking a watching brief on the legal developments in respect of the case – they wouldn't take an active part in proceedings but they would be monitoring them closely.

The first major hearing took place in Courtroom D of Davidson County Courthouse on Friday, 14 August 2015. The court was a breeze-block building we would later become intimately acquainted with during the murder trial. The clerk of Davidson County Superior Court, Brian Shipwash, was the presiding judge. An intelligent man with a kindly demeanour, he made us feel confident that he would leave no stone unturned in determining what was best for Jack and Sarah.

Molly was represented by Ray Grantham and Kelley Gondring of law firm Robinson & Lawing. Dave and I were represented by Kim

Bonuomo. Jason's will had been submitted to the court and it had already been processed. It was critical in that it underlined Jason's precise wishes for Dave and myself to be guardians of his children. Dave was to be the executor of Jason's estate while his children were minors. There was absolutely no mention of Molly. While under North Carolina law she would de facto inherit a share in the property as Jason's wife, having custody of Jack and Sarah would have effectively given her control of Jason's estate.

The details of the will were clearly a huge blow to Molly, as was evident from the ashen look on her face. I believe this is what caused the panic that prompted the ransacking of the house and going to MPS – I believe Molly wanted to find Jason's will. But my brother had kept it safely with his solicitor in Ireland.

Kim delivered an impressive summary of the reasons why the children should be placed in our care, not least the fact that both were Irish citizens, travelled on Irish passports and had no legal link to Molly. Jason's will was a clear indicator to the judge of what he wanted for his children.

The hearing was every bit as contentious as I expected it to be. I was called to offer evidence and spent five hours in the witness box. It was one of the most difficult experiences of my life. I was asked a series of questions that, I felt, were designed to portray me as the vengeful sibling and Molly as the victim. At one point, I was even asked why I had 'defriended' Molly on Facebook a few days after Jason had died. I was shocked at how anyone could ask such an obvious question. 'Because she told me she had killed my brother,' I replied. Molly might have insisted she'd acted in self-defence but, no matter what her claims, I knew she was responsible for Jason's death and that she and her father had killed him. I was convinced their story of acting in self-defence was nothing but a tissue of lies

Molly insisted it was she who had tried to stop the children calling her 'Mom' during her early days in Ireland but, over time, she said, they came to consider her their mother. Molly denied excessively disciplining the children – particularly Jack – if he didn't call her 'Mom' in public. She also, through her legal team, said the children would be better off in the US with her – and that they were very upset at the prospect of going to Ireland and not seeing Molly again.

Awful incidents were then recounted from 2011 to 2014, some of which, in my opinion, carried warning signs of what lay ahead, but none of us picked up the signals involved. They ranged from the effective collapse of Jason and Molly's relationship to the way the children were being treated by Molly. But these latter stories are Jack and Sarah's to tell.

Molly told the court that both Dave and I referred to her as Jack and Sarah's 'mom'. She also pointed to Paul, who was at the guardianship hearing, and said he too referred to her as the children's 'mom'. She told the hearing the children should stay in North Carolina with her. 'I am his mother – I have been his [Jack's] mother for eight years. I have raised and nurtured and taught him. I think it would be extremely detrimental for him to lose his mother.

'I'm (also) the only mother she [Sarah] has ever known. I have raised and taken care of her for – since she was a baby and I'm her mother.'

Molly called neighbours and friends to prove what a wonderful parent she was. One woman, Sara Neeves, actually referred to Molly as 'Supermom' in court. Jack had never heard of this woman and Sarah told us she vaguely knew the woman's daughter. Another, Shannon Grubb, said Molly was 'loving, very close to both kids'. In fact, there were multiple issues over how Molly treated both children, which we only learned about when Jack and Sarah came back to Ireland.

Molly also attempted to minimise her mental health issues. She said she had been diagnosed as being bipolar at 15 years old – but then claimed it was most likely a misdiagnosis. 'The last time I saw someone for bipolar depression was around age 17. Probably the last time I saw someone for depression was eight or nine years ago. I feel I probably wasn't bipolar – I was given antidepressants and they reacted physiologically with my body. So later on the diagnosis was changed to depression.' As it transpired, this was blatantly untrue. We also knew, thanks to her former fiancé Keith Maginn, that she had been on up to 16 medications daily.

Molly also denied that she ever had a box of lithium – despite my finding one lying around the bathroom of my home – and that she hadn't been prescribed anything for depression for over eight years. She made no mention of being in an Atlanta psychiatric clinic just months before she had travelled to Ireland to work as an au pair.

Critically, she admitted she had told an untruth to one of her friends who would later serve as one of her bridesmaids. In fact, she was caught out in many untruths and fabricated stories. Molly admitted in the guardianship hearing that she had told her friend she was going to Ireland to serve as an au pair for a family friend and that she had known the woman involved. In court, she acknowledged that she did not know the woman (Mags) – something I believe the judge took careful note of.

Our witnesses included myself, Dave, Lynn Shanahan, my sister Marilyn and Karen Gorey – the people who had had the closest contact with Jason, Molly, Jack and Sarah since 2011. Lynn had visited the US on holiday in 2013 and the fractures in Molly and Jason's relationship were all too apparent then. Lynn told the hearing that, just minutes after arriving in North Carolina, Molly had opened up about their problems.

> When we arrived Molly had said to me almost straight away that we had caught them at a bad time – that they weren't getting on at the moment. Molly was upset for the whole trip, crying. And told me she wasn't happy, that she felt like she was living in the shadow of Mags and it was very hard to know that obviously Jason had loved his first wife. [She] felt like she was trying to compete with that.

Critically, Molly revealed to Lynn she had sought legal advice about a separation and had been told that, if she split up with Jason, 'she was told she would only gain [child] visitation rights. She said she knew it was selfish of her because she was doing it for herself because she wanted the children to stay with her, but she didn't love Jason anymore.'

In hindsight, I believe this type of behaviour was to try and make visitors, particularly those from Ireland, feel uncomfortable so they would leave earlier than planned and probably decide not to return. It was, I am convinced, all part of a plan to isolate Jason.

Lynn also revealed that Molly had indicated that an old boyfriend had recently resumed contact with her. 'She said an old boyfriend had contacted her through Facebook and that we were [in the car] listening to a CD that he had given her. And that she would love to meet up with him for lunch but she didn't think that Jason would think that was appropriate.'

The submissions to the guardianship hearing revealed that if Lynn, her husband and two boys were hoping for a relaxing US holiday, they found themselves dealing with precisely the opposite. Molly, having raised the spectre of contact with an old boyfriend, suddenly told Lynn during a combined family visit to Myrtle Beach that she had secretly checked Jason's phone and suspected he was having a social media friendship with another woman. She never revealed details of the message she claimed she found on Jason's phone – and no one ever saw the message involved. It was bizarre.

'I looked around stunned,' Lynn told the hearing. 'I had just walked out. Jason came out of the bedroom behind her [Molly] and I said: "What is going on?" There was one or two upsetting incidences that had happened during my visit.'

The most alarming incident involved Molly losing control when Jack made a cheeky comment to her during a night out. 'We came out from a restaurant and Jack said something smart, as kids do. Molly was extremely upset saying that she wasn't getting the respect as his mother and that Jason needed to talk to him and to straighten him out.

'Jack then said: "But you're not my real mother." She just got – the behaviour was erratic, she was screaming and shouting.'

The group, standing outside the busy restaurant, were mortified and Jason had to walk Molly towards somewhere more private. Lynn and her husband moved their children away as they did not want them to observe the tribulations of their friend. But Lynn told the hearing that Molly was determined Jack should be punished over what had happened. 'It was Jack's turn to travel in our car and she made him go in Jason's car. [She] took all the electronics off him and was very upset about it. I felt like her behaviour after that was like a punishment to Jack.'

Lynn noted that Jack would be punished by Molly for the smallest mistake or transgression. When he forgot to bring his flip-flops for a beach visit, she refused to allow him purchase new ones – and refused to even allow him borrow spare flip-flops from his Irish friends. Lynn later noted that Jack's wardrobe was nothing like Sarah's – and when they flew home to Ireland, she deliberately left behind some of her own children's clothing that Jack had been admiring.

Lynn told the hearing that she was very distraught at the change in the relationship between Jason and Molly in 2013.

I tried to be a friend – I wanted the family to succeed as a family unit, for them all to be happy. When they were in Ireland I felt maybe the relationship was newer and they were happier. But when they moved back to America you could see the strain. I felt that the constant ups and downs, the constant levels of, you know, everything being so bad and [then] so right. I felt that Jason just couldn't cope with the situation that seemed to be blowing up. Everything was so explosive and dramatic. We wanted obviously for Jason to be happy but he couldn't be happy.

During the Myrtle Beach trip on 4 July, Lynn explained how Molly had packed beach bags for herself and the children but nothing for Jason. When Jason emerged from the sea and was standing on the beach covered in sand, he realised no clothing had been brought for him. 'I just felt so embarrassed for Jason because he had nothing, he had brought no clothes. He was standing there in wet, sandy gear – he had nothing with him. She [Molly] just said: "I'm not your keeper, you should have brought your own stuff." I just felt terribly embarrassed for Jason in front of everybody to be treated that way.'

Marilyn also told the hearing about an incident between Jack and Molly that had left our elderly father in tears. It happened during a US holiday in 2012 and was so upsetting no one who witnessed it ever forgot about it. Judge Shipwash was given an unvarnished, detailed account of what Molly was really like when she either lost her temper or was having one of her depressive episodes. Marilyn told the hearing that Molly's behaviour around Jack and Sarah could be both 'erratic and childish'.

Judge Shipwash reserved judgment in the case, clearly wanting the weekend to consider the submissions and reach his ruling. A case conference was scheduled for Monday morning with senior DSS officials. We didn't expect any developments until mid-week.

Dave and I had based ourselves in High Point, which was roughly 40 kilometres from Lexington. It was quiet, residential and ideal for our needs. Marilyn, Lynn, Karen and Paul had stayed and had been vital supports in helping us prepare for the custody battle. That was one of the longest weekends I had lived through since Jason's death. I was terrified the decision would go against us and that Molly would secure legal claim to the children. It would be the ultimate insult to Jason.

After the court hearing on Friday, we decided to pay a short visit to Dave's sister in Kansas. It would, we felt, offer some respite from the legal wrangles, the welcome support of some friendly faces, and it would give us a break from the four walls of the hotel. The drive took the best part of 16 hours in our hired car and we were exhausted when we arrived.

Early on Sunday, we got a phone call from our attorney to say we had to get back to North Carolina urgently. I was petrified it was something to do with the children's safety but all we were told was that we had to get back to Lexington as soon as possible. Ultimately, we ended up flying back and hiring another car to drive from the airport to Thomasville Social Services – while we had to leave our first hire care in Kansas. Marilyn, Paul and Lynn, God love them, had to drive that original rental car all the way back from Kansas to North Carolina.

Judge Shipwash had ordered that Jack and Sarah should be put into our temporary custody and he ordered DSS officials to remove the children from Molly's care.

Two DSS officials, including Shelly Lee, had travelled to Bobby's home outside Charlotte to pick up Jack and Sarah. They were greeted by Michael Earnest, Molly's uncle, who demanded to know why they were there. The two DSS officials were accompanied by two police officers from Union County.

Molly was in the swimming pool and clearly believed the visit was in connection with ongoing court matters and witnesses. When the court order for the return of the children to the custody of Dave and myself was produced for her inspection, she instantly broke down into floods of tears.

A DSS report, which was later supplied to us, revealed that Michael Earnest didn't take kindly to the development. 'Michael pulled [one official] aside stating that DSS had a part in this decision. [They] advised Michael that DSS had no input in this decision. That this was a surprise to our agency as well.'

The officials asked Molly to pack a bag for Jack and Sarah, after which the children were driven away to be brought to me and Dave. It makes for gut-wrenching reading but poor Jack and Sarah were distraught. The DSS report makes it clear that they both became emotional as the DSS staff and deputies did their job.

There are many things that, in years to come, I might forgive Molly for. I believe in repentance and forgiveness – it is part and parcel of an Irish Catholic upbringing. But I will never, as long as I draw breath, ever forgive her for what she put those two children through. She robbed them of their second parent and then manipulated a situation to make them distraught over being taken away from the very person who had just killed their father. There is word for this kind of behaviour and it is 'evil'.

Dave and I were asked to attend the Thomasville DSS office to take custody of Jack and Sarah. I was terrified of how the children would be, given all that they had gone through since 2 August. I walked through the door of the office and my heart was breaking as I looked at their innocent little faces as they waited there, playing with their toys. I quietly walked over and knelt down, with Dave by my side, and all we could do was hug them. That hug seemed to last an eternity. I simply cannot put into words how good it felt to have them back in our arms. My eyes welled up with tears at the sheer joy and relief of knowing they were safe. If a hug could protect children from hurt, sorrow and grief, Dave and I were determined to offer Jack and Sarah that kind of embrace. We simply didn't care who saw us. The following day, Monday, we got the news we had been praying for – Judge Shipwash had ruled that Jack and Sarah should be with us.

But even if we had won the legal battle, our troubles were still far from over. We had made it clear to everyone from the Davidson County Sheriff's Department to the DSS that we intended to return to Ireland immediately upon being granted guardianship of Jack and Sarah. Yet it quickly emerged that this might not be quite so straightforward. We were granted guardianship but the courts held the children's passports until the following Thursday pending the outcome of the custody hearing. Thankfully, Judge April Woods upheld the decision and we were given the passports and told we were free to return to Ireland.

What happened next was like something from a James Bond spy novel. Irish consular officials were outside the court to support us and verify the return of Jack and Sarah's Irish passports. Distraught with worry over how our attempt to bring the children back to Ireland might be frustrated, I asked one of the consular officials what we would do if somehow the passports weren't returned. He smiled at me, opened a briefcase at his side and revealed that brand new replacement passports for the children had already been prepared just in case.

There was still the possibility of Molly and her family issuing a legal challenge as a means of delaying our departure. But such a challenge would have to be physically served on me as a legal writ. So we needed to get out of the US as quickly as possible.

The next 36 hours were like torture for us – a vigil for news of what legal challenges we might face while desperately planning to get Jack and Sarah to the safety of their Irish home. Every time a phone rang, my heart seemed to miss a beat, as I could only imagine it was some dreadful news of a new legal problem. And all while we were trying to comfort and support two children who had suffered so much. It also underlined just how much Minister Flanagan held true to his promise to our family that Ireland would have our backs when we needed it most. Incredibly, we were alerted to the fact that Bobby Martens and Michael Earnest had already been at Charlotte Airport asking to check the passenger manifest for any flight to Dublin. Our fear was that they would somehow try any legal means to return Jack and Sarah to Molly's custody and that she would then flee North Carolina.

The Irish diplomats advised us to change our travel plans, with a Charlotte departure now deemed to be too risky. Instead, we would travel from Greensboro to Washington DC and make new plans for flying home. We arrived in Washington and were immediately accompanied to the ambassador's car to be driven to a hotel off Dupont Circle, which had been arranged by the Irish consul. No one could trace us to it and we were safe until the best way to fly home was decided. Incredible as it may sound, we even had to stay in Washington under assumed names. There was one moment of hilarity when Paul, who was with us and hadn't been told about the use of assumed names, tried to check out of the hotel under his own name and caused chaos as a result.

The following day, Irish diplomats arrived early to the hotel and advised that it would be better to fly home from New York, where two major airports (John F. Kennedy and Newark) both operate direct flights to Shannon and Dublin. This would make it difficult to the point of being impossible for anyone to intercept us and serve a writ. The consul had booked train tickets and we were escorted to Washington station to take the Amtrak train for the trip north to New York.

Since leaving court we had been mostly accompanied by Irish embassy personnel. While it was upsetting that such precautions were necessary, both Dave and myself remarked that we felt our government was looking out for us and ensuring our security throughout it all. It made me very proud to be Irish.

And the precautions were backed up by the stern legal advice given to both Dave and Paul. Under no circumstances were they to allow anyone to approach me – if anyone attempted to serve legal papers on me, Dave and Paul were to immediately intervene and take the document instead. If they took the legal papers, Jack and Sarah could still travel home with me. After a few tense hours at Newark Airport, we boarded the flight for Ireland and I felt like crying when I felt the bump as the wheels finally left the tarmac. Jack and Sarah were almost home.

We arrived back in Shannon Airport on 20 August with yet more incredible assistance from Clare airport officials, who ensured our transit through was smooth and fast. Not surprisingly, Jack and Sarah were physically exhausted and emotionally distraught. They had just endured three weeks that no adult, let alone a child, should have to suffer. One heartbreaking element was that Jack later told me he thought Jason might be waiting for them at Shannon and that all Molly had told them would turn out to be lies. They had been made orphans by the very person who portrayed herself as their loving mother. But they were home, they were safe and they were enveloped in the loving embrace of the Corbett, Fitzpatrick and Lynch families that Jason had so desperately wanted to return them to.

The healing process would take time and tears – lots and lots of tears. It wasn't helped by the fact that we now had Jason's funeral to attend to. But my brother had raised two wonderful, brave and resilient children and they would now surprise us all with their capacity to respond to the love, kindness and understanding that was showered upon them by relatives who would do anything to shield them from further hurt.

Jason's funeral notice was released to the Irish newspapers on Sunday 23 August, three weeks to the day since his murder. Thousands attended his removal at Cross's Funeral Home on Lower Gerald Griffin Street in Limerick the following Tuesday. It was a tribute to the esteem in which he was held. People who knew Jason from primary school, secondary school, from his days working in Limerick right up to his time in the US, arrived at the removal and Mass to show their support and solidarity. His colleagues travelled from across Ireland and the UK. The stories about Jason, about his kindness and humour, brought tears and smiles alike to our faces.

Jason's Requiem Mass was celebrated at Our Lady Queen of Peace Church in Janesboro at noon on Wednesday. It was the church where Jason had made his First Holy Communion and his Confirmation. None of us thought Jason would begin his final journey from the same church in such a short time. The Gardaí blocked off local roads to facilitate the passage of the funeral cortège as Jason's coffin made its final journey from Janesboro to Castlemungret, with a brief pause as a mark of respect outside his childhood home.

I wrote the eulogy, which was delivered by Dave. He had also had to deliver the eulogy at Mags's funeral and, on both occasions, my husband did us proud. He thanked the many people who had stood by us over the nightmare of the previous few weeks. But I wanted everyone to have a sense of the person my brother was – and it wasn't helped by the fact that this was the very day Jason should have flown back to Ireland with Jack and Sarah.

'I hope that Jason will continue to live on within our hearts and minds where our memories will always stay protected,' I had written.

Jason had a wonderful life and was at his happiest when he met and married Mags and had their two beautiful children together. For a time he was as happy as any man can be. After Mags died, he lived his life with dignity but was a lost soul and the light and spark was never fully replaced. If Jason couldn't be here, I know that in my heart he wanted to be with Mags. Right up until he went to America he would spend every single day at her grave. She was his world and he felt blessed to have had that kind of love in his life.

I finished the eulogy with one of Jason's favourite sayings: 'How lucky am I to have had something that makes saying goodbye so hard.'

That thought gave me comfort because I knew just how difficult and painful the road ahead would be.

After the Mass, where it was standing room only in Our Lady Queen of Peace Church, we reunited Jason with the love of his life, Mags. He was buried beside her in Castlemungret Cemetery, with the Irish media respecting our wishes that the graveyard element of the funeral should be strictly private. For me, it was the hardest part of the day. I felt I hadn't any tears left to weep but, standing at that graveside, I found yet more to shed as I looked at my parents and their broken spirits there for all to see.

Catherine admitted the Fitzpatrick family found the burial ceremony very difficult as it brought back so many memories of Mags's loss.

Standing there with the grave opened again was very upsetting. We were all heartbroken at Jason's death but it also brought back so many painful memories of November 2006. Then, just as the burial was about to take place, two white butterflies appeared from nowhere and began flying over the grave. I will never forget it – it was almost a sign that Jason and Mags were back together again. Mags always believed in those kinds of symbols and signs.

Months after Jason's murder, a work colleague found a computer memory stick that had belonged to Jason and sent it to us. All it contained were several poems he had written after Mags's death in 2006 and some video footage of Jack and Sarah. Reading them, I realised that Jason had returned, earlier than any of us would have wanted, but returned nonetheless to Mags's arms. His nickname for the mother of his children was 'Mag Mag'. One poem he wrote was entitled 'I Miss You Mag Mag'. It reads:

Each time I miss you, a star falls down from the sky,
So if one looked up at the sky and found it dark,
With no stars, it is all your fault,
You made me miss you too much!
When you didn't come back,
My heart crumbled,
All my fears were a reality,
The love I have for you was heightened,
Was out of control,
I was angry, scared, confused,
I was alone
I never felt more alive than when you were here,
It was happy then,
Looking forward to each day,
When you'd phone and ask,
Are you on your way?
My home was being with you Mag Mag.

I had made three promises to my brother that emotion-charged evening in Cumby's. With the support of my family and Jason's friends we had brought him home to be buried in his beloved Limerick. We had also secured custody of his children and brought them safely back to Ireland. Now I would devote my every waking moment to delivering on my third promise – that I would see Molly and Tom Martens face justice for the evil they had visited on my brother.

6

Character Assassination

My brother's body wasn't cold in the ground when I discovered the lengths to which Molly and Tom were now prepared to go to avoid being held responsible for his death. Worse still, despite having lost the custody battle for Jack and Sarah in North Carolina, they switched tactics and began an alarming campaign of trying to contact the children in Ireland.

We received a phone call in September 2015 from a firm that operated from Shannon Airport and specialised in aviation advertising – basically the firm would fly small Cessna planes trailing banners around major festivals or sporting events in Ireland to promote goods or services. The man on the phone rather delicately asked what our family's position would be on them taking a contract from the United States to have one of their planes fly a banner over Limerick city and the school in which Jack and Sarah were now enrolled. It was to wish Jack and Sarah happy eleventh and ninth birthdays respectively. The message – and the contract – was from the Martens.

I was dumbfounded. At this point, I thought I was beyond being shocked but this was something I simply couldn't believe anyone to be capable of. I thanked the person for having the consideration to contact us for our opinion rather than blindly accepting the contract. They had their suspicions that something strange was involved and, when I outlined what had happened in the US, they immediately agreed that accepting the contract wouldn't be appropriate.

It is at times like these you realise just how respectful a place Ireland can be. I'm sure there are plenty of other countries where a firm would simply have put profit before acting responsibly. The word spread quickly and other aviation firms adopted the same position that flying such a banner over Limerick would not be correct given all that had happened to Jack and Sarah.

Our local newspaper, the *Limerick Leader*, was also contacted to place half-page adverts. They refused the contract. Limerick is a place where loyalty is taken very seriously. But advertising wasn't our only concern. We quickly learned that social media posed its own risks for Jack and Sarah.

Over the coming months, we received and were told about 'friend requests' over social media that families and teens in the general area of Raheen had received from the US. All were unsolicited and all originated from places within a few hours' drive of North Carolina. In all cases, it quickly emerged that the individuals involved were trying to glean second-hand information about Jack and Sarah. It became an entirely new – and deeply worrying – front in what had become a psychological and informational war of attrition now being waged on us.

We weren't the only ones concerned. Limerick Gardaí debated placing both Jack and Sarah on their CRI alert system. This is a rapid response police system aimed at protecting children who are deemed to be at risk either from estranged parents or family members. An undercover detective performed security screening around our Raheen home. We were assured that if we ever raised an alert over the children, the entire area would be in total lockdown within minutes. All ports and airports would also have full details on Jack and Sarah.

By late September, about seven weeks after Jason's death, I got the first indications that the Davidson County Sheriff's Department were increasingly sceptical of the explanation offered by Molly and Tom for the precise circumstances of Jason's death. I didn't know it at the time, but they had by now received the detailed pathologist's report into the fatal injuries that Jason had sustained. The appalling scale of the injuries suffered by my brother – which you will read about later – and the total lack of any injuries to Molly and her father gave them pause for thought. The toxicology findings added further to their suspicions.

Police had also received the initial forensic reports and the overall breakdown by detectives of what the father and daughter had claimed occurred on 2 August – and how it tallied with the physical evidence. This prompted the Davidson County District Attorney's Office – in a move that would prove of critical significance in the trial to come – to contract with a Florida-based blood-spatter expert for his assessment of precisely what had happened in the master bedroom.

The Davidson County investigation team, led by Detectives Michael Hurd and Brandon Smith and supervised by Lt Det. Thompson, were painstaking in their research. I got the impression they were increasingly suspicious about the overall circumstances in which Jason died. I also believe that Molly and Tom's actions at this point backfired – making detectives look long and hard at them rather than believing the outlandish claims they had by now levelled against Jason.

Within hours of arriving in North Carolina after Jason's death I knew Molly was painting my brother as the stereotypical drunken Irishman. Her story was effectively that a drunken thug got what he deserved after a 'hero' father bravely intervened to protect his innocent little princess. I understood that, at all costs, I had to show Jason for the person he was and not what Molly and Tom claimed him to be.

I couldn't believe it when I was contacted by Davidson County police and told that Molly was alleging that Jason was an associate of the IRA. Detectives had been informed that he had a long and troubled history of violence, dating right back to his teenage years.

Even more bizarrely – and I would have laughed but for the fact that it was so deadly serious – Molly had even claimed that Jason was a mixed martial arts (MMA) fighter.

Jason loved sport – but it was golf, football and rugby, not the MMA that Conor 'Notorious' McGregor has made so famous. My brother's weakness was his love of food and it showed on his waistline, as it does for so many people when they enter middle age and work long, demanding hours. But it wasn't sufficient for us to dismiss each claim as ludicrous. We had to provide physical evidence to the Davidson County police that what Molly was claiming was totally untrue. We began a year-long and painstaking campaign of securing statements and testimonials from teachers, school principals, senior Gardaí and even work associates of Jason as to his character, interests and involvements. Those who have made statements include Ann-Marie O'Connell, Karen Gorey, Mike Edwards, Catherine Fitzpatrick, Lynn Shanahan, Joanne Sheehan, Sarah Fitzpatrick, Morgan Fogarty, Michelle McCormack, Simone Dillon, Michelle O'Callaghan, Mark Wenham, Jane Woods, Chris Dears, Bobby O'Connor and Brad Tackaberry, who was Jason's most senior boss in MPS. I want to thank them from the bottom of my heart for their support.

Some of the statements must have set alarm bells ringing for the North Carolina detectives. Mags's sister, Catherine, was scathing in her comments about Molly. She bluntly described Molly as 'a compulsive liar'. That was hardly surprising because Molly had sent a text to Catherine and the entire Fitzpatrick family on 6 August 2015, as the Martens family tried to organise an adoption for Jack and Sarah before Jason was even buried. In a cruelty beyond words, adoption papers were even sent to my elderly parents to compound their agony. Molly's text read:

I just wanted to let you know the kids are doing OK. We have the memorial today and they are going to see a counsellor. I don't know what you are thinking about me with so much slander out there but I realise I have no control. If the Corbetts have, for whatever reason, led you to believe that I am keeping them from Jason, I assure you this isn't true. He had to undergo an autopsy and after finally making it to the funeral home he has not yet been released for viewing. I am trying to get whatever signed possible for his family to see him and take him back to Ireland.

In regard to speaking with them, I cannot do it because of the threats they have made. I implore you to consider the kids. They have lost one mother and now they have lost their father. Please do not aid in taking them from the mother that has nurtured and raised them for the past seven and a half years. Would you truly think that is best for them?

Catherine had rung Molly immediately after Jason's death to find out what had happened and to make sure Jack and Sarah were OK. Molly had told her she was 'upset but more frightened of the Corbetts'. Catherine knew the claims being levelled against Jason made no sense – and was baffled by the allegations Molly was now levelling against us.

Catherine recalled:

I knew that wasn't Jason – he just wasn't that kind of man. Then, a few days later, papers arrived from the US about Molly wanting to adopt Jack and Sarah. What Molly didn't know was the subject of adoption had cropped up sometime earlier when Jason was in Ireland and visited my parents. We knew Molly was pushing to be allowed adopt Jack and Sarah. But my mother told Jason: 'Don't ever let that happen.' He promised he wouldn't let any adoption go ahead.

There was something about Molly – something that made us all think twice.

I suspect detectives also noted the fact that Molly's medical records in North Carolina made absolutely no reference to her being treated for mental health issues. Molly had been very careful to keep her Tennessee, Georgia and North Carolina medical records totally separate. But I was able to provide detailed information to support my assertion that she had a very troubled medical past and wasn't being totally honest with the authorities about it.

In this regard, we were very grateful to Molly's former fiancé, Keith Maginn. A native of Cincinnati in Ohio, Keith had met Molly via a dating site in 2006/2007 and their relationship blossomed. They got engaged but Molly's mental health problems gradually escalated. Keith didn't want to get involved in the North Carolina proceedings but agreed to do so for two reasons. Keith recalled:

> The first reason was that Tracey asked me to help. The second reason was because of the children [Jack and Sarah]. I realised that Molly had lied about her mental health issues and I was naturally concerned that she might get custody of the children. We were still engaged when she suddenly flew to Ireland in 2008.
>
> After that, I heard nothing.
>
> She went to Ireland not long after she was released from the [psychiatric] clinic in Atlanta. I had first met Molly through a dating site. She was very free-spirited. I had never met someone like her before. She was fun and carefree – there was something very special about her.

But, Keith admitted, the relationship became troubled due to Molly's increasingly serious mental health issues.

> She had told me she was bipolar. I didn't think much of it at the time because she was so carefree, happy and fun to be around. But that was because her medications were balanced. When the medications weren't balanced, she was a totally different person. There were occasions when I would find her crying in the apartment and refusing to go outside, sometimes for days. Eventually, it got so bad that she had to be taken to Atlanta [for medical help]. She was taking up to 16 different medications a day – it was just astounding.

Keith's help proved invaluable to us and we are deeply grateful to this day. The scale of what he endured was borne out by the fact that he eventually wrote a therapeutic memoir that, in part, dealt with his relationship with Molly. It was entitled *Turning This Thing Around*.

His assistance to us – and honesty about what Molly was really like – also came at a cost. Molly took to social media and challenged him: 'How could you do this to me – you know how good a mother I was.'

The closer the police looked into her stories and claims, the more inconsistencies they found. Some were simply strange. Others were so bizarre they hinted at someone living an almost Walter Mitty-like existence. Crucially, they also worked to undermine her credibility and the reliability of what she told the police.

We also discovered that, within 24 hours of Molly being released by Davidson County police, after making her voluntary statement on 2 August, she had spent a staggering $5,500 from the joint bank account she'd held with Jason on what we were told was 'a forensic clean' of their Panther Creek home. As she was leaving the police station she turned to one officer and said: 'Is my house clean?' The officer, given the circumstances and that they were dealing with the death of a young father of two, was initially dumbfounded. But they then bluntly told Molly: 'We don't do that.'

The professional sanitation firm contracted by Molly scrubbed the house from floor to ceiling. They left the property spotless. It meant that, after 4 August, further forensic tests by police at the property were near impossible.

Within hours of my arrival in North Carolina, I had asked police about doing a floor-to-ceiling forensic analysis of the property. I particularly wanted them to examine every room using Luminol, not just the bedroom, bathroom and hallway, where blood was clearly visible. Luminol is a compound that exhibits 'chemiluminescence', a blue glow, when mixed with an oxidising agent and is a critical tool for forensic scientists in detecting trace amounts of blood.

I wanted Luminol surveys of all the rooms in the property because I was convinced it would help unravel Molly and Tom's explanation of what had happened to Jason. My suspicions were underpinned by the fact that I was familiar with the property and realised immediately that items were missing, including Jason's home computer.

A shocking development came from something Jack told us. He saw Jason late on the evening of 1 August, just as he went to bed. Jason was in bed alone watching a Japanese golf tournament – something Dave later confirmed via US TV listings. But Jack also spotted a suitcase packed and standing next to Jason's bed. It contained items of Jason's, Jack's and Sarah's clothing. I am convinced the humiliation of the Friday evening had been the final straw for my brother and he was now about to bring his children back to Ireland. We also learned that Jason had told Jack and Sarah they were moving back to Ireland. When they asked if Molly was coming too, Jason said he didn't think so.

I firmly believe that is why Molly made multiple calls to her parents on Saturday. It is also hugely significant that no such packed suitcase was found in the house just a few hours later, when Jason had been bludgeoned to death and Davidson County police officers arrived at the scene.

Adding further to the mystery was that a neighbour told us they spotted a vehicle pulling out of the driveway at Jason's house in the early hours of that 2 August morning, before emergency services arrived at the scene. Frustratingly from our point of view, the vehicle could not be traced.

Another issue was the fact that my brother never slept naked – everyone in our family knew that, as a traditional Irishman, he wore not only boxer shorts but sometimes pyjama bottoms or even a T-shirt when sleeping. So why was he found naked? Where was the underwear we were all convinced he had been wearing that night? Where was the clothing Molly was wearing before she changed into those pyjamas?

I also realised that another of Molly's stories was also total fiction. She had told us shortly after her arrival in Ireland that she had a sister called Grace who died tragically in childhood from leukaemia. Grace was a name that often cropped up in Molly's writings – a Grace even featured in Molly's 'Inferno' story as a baby sister who, despite an early death, had failed to make it to Heaven. But, we now discovered, there had never been a baby sister called Grace in Molly's life.

Molly, in her brief time at Clemson University, had shown her roommate a framed photo of a young girl and said it was her sister, Grace. The roommate then discovered it was a generic photo that came with the photo frame.

Other friends, Damian and Michelle McCormack, revealed that Molly's struggle with the truth even extended to her own family. They recalled how, on 3 August 2013, they met Molly with Jason, Dave and myself at Spanish Point. Molly told them her father was battling testicular cancer and that her mother had a condition that would eventually leave her blind. Damian and Michelle were understandably horrified for Molly – and Jason, noting their reaction, asked what was wrong. Molly instantly changed the subject. Damian and Michelle thought she was simply upset but it later emerged her stories about her parents were fabricated.

Police looked long and hard at Molly's actions over the 48 hours following Jason's death. She had been accompanied by family members to the MPS plant to collect my brother's personal effects on 4 August. The plant officials, having no idea about the circumstances of Jason's death, handed the effects over in the plant lobby. Among those with Molly that day was her uncle, Michael Earnest.

The previous day, he had phoned MPS and spoken with Jason's colleague and friend Melanie Crook. 'He called several times. That was Monday, August 3. What I remember most is that he was particularly aggressive [in tone],' Melanie recalled. 'Eventually we arranged that he would call to the plant the following day for Jason's personal items. That was the visit in which he accompanied Molly to the [Lexington] plant.

But, sometime later, I was contacted by two federal agents who wanted to talk to me about those calls I received on August 3.'

Michael Earnest was subsequently the focus of an administrative inquiry by the Special Inspector General for Afghanistan Reconstruction (SIGAR) over precisely what contacts he had with MPS on 3 and 4 August. These were the agents who contacted Melanie at MPS. Molly's uncle vehemently denied identifying himself as a federal agent as he sought Jason's belongings. In an interview with Wayne O'Connor of the *Sunday Independent*, he flatly rejected any suggestion that he had linked his employment to his role as Molly's uncle at MPS. 'It was purely routine … it was simply in line with procedures and protocol,' he said. Mr Earnest insisted he was cleared of any wrongdoing by SIGAR.

> Yeah, well absolutely. What I have to defer on that is my organisation, because of the complaint, they had to investigate it and they did it thoroughly. They conducted a very thorough investigation as far as I understand and I am still employed. Had I done that [there would be] a number of things [resulting from the allegations being proven]. Number one, I would not be employed and, number two, had I done those things the Davidson County Sheriff's Office would have rightfully been able to charge me with obstruction of justice. None of those things happened so you can make your own conclusions.

Jason's home computer had also vanished. There was no trace of it at Panther Creek Court. His work laptop was recovered. It was the same story with Jason's phone, which had vanished into thin air. But, thankfully, I was able to recover a lot of Jason's email traffic – some of which would prove vital in highlighting the background to the case to police.

Shortly after Jason's death, and by agreed consent order when the property was effectively sealed under court control, Molly's attorney informed our legal team that she wanted to recover a few personal items from the Panther Creek Courthouse. Permission was given. We had no idea of this at the time. But I got a phone call from a neighbour to tell me that a large number of trucks had arrived outside the property and it was being emptied. I immediately contacted Davidson County officials as well as our North Carolina lawyers and asked what was going on. To his credit, the instant Judge Brian Shipwash was made aware of the incident he got involved. It transpired that Molly had arranged for seven trucks to arrive at Panther Creek Court at 6.30 a.m. and they began loading everything, from furniture to clothing and even kitchen appliances that she had marked with stickers. The only things left in the 4,000-square-foot house were items of furniture that Jason had shipped over from Ireland, including a bed, a dresser and an old patio set. Molly intended to bring everything to Tennessee and sell them off. This is what one storage official had told us he was instructed to do.

Nothing had been left in the house but rubbish and dust.

Davidson County Court immediately ordered that, pending the conclusion of legal matters, all the belongings needed to be placed in secure storage under court control. They are still there under lock and key, though most likely deteriorating to the point where they will largely prove valueless when finally released.

Between 4 August 2015 and 17 July 2017, the day the Davidson County Superior Court murder trial of Molly and Tom Martens opened, Dave and I had to undertake 13 trips to North Carolina to support either civil or criminal proceedings arising from Jason's death. Each time felt like we were walking into a psychological war zone.

Jason drove a Honda Accord. It had also vanished from Panther Creek Court when we arrived in North Carolina on 4 August. Days after Jason's death, I discovered that Tom Martens was now driving the car. On the occasions we would arrive for court hearings over the next year, Tom would arrive driving Jason's car. He would park the car, deliberately look over towards us if we were in the car park and smile. It dawned on me that this was all about playing mind games and trying to upset us. It was a similar story with Mags's old jewellery. Her favourite rings – including her engagement and eternity rings, given to her by Jason on the births of both Jack and Sarah – were among the items that Jason cherished most. He had always promised them to Sarah as a keepsake of her mother. They were among the items that we discovered were no longer in Panther Creek Court. But I'm nothing if not determined and I wasn't going to let the rings go without a fight.

Our North Carolina lawyers, fighting a civil action on our behalf, given that Dave had been appointed executor of Jason's estate in his will, were told to specifically request the return of the rings for Sarah. For a time, the rings' whereabouts were supposed to be unknown to Molly. At one point it was suggested to us that they were lost. On another occasion Molly hinted that we had stolen them from the house. Then, out of the blue, Molly had them in her possession in court. Jason's items were never returned.

Back in Ireland, we had decided it was very important for Jack and Sarah to receive every possible support, including counselling for what they had gone through. Both Dave and myself had undergone training as foster parents and one of the most important things we'd learned was how vitally important it was for children to be listened to. Thus began a slow, painstaking process of recovery and healing for the children. Unfortunately, it also brought to light a lot of things that made my blood boil. Most disturbing was that Molly had repeatedly told the children that Jason had suffocated Mags. Sarah was just six years old when Molly first told her: 'Daddy killed your mom.' She wanted to maintain her control over the children by making them afraid of the person determined to protect them. And worst of all, Jason never knew what Molly was secretly telling Jack and Sarah.

She said she was their protector in the US and it was vital the children did everything that she told them. But children are also shrewd observers and they witnessed what Molly was doing to Jason and were scared of her.

Four sets of twins started in the Junior Infants class at Janesboro national school in Limerick in September 1980. Jason and Wayne are pictured (*far right*) in a photograph that appeared in our local newspaper, *The Limerick Leader*. My brothers weren't impressed by being dressed in short pants. (Photo: Tracey Corbett-Lynch)

I'm photographed here (*back left*) with my sister, Marilyn, and twin brothers, Jason and Wayne, in the back garden of our Janesboro home in Limerick. (Photo: Tracey Corbett-Lynch)

Our house was always full of laughter. Here I am photographed with my mam and dad, Rita and John, as well as Jason and Wayne in the kitchen of our home around 1983. (Photo: Tracey Corbett-Lynch)

Jason was exceptionally close to mam and dad. He is socialising here with dad in Limerick around 2003. (Photo: Tracey Corbett-Lynch)

My mother was a 'typical Irish mammy' and so proud of all her children. She is pictured here dancing with Jason at his 21st birthday party. (Photo: Tracey Corbett-Lynch)

Jason and Wayne are photographed during one of our family's beloved summer holidays in Clare. The world famous Cliffs of Moher form the backdrop. (Photo: Tracey Corbett-Lynch)

My brother adored Margaret 'Mags' Fitzpatrick from the moment he set eyes on her. Here they are pictured on a summer break together. (Photo: Tracey Corbett-Lynch)

Mags's sister, Catherine (*left*), with Mags and Jason. She lived with them for a time and was with them the evening Mags had her fatal asthma attack. This photo was taken the day after their wedding as both families gathered again with friends in Pallaskenry. Note the watch Jason is wearing – it was a gift from Mags. It is the only piece of his jewellery we have left. (Photo: Tracey Corbett-Lynch)

All my brother's dreams came true when he married Mags in 2003. He is all smiles here (*second from left*) as he poses on his wedding day with (*from left*) my husband, David Lynch, his best man, Damian McCormack, and Wayne Corbett. (Photo: Tracey Corbett-Lynch)

The perfect couple. My brother, Jason, proudly photographed on his wedding day with Mags Fitzpatrick. (Photo: Tracey Corbett-Lynch)

Jason takes Jack and Sarah to see Santa Claus at the Field Boxmore (later MPS) Christmas event in December 2006. My brother lost his beloved Mags just three weeks earlier. (Photo: Tracey Corbett-Lynch)

Jason out with his friends in his beloved Clare during a trip home from North Carolina in 2014. He couldn't have asked for better pals. Pictured are (*from left*) my husband, David, Paul Dillon, Jason, Brendan O'Callaghan and Wayne. (Photo: Tracey Corbett-Lynch)

Molly always insisted on opening her Christmas gifts after everyone else. She is pictured with her parents, Tom and Sharon, and brother, Connor, in the background. My brother, holding a cup of coffee at the left, patiently watches on. (Photo: Tracey Corbett-Lynch)

We organised a special girls-only dinner party in Limerick's Cornstore Restaurant for Molly to mark her forthcoming wedding to Jason. Pictured are (*from left*) Marilyn, myself, Simone Dillon, Molly and Michelle O'Callaghan. (Photo: Tracey Corbett-Lynch)

I think the look on my brother's face speaks volumes about how his wedding day to Molly was tension-filled rather than blissfully happy given her bizarre antics. Tennessee's imposing Bleak House is in the background. (Photo: Tracey Corbett-Lynch)

After Jason's move to North Carolina, we visited the US as often as possible to maintain contact. Here I am photographed with Jack and Sarah on a 2012 visit. (Photo: Tracey Corbett-Lynch)

Jason's life revolved around Jack and Sarah. Here he is taking the children for a walk behind their new Panther Creek home in the Meadowlands area of North Carolina. (Photo: Tracey Corbett-Lynch)

Jason with his good friend and neighbour David Fritzsche (*right*), as both enjoy a cold beer having mowed their lawns at Panther Creek Court on 1 August 2015. This was the last photograph ever taken of my brother. He was murdered just over eight hours later. (Photo: David and Michele Fritzsche)

Hundreds took to the streets of Limerick to support our 'Lighting the Way Home for Jack and Sarah' campaign at the height of the bitter custody battle in August 2015. We were absolutely overwhelmed by the support. The front row includes members of the Fitzpatrick family, Brendan O'Callaghan, Damian McCormack, Wayne, Mam and Dad. (Photo: David Woodland Photography)

Jason's funeral left us all broken-hearted but my husband, David, did us all proud with an emotion-charged eulogy. David (*far right*) shoulders Jason's coffin from the church en route to Castlemungret Cemetery. To the left are (*from the rear of the coffin*) my son, Dean, Jason's close MPS friend, Morgan Fogarty, and Brendan O'Callaghan. (Photo: Tracey Corbett-Lynch)

Molly Martens photographed in the early hours of 2 August 2015 outside the Panther Creek Court property by Davidson County police immediately after my brother's murder. Note Jason's blood spattered all over her face and hair. (Photo: DCSD/Ralph Riegel/*Irish Independent*)

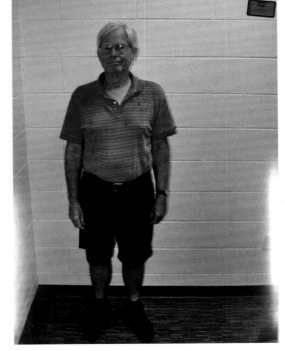

Tom Martens pictured at a Davidson County police station just hours after my brother's murder. The stains on his red polo top are from Jason's blood. (Photo: DCSD/Ralph Riegel/*Irish Independent*)

Molly Martens photographed at a Davidson County police station just hours after Jason's murder. Her clothing was found spattered with my brother's blood and tissue. (Photo: DCSD/Ralph Riegel/*Irish Independent*)

A close-up photograph of Molly's neck. The dark mark below her ear is believed to be another spatter of my brother's blood. (Photo: DCSD/Ralph Riegel/*Irish Independent*)

The metal Louisville Slugger Little League baseball bat used to beat Jason to death. (Photo: Ralph Riegel/*Irish Independent*)

The heavy concrete paving brick found by police in the master bedroom of Jason's Panther Creek Court home. It was covered on all surfaces with Jason's blood, tissue and hair. (Photo: Ralph Riegel/*Irish Independent*)

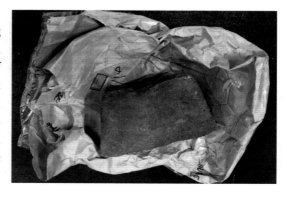

Molly Martens walks into Davidson County Superior Court in Lexington, North Carolina, for jury selection on the second day of her second degree murder trial. (Photo: Ralph Riegel/*Irish Independent*)

Just over an hour after being found guilty of second degree murder by a jury, Tom Martens is led in handcuffs by Davidson County Sheriff's Department officers to a waiting van for transfer to prison outside Raleigh, North Carolina, on 9 August 2017. To the right, his daughter, Molly Martens, is led in handcuffs and shackles out of the court for transfer in the same van to a Raleigh women's prison. Both are now serving sentences of 20–25 years. (Photo: Jerry Wolford /Polaris /eyevine)

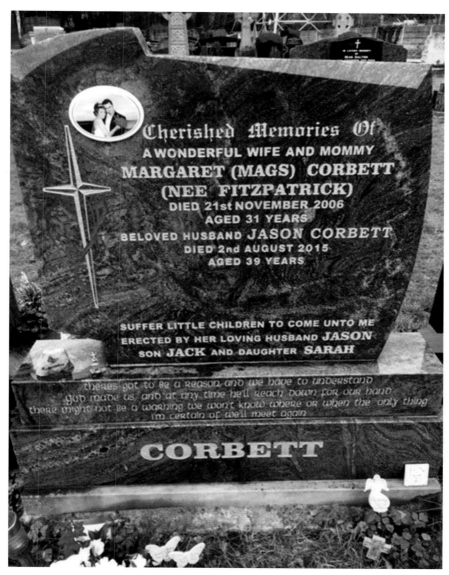

The headstone at Castlemungret Cemetery in Limerick, which marks where Mags and Jason now rest in each other's arms. Note the small tokens left on the headstone plinth as remembrances. (Photo: Ralph Riegel/*Irish Independent*)

An image which perfectly captures the type of generous, warm and happy person that Jason truly was. (Photo: Tracey Corbett-Lynch)

Jack and Sarah revealed that Molly would hide Jason's car keys when he came home. It was all part of an elaborate campaign to wear him down psychologically – the 'gaslighting' I mentioned earlier. Jason, late for a meeting, would end up frantically ransacking the house for his keys and doubting his own sanity over how the keys had vanished from where he thought he had left them. Just when he was at his most agitated, Molly would 'discover' the keys and hand them over to Jason. Or she would put them somewhere Jason had just searched. On occasions, she would speak to the children and ignore Jason, treating him as if he wasn't there.

Molly would also deliberately omit key articles for Jason when they were heading to the beach or going on social outings. The children told us she might deliberately remove or leave behind his beach towel, his swimming trunks or even his socks – enough to make him doubt himself and play with his confidence. They were small things but all part of what I believe was a psychological campaign to wear down my brother.

She would even give him the incorrect times and venues for sports events Jack and Sarah were involved in – thereby adding to the public appearance that she was effectively operating as a single mother and married to an uncaring husband.

On 25 May 2014 Jason resorted to sending Molly an email, in her official capacity as swim-team coach, to insist on being notified of events involving Jack and Sarah. The email read:

Going forward as swim team parent who helps pay for our kids to attend, I would like to be included in correspondence so I know what is going on with the team. My wife does not tell me. I have asked you to communicate prior to this and it is with great sadness that I now have to resort to email for communication regarding our kids. I would also like to be included in school events. It was brought to my attention the other day about upcoming events regarding fathers that was also kept from me for some reason. I would just like to know what is going on and since you will not or forget to tell me, maybe copying me on email might help.

The children also revealed that, for the last year of their marriage, Molly had hidden recording devices throughout the house – behind pictures, in the children's bedrooms and in the sitting room – and even in Jason's car. Molly monitored his every movement. I can only presume she was hoping to secure something that would help her in her legal battle to secure Jack and Sarah in any divorce. But, knowing Jason, there was nothing to find – his life was his children, his family and his work.

The recordings came to light when Jason, eager to impart his work ethic to his son, agreed to pay Jack $5 for cleaning his car. Jason wanted Jack to learn that money had to be earned. Jack took to the job with enthusiasm but, as he was cleaning Jason's car on the front driveway, he found what he thought was a mobile phone stuck under the driver's seat. He handed it to Jason, who immediately knew it was a recording device.

Jason told Jack and Sarah to play in the garden and he went into the house to talk to Molly. I have no idea what was said – neither do the children – but I think it is worth noting that this happened just weeks before Jason's murder.

When we had received legal permission to visit Jason's home, we found Molly had left a stack of empty packaging – all from recording devices. Molly had realised we knew about her hiding recording devices around the house and, I can only surmise, was now trying to play mind games with us. I couldn't help but wonder if she was trying to hint that she had even placed recording devices in the bedroom used by Dave and myself when we had stayed with Jason between 2011 and 2014.

Our greatest horror was over the revelations about how Molly had been treating Jack. The little boy would be punished if he didn't call Molly 'Mom' on all occasions. He also faced punishment for the smallest things that Molly didn't like. Once, Jack fell ill while Jason was away on business. Unable to reach the toilet in time, he got sick into the sink. He called Molly for help but she was angered by what had happened and made him scoop the vomit from the sink with his hands. She told the poor child he had to learn how to control such illnesses in future.

On one occasion, Jason was asleep upstairs when Molly, angered by something Jack had said or done, confronted him and grabbed him by the neck. The child let out an involuntary cry. Jason, alarmed, came down the stairs and a row erupted over what Molly had been doing with Jack. Molly left the house and, according to the children, only returned the following day.

After the incident between Molly and Jack, Jason began trying to spend more time alone with Jack. Every bruise or scrape that Jack had, Jason would want a detailed explanation of how it had been sustained. Again, this happened in the early summer of 2015 and, I believe, was another factor that persuaded Jason it was time to bring the children back to Ireland.

Throughout we were buoyed by incredible public support in Limerick and throughout Ireland. A special 'Justice for Jason' campaign was launched by Mary Fitzpatrick, Simone Dillon and Richard Lynch, who is best known for his 'I Love Limerick' initiative. The Facebook section of the campaign was then taken over by my first cousin Nuala Galvin.

They were tireless in supporting our campaign for justice – and performed miracles in highlighting the case, keeping the pressure on the authorities for action and ensuring that Irish politicians stayed active in supporting us. They also built up an incredible worldwide network of contacts, which allowed us to uncover vital details of Molly's past and her behaviour at Panther Creek Court since 2011.

Nuala recalled:

Tracey and I both come from very large families. My mother [Mary] and Rita are sisters and are very close, always keeping in contact. They are always keeping us up to date on what is happening in our cousins' lives. When the news of Jason's death broke, I immediately went with my mother to Rita's house to offer whatever support we could. Over the following weeks and months, I became very close to Rita. Now, almost three years later, I count Tracey as one of my closest friends.

I was asked to help out with the 'Justice for Jason' campaign and the Facebook element of it was something I could do. It grew to the point where it was absolutely incredible. In August 2017 at the height of the North Carolina trial the Facebook page had 378,434 page engagements. For the most part, people were very supportive and very kind. The 'Justice for Jason' page became a community of people who not only showed up every day to support the Lynch–Corbett family but to support each other as well. Many lasting friendships were formed. A lot of people who had lost loved ones in similar circumstances found great support there. I was posting updates on the page twice a day and I tried to focus on justice and the truth of what happened as well as being positive and respectful towards everyone.

The network of contacts the page helped develop was just astonishing – there were people all over Ireland, the US and the world who wanted to help. Of course, the page also helped to counter some of the material being posted on social media about the case that was blatantly untrue and, on some occasions, vile and hurtful.

A special vigil organised by Simone, Richard and Mary was held in Limerick on 18 August 2015 as part of the 'Justice for Jason' campaign. It was the eve of the custody decision in North Carolina.

The speakers included Fr Pat Hogan from Southill and former minister and Limerick TD Willie O'Dea, Senator Kieran O'Donnell and Mayor Jerry O'Dea. Fr Pat's address was nothing short of inspirational. More than anything, it helped steel us for the legal battles that lay ahead.

By October 2015 I knew that Davidson County police believed that Jason had been unlawfully killed by Molly and Tom Martens. There were simply too many holes and contradictions in their story. In repeated phone calls and meetings with police and Davidson County District Attorney officials I had learned there was a growing body of forensic evidence that cast major doubt on Molly and Tom's version of events.

In the weeks after Jason's death, I had been swamped with contacts from people across Ireland, the United States and even Europe. Many just wanted us to know how highly they had thought of my brother. But others had valuable information they wanted us to know. Particularly important for us were the number of people in North Carolina, Tennessee and Georgia I was able to make contact with and who were able to shed light on Molly's past.

This is how I discovered so many of the stories Molly told us were complete fantasy. I have never been a big fan of social media but it provided an invaluable tool in tracking down information I felt was vital for the Davidson County police. The downside was that social media was also an avenue by which people could direct poisonous, malicious and false commentary towards us. Thankfully, we were blessed to have Nuala, who operated single-handedly as a filter to protect us from the most vicious of the comments.

Piece by piece, we were able to put together the jigsaw of Molly's lies, half-truths and fantasies until there was no doubt in the minds of investigators as to the type of person they were dealing with. For instance, Molly was an avid reader and joined a local book club. Hard as it is to believe, in the months before Jason's murder the two books she had recommended were Robert Tine's *The Hand That Rocks the Cradle* and Gillian Flynn's *Gone Girl* – both books with a deranged woman as the central character.

Through emails and correspondence, we could also see that Jason had desperately tried to control Molly's spending issues. She was a compulsive shopper. When Panther Creek Court was examined, there were virtually three rooms full of her clothing. We learned that Jason, trying to balance their family finances, had been attempting to make Molly adhere to a spending budget. She had spent $90,000 in the eight months before Jason's death.

Money always seemed to be important to Molly, as borne out by a letter she had written many years before. When Molly had worked at the Visage beauty salon in Knoxville, she had fallen ill and the staff had kindly fundraised to buy her a gift. In her letter thanking Visage staff, Molly had written: 'They say money doesn't buy happiness – well, I beg to differ. At the very least, it takes care of one enormous worry, paving the way towards a happier future.'

We also learned that some neighbours in Panther Creek Court had also seen Molly's darker side. Tom and Jerusha Maddock lived locally and had become very friendly with Jason and Molly. I got to know them after 2015 and discovered what a wonderful couple they are – genuinely warm, caring and family-orientated people. But Molly had, for her own reasons, effectively waged psychological warfare on Jerusha. Jerusha recalled:

We met Jason and Molly in early summer of 2011. Jason was fun loving and charming. He had a great sense of humour and was very self-deprecating. He was sincere, was a proud dad and a good friend. Our opinion of Molly definitely changed over time. Initially, she seemed very bright, outgoing and fun. It wasn't long before we noticed certain incongruities in her relating both the inconsequential happenings of her daily life and more meaningful stories regarding her past. The inconsistencies raised our suspicions. When her manipulating and lies started to take a more nefarious turn, I questioned or challenged her. That was a huge mistake on my part. That put a target on my back.

At first, I was simply frustrated. I didn't understand the depth of her depravity. Then Molly began to attack my character and played mind games that hinted at her capacity for malice. It's important to understand she did this with guile and tried to maintain her mask of charm and often played the victim to everyone else. Close friends did not all see or know the same Molly. It is extremely difficult to defend yourself against someone with no moral boundaries. You cannot win. Eventually my frustration turned to fear and I started withdrawing from certain social occasions I knew she would attend. I hoped my absence would convey a sense of victory to her. I was no longer in her way and therefore no longer needed to be undermined within our social circle and community. The bottom line – Molly threatened my sense of security and she scared me.

Honestly, to us, there were no revelations during the [2017] trial. The shock came when we first learned Jason had died and the horrific details of his death. By the time the trial began, we were set in our beliefs regarding the rage and torture Tom and Molly had inflicted upon Jason. We have had no personal contact or interaction with Molly since Jason's murder. We were aghast and extremely worried when she pursued custody of Jack and Sarah. We believed her posts on social media after Jason's death reflected her inability to feel true sorrow and compassion for Jack, Sarah and the rest of Jason's family. They were carefully crafted to elicit a specific response from an intended audience. All of Molly's words and actions were self-serving.

Other neighbours were equally supportive and the kindness they showed us will never be forgotten. Tony Turner was an Englishman who supported Manchester United – Jason was an Irishman who supported Liverpool, United's fierce rivals. They became firm friends in Panther Creek Court and the banter, or 'craic' as we say here in Ireland, between them was hilarious. Tony recalled:

Jason was a true friend who I could turn to, a kind and caring man. I valued his friendship and respected him as an individual. Although he had a very high and responsible work position, he never let it go to his head. Jason was a great joker with a dry sense of humour that didn't get lost in translation between us, a humour sometimes a little too dry for some of our American friends … He was a tremendous father to his children and did everything possible to spend quality time with them. He ensured they got to their sports events on time and he chastised them in a loving way when they did something wrong. Once, he had an opportunity for a work promotion and turned down the position, believing he was travelling enough and didn't want to be away from his family any more than he already was.

When I was going through my divorce, Jason came over to make sure I was okay. We chatted for an hour or so over a cold beer, dancing around the subject until he realised I was actually okay and handling the situation. After that we talked freely.

In the beginning, we were friends with Jason and Molly as a couple, although I never had any personal conversations with Molly. She was a great swim coach for the neighbourhood kids but there were a lot of things I heard second-hand that made me feel wary about her. There were also a lot of rumours and innuendos about Jason and Molly's relationship, but I withheld judgement since there were no indications that the gossip was true. Afterward, I just felt sad. Molly had everything – a great husband, a great family and a good life. She just let it slip away with an atrocious ending. I was horrified that someone like Jason could be subjected to such a horrific end to his life. Nobody deserves to go away like that, but violence towards a person so gentle, kind and thoughtful leaves me lost for words and without forgiveness of the brutality he was subjected to.

Another of Jason's great friends, was Charles 'Chip' McDonell, a senior US business executive who was drawn to my brother because of his kindness, good humour and family-oriented life:

I knew Jason for around eight years after he moved to North Carolina and into our community. In that time, we became very close friends. Jason was the type of guy that would do anything for his friends. He stepped up whenever he was needed to help our fellow neighbors or friends and would give you the shirt off his back if you asked.

Jason was one of the best fathers that I knew in the neighborhood. He was a very important man at work and was required to travel a fair amount due to his job. When he was at home, however, he was devoted to his family. He always made it a priority to make it to his children's swim events, baseball games and soccer games even if it meant that he had to leave work. He was very involved with his kids' sports as a coach or in helping to better the team by being part of organizing and fund raising. He thoroughly enjoyed playing golf with Jack or with another father/son pair like my son and myself. I loved hearing stories about how funny Sarah and Jack were. It was obvious how much he loved and respected them both.

Jason was the all-around great guy that everyone respected. Even with his responsibilities at work, he found time to be part of the community. I used to love coming over to his house to play pool with some of the fathers in the neighborhood. Other times, we would just sit around a fire pit over a beer with some of the neighbors while watching the kids play. He always had a joke and always made the atmosphere more entertaining. I miss my friend.

It was a similar experience for Dave and Michele Fritzsche, who were Jason and Molly's next-door neighbours. Michele recalled:

We met Jason and Molly in May 2011 immediately after they moved in. We found Jason to be very pleasant and friendly – over time, we became better acquainted and our opinion only improved. Jason was a good, loving father who was devoted to his family and was hard-working, friendly, likeable, funny, appreciative and overall a good guy. Our initial opinion of Molly was also a positive one. She was also friendly, likeable, loving towards and focused on her family. Over the course of that first year as she began to meet other neighbours and form new friendships, my opinion of Molly began to waver. We shared several friends and socialised in groups together. Many times, I felt Molly had a story or an experience that was either equal to or greater than the one someone else was sharing about themselves. Although that can be annoying, you brush it off and consider it a quirk. However, I realised after some time and after many casual conversations with mutual friends and neighbours that we were also being told different versions of things – the topics varied and some were more serious or concerning in nature than others. In my opinion, the stories I was aware of became increasingly hard to believe, almost far-fetched, contradictory and potentially dubious.

My opinion of Molly changed slowly over time and I found myself limiting the amount of time I allowed myself to be alone with her to limit the possibility of being confided in. Molly was a nice person, a friend and a good neighbour but it was impossible not to question her honesty and wonder if she was a compulsive liar.

Michele admitted her greatest concern revolved around Molly claiming to some that she was Sarah's biological mother and that Jason was abusive.

It makes one question many things. Molly was telling different versions to different people. As for her claims that Jason was abusive, we only heard those second-hand from mutual friends whom she had told directly. Dave and I did not believe the allegations to be true. But I found myself looking for signs of abuse to help us decipher what was going on.

Dave and Michele found nothing to indicate any type of abuse as alleged by Molly. In fact, Molly's behaviour seemed to flatly contradict what she was telling her close circle of friends. 'I often wondered why she would say certain unflattering things to him [Jason] in public because if he was abusing her I would have thought she would be more reserved with comments that could potentially cause a disagreement. We really believed this was all about getting the attention that she seemed to enjoy and need.'

Michele and Dave had no major contact with Molly after 2 August. The couple admitted they were 'deeply shocked' to learn of the horrific injuries that Jason had sustained that night. Watching the US TV interviews that Molly and Tom had given on the eve of the trial left them both troubled. 'We do not think she or her father were genuine or remorseful for what happened. Molly portrayed a meek woman and that is not how we knew her.'

Another neighbour, Katherine 'Katye' Oliver, was also very wary of Molly. In 2017, Katye would attend every day of the Davidson County trial.

Molly and I were in Book Club and Bible Study together and my daughter babysat for Jack and Sarah. I had some suspicions about Molly, both first and second-hand, that caused me to keep an arm's-length relationship with her. For at least three years prior to the murder, several of us would have regular, private conversations about Molly's wild stories.

If I could use one word to describe Molly, it would be 'unbelievable'. No one had more life experiences, career paths, Forrest Gump-like stories, than Molly. She could 'one up' any story you told, and she had experienced it all, even though she was only in her late 20s. She used her looks and her seemingly well-educated mind to manipulate and create the picture of herself that she wanted others to believe. Her 'wild stories' destroyed her credibility. To a private circle of people, she was the growing joke for all outlandish claims.

I found it very interesting in my messaging back and forth with Tracey Lynch and Catherine Fitzpatrick that the Molly of

Meadowlands was so different than the Molly of Ireland. I gathered that Molly was quiet, removed and did not make efforts to reach out and develop relationships with any of Jason's friends or family while she was in Ireland. Yet, the Molly I knew was a leader in the community, a swim instructor for the neighborhood swim team, and a 'room mom' in the children's classrooms. She led our Book Club in every book discussion. She fit, for all purposes, the anti-abuse victim profile. She was not a 'wallflower', shirking from conversation or attention of others. Molly commanded attention with her voice and her showy clothing choices. There was no denying when Molly entered the room.

Molly regularly attended a Bible Study I led out of my home for most of one year. She was outspoken in this environment also, though she shared very little personal struggles or prayer requests. She never shared or hinted of any marital discord of any kind. I felt conflicted by my behind-her-back suspicions of Molly UNTIL one particular evening. One Bible Study attendee was sharing the news of her recent pregnancy. Ladies began chiming in about their own pregnancies and deliveries. Several of us in the room nearly fell out of our chair when Molly casually shared about her discomforts with pregnancy and stretch marks, etc. She even spoke about her delivery and episiotomy!

We were flabbergasted that she would discredit Sarah's mother's role in Sarah's birth and replace it with her own story as the birth mother! We knew there were some women in the room who had no idea that Molly was not Sarah's mother. We were so shocked by Molly's seemingly believable claims that we did not confront her on this untruth.

Not everyone was as supportive to us as the Olivers, Fritzsches, McDonells, Maddocks, Turners, Viers and many other families in the Meadowlands, the area in which Panther Creek Court is located. As Tony

Turner acknowledged, the local community was split – many simply didn't know what to believe. That being said, the one person I was deeply disappointed in was Charlie Grubb. He was a neighbour and Jason had considered him a trusted friend. In fact, Jason had gone out of his way to help steer work towards Charlie through his MPS business.

But, after Jason's death, it was as if Charlie simply didn't want to get involved. We knew Jason had spoken with him about his plans to return to Ireland – Melanie Crook of MPS had confirmed that to us. But Charlie was reluctant to get involved. He appeared more concerned about the fact that his wife, Shannon, was Molly's closest friend. My belief is that any ties of friendship Charlie had with Jason appeared to end with my brother's death.

By now, we had gotten to know Davidson County Sheriff David Grice and District Attorney Garry Frank and his team, not to mention Lt Det. Thompson and the police officers who were carefully building the case against Tom and Molly Martens. In the weeks and months after Jason's killing, I realised just what a dedicated group of professionals they were. But I also discovered what truly kind-hearted people they were.

The District Attorney, on reviewing the police file, immediately dismissed the story of self-defence. When he received the post mortem report, he knew the Davidson County team were dealing with something far more sinister. 'That is a critical factor, in my opinion,' Mr Frank said. 'To argue that it was necessary for this [Jason's battered skull] when you wind up looking like this [Tom and Molly totally uninjured] after the incident is a very incredible leap in my opinion.'

That Christmas was our first without Jason. It may officially have been the festive season but none of us felt like celebrating. We couldn't escape the dark pall of grief that had been cast over us.

Going to the grave that now held Jason and Mags that Christmas was one of the hardest things I ever had to do – we were all still so raw from the events of August.

It was particularly hard for Jack and Sarah because Christmas brings its own reminders of all that is lost. They were swamped with presents from family, friends, neighbours and well-wishers. I don't think two children were ever hugged as much over Christmas by doting grandparents, aunts and uncles. Our family had closed ranks and were surrounding Jack and Sarah with a protective wall of love. But there was no hiding the fact that they had been orphaned.

Christmas was also dominated by thoughts of what 2016 would bring. We had done our part in getting every possible piece of information to assist the Davidson County police investigation into Jason's killing. I wanted the North Carolina authorities to now do their part and press charges against Tom and Molly for what they had done. We did not know at that point that the decision to charge had been made, but had been legally sealed by the District Attorney until January.

7

Molly and Tom Charged

I finally got the only New Year's wish I wanted – an indication that charges would be brought in North Carolina over Jason's death. On 4 January 2016, Molly and Tom Martens were ordered to appear before a Lexington court, where they were formally charged with second degree murder and voluntary manslaughter.

Molly and Tom both faced the two charges. We knew the voluntary manslaughter charge was simply a fall-back option for the trial if something disastrous happened to the prosecution case. The main charge was that of second degree murder – essentially, murder without premeditation. It differs from manslaughter in that, for second degree murder, the defendant must have used malice in the fatal assault. In North Carolina, the heaviest sentence for a second degree murder conviction would be life imprisonment. And, in the US, life means life.

After being charged, both Molly and Tom were released pending their trial. They were never remanded in custody at any stage, either after the initial charge or during the entire trial process.

I knew that this was only the end of the beginning. But I felt that the decision to charge Molly and Tom was an important first public vindication of Jason – it was almost a message to the world that the story about a hero dad defending his little princess from the drunken Irish brute was a fiction.

While part of me was delighted with the charge, another part was disappointed. I had hoped the pair would be charged with first degree murder, which is the killing of someone with premeditation or intent. In North Carolina, a conviction for first degree murder carries the death penalty. It wasn't that I wanted the death penalty for them but I was convinced the killing of Jason didn't occur on the spur of the moment. I feel that if Molly had taken the stand, this would have been abundantly clear. The more I learned about what the police had found, the more I believed there had been intent in Jason's murder, at least by Molly.

I learned that the entire District Attorney team had studied the merits of a first degree murder prosecution. They felt the forensic evidence was very persuasive. But it ultimately proved to be a decision taken on the finest of margins.

Reluctantly, they decided to go with second degree murder given the evidence available to them. Securing a first degree murder prosecution is difficult at the best of times and, in Jason's case, they felt the available evidence meant a second degree murder prosecution was the correct call. That would be joined by a voluntary manslaughter charge. But, to this day, I believe it was a decision only taken by a hair's breadth margin. Our family certainly felt there was sufficient motive and intent to justify the higher charge.

I knew Molly and Tom would be absolutely furious over the charges. What I understood about Tom was that he was a very proud, arrogant man and would be privately seething over the suggestion that he could ever be associated with anything of such a criminal nature. He would also loathe the media coverage, which he would view as an invasion of his privacy. By this point, I honestly feared that Molly was believing her own lies – so God only knows what she felt about the charges.

Just hours after being charged, Molly took to social media to make her feelings known. She launched a scathing attack on what she termed 'the level of slander, harassment, lies and absolute corruption' that she and her father had been subjected to. But I wondered whether she was now getting a high out of the media attention. Her Facebook page was on a public setting and, over the years, she had engaged in a series of public rows over the events of 2 August.

Molly seemed to have a relentless fascination with social media – she was constantly posting material about herself, about Jack and Sarah and, occasionally, about the ordeal she was going through. There were times when I felt my family was at the centre of a hurricane of media attention.

There were many examples. Molly took to social media to complain that we had deliberately ensured all of Jack and Sarah's toys and personal belongings from the US were kept from them. Then Molly slated the Irish media. 'The Irish press has printed many inaccuracies … there are [so many] inaccuracies and falsehoods out there. The lies that have been told that I have aforementioned can be proven with documentation … poor journalism … doesn't anyone care about fact-checking their stories?'

I firmly believe that a close study of Molly's social media postings gives a hint as to her mental state. On the one hand she seems to revel in the attention and controversy her postings generate – but the bizarre claims, the rambling posts and even the spelling and grammatical errors indicate someone under severe mental strain. She even claimed we were using Jack and Sarah to fundraise just to ensure she was falsely prosecuted.

Molly posted:

As the money is apparently being used for the family [Lynch-Corbett] to publicize fabricate and perform an investigation of a crime that did not happen, to incriminate the children's mother (sorry, the person they called 'Mom' as we are not blood-related) then, yes, I would say that is most inappropriate. Has anyone actually wondered where that money is going? Maybe that money was used to hire the locksmith to break into my house so they could go through my underwear drawer and nightstand as they did last week.

Molly repeatedly used social media to complain about the 'lies' being told about her and to plead for contact with Jack and Sarah. She also kept posting photographs of the children, which was something we greatly objected to. We were determined to shield the children from the legal maelstrom in which they found themselves and I issued a stark warning to Molly and her family to desist from posting such photographs. My appeal was basically ignored.

Molly's uncle, Michael Earnest, also used social media to advance Tom and Molly's case. He stressed that the father and daughter had co-operated fully with the police and had acted only in self-defence. 'Tom and Molly need our help to exonerate them from these charges.'

But, in one critical posting, he also wrote: 'In the early morning hours of 2 August 2015, Tom and Sharon were awakened suddenly to the desperate screams from their daughter Molly.' That post was removed within a couple of hours. The reason that is important is because he insinuated that Sharon Martens was awakened by the noises from the bedroom overhead. As you will read later, the defence emphatically stated in the Davidson County Superior Court trial that Sharon Martens did not wake up and never left the basement bedroom on 1–2 August.

We had been advised not to undertake any interviews or participate in any TV programmes lest they might unintentionally impede the prosecution or cause problems for the Davidson County authorities. There were times when I almost screamed in frustration at being unable to reply to some of the claims from the Martens family – but I also understood that the murder trial would be our forum for having the truth confirmed.

It wouldn't be a quick prosecution. I was informed that an enormous amount of work was still required with the case file. The trial wouldn't see the inside of a courtroom in North Carolina in 2016. The prosecution would likely take place before the Davidson County Superior Court sitting in Lexington, most likely in early or mid-2017. The wait was excruciating – our lives were on pause for two years.

I also learned some key facts about such cases in North Carolina. A conviction could only be recorded by unanimous verdict of a 12-member jury. Unlike in Ireland, where majority verdicts of 11–1 and 10–2 are allowed for every jury, just two states in the US allow such majority verdicts – and North Carolina was not one of them. If just one jury member disagreed with their colleagues, it would be a hung jury and no verdict could be recorded. In that scenario, it was either a fresh trial or no new prosecution would be ordered.

While I would have preferred an early trial date, the delay at least afforded us the opportunity to help Jack and Sarah get some kind of normality back in their lives and to begin saving for the mammoth costs involved in attending a North Carolina trial. When I flew to North Carolina immediately after Jason's killing, I had never been away from my children for more than a couple of nights. But it was almost three weeks before I saw them again after that awful 2 August day. I knew that, if anything, the murder trial would prove an even greater undertaking. Murder trials, particularly complex ones, can last anything up to seven weeks in some US states.

The travel costs over the two years were also mind-numbing. Dave had signed up for a loyalty programme with the hotel chain we stayed with in High Point. By the time we left, we had built up so many loyalty points we were able to qualify for several free nights when we returned to North Carolina.

The multiple trips from Ireland to the US were a huge drain on our finances. Between the custody, guardianship and estate battles in Ireland and the US, legal bills were in excess of $500,000 (€400,000). But supporters across Limerick and all parts of Ireland, as well as Jason's US friends and MPS colleagues, rallied to help us. They staged fundraising events from tea parties to cake sales and from sponsored walks to film nights at local cinemas. They helped raise €52,000 ($65,000), which kept us going. We were so thankful and grateful for this support in 2015. We tried to cut costs as best we could by planning trips with almost military precision. If we had a court appointment at 3 p.m. in respect of Jason's estate or a key briefing on the prosecution case, we would fly into

Charlotte that morning, drive up to Lexington for the afternoon meeting and try to be ready to fly home the following day. On occasion, we would fly directly to Washington and then drive the six hours to Lexington just to save on flight costs. It was gruelling and exhausting but it kept costs down. We also had to keep our jobs, though our firms were incredibly understanding of the plight we found ourselves in.

In the meantime, our civil actions to defend Jason's estate for the benefit of his children continued apace. At almost every single stage, the Martens fought us. Very little was conceded and, in one particular court proceeding, Molly even insisted that she be referred to as 'Ms Martens Corbett'. I understood immediately it was her way of trying to unsettle me and play mind games.

But Dave brought his business acumen to bear and, with the support of our able North Carolina lawyers, we began to score notable legal victories, particularly in relation to protecting Jason's assets and possessions. Our aim was to have everything secured until after the criminal trial was concluded. Eventually, we were even able to get Jason's Honda back from Tom Martens.

The courtesy and kindness shown to our family by the Davidson County authorities, both from the District Attorney's Office and the Sheriff's Department, was beyond words. If a meeting ran late into the evening, we were swamped with offers of hospitality including invitations to attend people's own homes for meals. Garry Frank, Greg Brown, Alan Martin and Ina Stanton went above and beyond their duties in looking out for our interests. The kindness and generosity we were met with did a lot to reinforce my faith in humanity and kindness.

Eventually, we were told that, before the murder trial could open, a special pre-trial hearing would be necessary. This would resolve a lot of the issues over how the trial would operate on a day-to-day basis as well as what evidence and witnesses could be called. More than likely it would take two days. I understood that two key issues would dominate the pre-trial hearing – whether statements made by Jack and Sarah in August 2015 would be allowed as evidence and whether Tom Martens would be allowed to introduce a statement that raised major questions over the manner of Mags's death. It was despicable. I also learned that we wouldn't be any wiser as to whether Molly and Tom would take the stand and offer sworn evidence in their own defence.

I expected Jack and Sarah's statements to be an issue. But I was genuinely shocked at the attempt to suggest Mags's death was anything other than a natural tragedy. I wasn't the only one. The Fitzpatrick family, once made aware of what was happening, weren't just shocked – they were appalled, as I knew they would be. Michael Fitzpatrick, Mags's father, insisted on going to a Limerick solicitor to make a sworn statement that he had never made such comments to Tom Martens as were now alleged by the former FBI agent. Michael became seriously ill and died before the 2017 trial. It was unforgivable that his grieving wife should have had to cope with such outrageous claims about the loss of her daughter at the very time she was mourning her husband. Marian Fitzpatrick is one of the nicest ladies I have ever met and reminds me so much of Mags.

Tom claimed that Michael had suggested he held Jason responsible for his daughter's death. Tom alleged he was left shocked by the remark – and, in hindsight, it made him fear for the safety of his own daughter. In other words, it played – as he understood from his legal training – towards his state of mind at the time of Jason's killing. He claimed these comments had been made to him at Jason and Molly's wedding. The only problem was that, as we pointed out, Michael had not attended the wedding. This was quickly explained away as a typographical error and the comments were suddenly attributed to a different occasion. But Michael was adamant he had never said anything of the kind to Tom. He had only met Tom Martens once and that was in company. Prosecutors were now provided with a sworn statement to that fact.

What I wasn't surprised at was Tom and Molly's attempt to introduce statements made by Jack and Sarah in August 2015 in the days before we were able to bring them back to Ireland. Having been in the Martenses' custody for weeks, I knew that they were simply repeating what had been said to them. Any child in their position would have reacted similarly, particularly after such a traumatic event as the loss of their father and their desire to co-operate with their sole remaining parent.

In Ireland, Jack and Sarah had received counselling. They also made disclosures about what had happened in the US. They explained not just what had happened in August 2015 but the behaviour that Molly had engaged in with Jason in the days, weeks and months before his death.

If Tom and Molly attempted to introduce the August statements, we would fight to ensure that detailed Irish statements would also be available to the judge and jury.

On 8 and 9 June 2017, Judge David Lee held the pre-trial hearing in Davidson County Superior Court. He would now rule on all aspects of the forthcoming trial, which was scheduled to open on 17 July. After almost two years of waiting, I couldn't believe the final battle for justice for Jason was upon us. Dave and I travelled over for the entire pre-trial hearing and were to offer evidence. For the trial itself, most of my family would attend. Several of Jason's friends, including Paul and Lynn, would also travel to North Carolina for the trial.

In Davidson County courthouse, Judge Lee opened the preliminary proceedings by introducing himself. He was a reserved man but with a ready smile and distinctive southern accent. We would later discover he also had a keen wit and a razor-sharp sense of humour. Within a few minutes of the hearing's opening, we also realised he boasted an exceptional legal mind and was determined that the murder trial would run in a careful, efficient and meticulously planned manner. Judge Lee was not a justice who tolerated surprises when it came to a murder trial.

Tom Martens was being defended by David Freedman and Jones Byrd. They ranked among the best defence attorneys in North Carolina, with Mr Freedman specialising in serious criminal cases such as murder. Molly was being defended by Walter Holton and Cheryl Andrews, also considered among the best legal advocates in the state. Both boasted impressive track records in terms of trial successes.

But, over the previous two years, we had learned to greatly respect the abilities of District Attorney Garry Frank and his team of Assistant District Attorneys including Greg Brown, Alan Martin and Ina Stanton. Mr Frank would not play an active part in the trial – the lead role would be assumed by his three assistants.

Judge Lee quickly found himself besieged by motions, mostly from the defence. The first was for the trial to be moved out of Davidson County. Both Mr Freedman and Mr Holton asked for the trial to be transferred to Mocksville in neighbouring Davie County. They argued that the vast amount of publicity generated by Jason's death and the subsequent investigation made it impossible to select an unbiased jury in Davidson County. But it all ended in farce when Mr Martin pointed out that Mocksville Courthouse was undergoing construction work in July – rendering any trial there 'a practical impossibility'.

Judge Lee also noted that he was 'having a hard time' in seeing the local prejudice claimed by the defence.

The defence also called for submissions from a private investigator, Robert Spillman, a retired Winston-Salem police officer, and Shannon Grubb, who described herself as Molly's 'closest and best friend'. Ms Grubb cited local commentary as indicating to her that Molly wouldn't receive a fair trial in Davidson County. But she also took issue with the investigation itself.

It is my belief – I don't believe she would get a fair trial in Davidson County if the same people were responsible for taking my statements and all the information that was obtained. The statements from the Sheriff's Department was [that] my statements were incorrect, not written down, not properly the process.

I want the truth to be my words to be in the record ...

The pre-trial hearing was front page news locally in *The Dispatch*, Lexington's own newspaper, a hint of the huge interest the trial itself would generate. Both defence legal teams argued that the media in North Carolina and in Ireland had published 'initial inaccurate and misleading allegations'. Submissions also alleged that 'the family of Mr Corbett has undertaken an extensive social media campaign to sway public opinion against the defendant(s)'. This had allegedly extended to 'include direct threats to the defendant and her family as well as Facebook and website postings critical of the defendant'. They further claimed that the cumulative publicity, from Jason's death through the custody battle to the pre-trial coverage, had led to 'word of mouth' commentary throughout Davidson County that would adversely impact on the prospect of a fair trial.

If I wasn't seething inside, I probably would have laughed with contempt at such a claim. Starting within days of Jason's death, Molly and her family had conducted a remorseless campaign to endorse their version of what had happened at Panther Creek Court. Molly was ceaselessly placing material on Facebook, particularly about her love for Jack and Sarah. 'Wherever you are, my love will find you,' she posted. They had even given interviews – something we avoided after the week of Jason's death. The only newspaper interview I gave was to the *Limerick Leader* and that was solely to thank everyone who had supported us in our battle to get Jason's body home for burial and to secure custody of Jack and Sarah. It was also to thank the people of Limerick for the manner in which they had sought to honour Jason's memory during his funeral arrangements and for their fundraising campaign.

I also found it highly ironic that they were citing media coverage as a potential interference factor in the case when Tom and Molly either already had or were shortly about to conduct a major pre-trial interview with US network ABC for their crime programme *20:20*. In Ireland, we have a phrase for this: 'running with the hare and hunting with the hounds'.

The Davidson County prosecution team urged the court to dismiss the submission as without merit. One Assistant District Attorney described the argument as 'irrelevant and unpersuasive'. It was pointed out to Judge Lee that the Martenses' legal teams had engaged in the very type of pre-trial publicity that they were now formally objecting to. 'Counsel for the defendants have participated in local, national and international interviews discussing the facts and circumstance of the killing of Jason Corbett,' it was pointed out.

The Davidson County prosecutors further argued that the defence team had filed documents in advance of the pre-trial hearing for the very purpose of ensuring that allegations against Jason were publicly available to both the US and Irish media. 'The defendants have used a pre-trial motion filed months prior to any hearing as a strategic tool to transform potentially inadmissible evidence into public record. If the defendants are prejudiced by their own conduct, they cannot be heard to complain,' it was stated.

I had no prior experience of criminal trials. We were like babes in the wood when it came to matters like this. Every single development in the trial process appeared to us to be a potential threat or cause for concern. While I didn't know it, these types of submission were commonplace in such murder cases. But Judge Lee wasn't having any of it. Without specific proof that a fair and impartial trial was under threat, he was not ordering the trial out of Davidson County. 'The defence has failed to find existing community prejudice that they can't receive a fair trial. There is no showing of prejudice in the investigation or proceedings … to preclude selection of a jury,' he ruled.

That brought us to the key element of Jack and Sarah's statements. According to the defence legal teams, these statements corroborated Molly and Tom's contention that there had been a domestic-violence scenario in the Panther Creek home. But the children's statements, if you study them closely, simply reveal two shocked and traumatised youngsters repeating precisely what Molly, Tom and Sharon told them and nothing more.

I was called to offer sworn evidence as to the issue. I explained that we had organised counselling for both Jack and Sarah when they arrived

137

back in Ireland. Shortly into this process, Jack was very upset one day and explained to us that what he had said during an interview with DSS and Dragonfly House officials in North Carolina was not true. When questioned via Skype by Assistant District Attorney Ina Stanton months later, Jack confirmed that he had not witnessed or heard of any domestic abuse between Jason and Molly. He felt so bad about the incident that he wanted to contact Davidson County police to explain what had happened and apologise. The poor child was terrified the entire world he knew was about to be taken away from him and so said what he felt had been demanded of him.

'He said he felt really bad about it. [Jack] said he wanted to tell the police that he had lied,' I told the court. To support the matter, I confirmed that sworn statements had been taken from both Jack and Sarah in Ireland that totally contradicted what they had told DSS officials in North Carolina. Our position was that we didn't want the North Carolina statements introduced into evidence. If they were, we only wanted the Irish statements introduced to clarify them. Our overriding priority was protecting Jack and Sarah. We refused to allow them to endure the trauma of offering evidence at a criminal trial. Jason would not have wanted it – no matter what the outcome.

Needless to say, the defence vehemently objected to this. They made a major issue about the fact that we had not brought Jack and Sarah to the US to potentially offer evidence. Now, they demanded that the North Carolina statements be allowed into evidence. Both defence attorneys argued that staff at the child advocacy centre followed national protocols as to whether a child knows the difference between a truth and an untruth.

However, Judge Lee reserved his position on the children's statements and said he would prefer if arguments over those specific statements were handled by the trial judge. It wasn't quite clear yet that he would handle the trial the following month. It was a similar matter in respect of Michael Fitzpatrick's disputed statement to Tom Martens. That would also be resolved by the trial judge.

But the defence still weren't done. They now turned their sights on the District Attorney's Office and the Davidson County legal office itself. They alleged that the clerk of Davidson County made improper contact with our family in Ireland on the issue of the estate and the guardianship proceedings over Jason's two children.

They also alleged that the Davidson County Sheriff's Department 'have developed an inordinately close relationship to the family of Mr Corbett and the Irish media'. Specific elements of media coverage were singled out to Judge Lee – and, it was complained, we had made an inappropriate gift to the Davidson County prosecution team in the form of a box of Irish tea bags. We had given them as a gesture of thanks for their kindness.

When I asked about it, I was told that the defence complaints were in response to a discovery motion they had filed for communications between our family and the Davidson County authorities. Part of me was shocked. But the more I thought about it, the more I began to realise that Tom and Molly must be worried about the strength of the prosecution case if this was the kind of nonsense they were willing to engage in.

But I also knew that Molly was under increasing mental and emotional strain. Proof of this came when she was involved in a minor traffic accident in Davidson County where she clipped a parked car. However, Molly left the accident scene without waiting for the police to arrive – only to be recognised and identified by the householder involved who had gone to investigate the noise. However, no prosecution was taken in light of the more serious criminal matters pending. Similarly, Molly wasn't prosecuted for a blatant case of perjury over sworn evidence she had given about her mental health history.

8

The Trial Opens

After all the waiting and praying, the trial date was suddenly upon us. I had mixed emotions – I knew the court case would be traumatic and painful for us all. Not just because of what had been done to Jason but also because of the lies that Molly and Tom Martens were still trying to persuade people were the truth of what happened that awful night.

What I found every bit as difficult was the prospect of being separated from Dean, Adam, Jack and Sarah for so long.

I knew Dave, myself and other family members would be in North Carolina for several weeks. My fear was that we might be there for several months if the trial proved protracted and the jury took an extended period to reach a verdict. We had set up Skype so we could talk to the children every single morning before court. It made it easier to appear upbeat for the children because most evenings I was so emotionally exhausted and traumatised by the evidence of the day I would probably have broken down and wept at the sound of their voices.

We had planned as exciting a summer as possible for the children to ensure Adam, Jack and Sarah wanted for nothing and were kept busy and entertained. Our eldest son, Dean, who was in his twenties, assumed the parental role. Dave's sister even flew home from the US to help out.

It meant that we could travel to the US to see justice done for Jason while knowing that Jack, Sarah, Adam and Dean were surrounded by those who loved and cared for them.

It would also be a difficult separation from my parents, who I knew had placed all their faith and hope in Jason's killers being convicted. Mam and Dad were now quite elderly and it was equally difficult for them being at home and unable to travel to North Carolina due to their health. Sarah, in particular, did not want my dad (her grandfather) to go. Those last hugs and saying goodbye were like a knife through my heart. I hadn't even left Limerick and I was already missing them. But I felt it was critical we were in Lexington throughout the entire trial for justice to be served for Jason.

I wasn't the only one upset – our friends who accompanied us had also left their young children. Paul's wife, Simone, had given birth five days before he left. Words can't convey how grateful we were for their support.

My only comfort was that all the children would be together for the summer holidays – and my eldest son, Dean, with his girlfriend, Kelly, would go above and beyond to ensure that the youngsters were spoiled for everything while we were away.

We flew from Dublin to Washington several days before jury selection was due to begin on 17 July in Davidson County. I knew we needed time to sort out whatever last ditch issues arose with the District Attorneys. On arrival in Washington, we hired a large SUV and drove the eight hours south to North Carolina. Travelling with us were Paul, Lynn and her husband, Tim. My sister Marilyn would fly out to Charlotte with her partner, Wayne. We would also be joined by other family members and friends.

We all met that evening at our hotel, a budget-friendly three-star hotel in Archdale that Dave and I had discovered during our previous trips. It was discreet and set back from the road and we felt secure there. It was close to restaurants, supermarkets and all the facilities we would need during our stay. The staff were also wonderful and friendly but not intrusive.

A further boost came from Dave's sister, Linda, who lives in Kansas. When we arrived at the hotel, we found that she had left special 'care packages' in the bedrooms for everyone. These included everything

Linda thought we might need in the US ranging from iPhone charging cables, US power adaptors, calming oils, mosquito repellent and even antihistamine creams. It was a gesture that meant so much, particularly as Linda was now flying to Ireland to help with the children.

That Sunday, we faced one of the ordeals that I dreaded most. The District Attorney's Office had asked multiple times if Dave and I wanted to view the photographic evidence that they intended to present during the prosecution. I repeatedly declined because I was terrified of the effect they might have on me. My overarching fear had been that my upset at viewing crime-scene or pathology photographs might impede my ability to function, care for the children and work from Ireland to support the North Carolina authorities.

Now, I knew I didn't have a choice. I reasoned I had three to four weeks to process it before going home. How naive I was. Once you view such horrific images they never leave you. But I realised that viewing the material was important both for ourselves and for the prosecution team. The last thing the prosecution wanted during the trial were scenes of upset and high emotion from Jason's family – particularly if it served to distract from the issues at hand. They had enough to worry about without us adding to their avoidable concerns. The searing heat of the day stood in stark contrast to the icy chill of inevitability I felt as we arrived outside the District Attorney's Office in Lexington for the briefing. We were all still struggling to shake off the effects of jetlag, not to mention exhaustion after the 20-hour journey.

District Attorney Garry Frank's office is a nondescript building just across the road from Davidson County courthouse in the centre of Lexington. Almost all the buildings and homes in Lexington had US stars-and-stripes flags displayed, with Independence Day just a couple of weeks past. But we were feeling anything but festive. Scattered around the office were boxes of files and documents, each of which I was almost afraid to stare too closely at. I knew they contained all the harrowing details of what had been done to my brother.

Over the course of the next few hours, I tried to contain myself as I heard Molly Martens's voice reveal via a recorded police interview how she had struck Jason with a large garden paving brick. It seemed almost matter-of-fact to me – as if everyone had a concrete paving brick on their bedside table. Then, to my amazement, I heard that her father had no recollection of the brick being used in the bedroom assault at all. It was as if the brick didn't exist for Tom Martens.

He readily admitted hitting Jason with a metal baseball bat but kept insisting it was in self-defence. Tom kept repeating that Jason had been attacking Molly. I couldn't believe it – this was their story?

What on earth was a concrete paving brick doing in the master bedroom that night? If it was self-defence, why were both Molly and Tom totally uninjured at the scene? What about Sharon Martens? What had she heard? Where was she while all this was going on?

Nothing could have prepared me for the horror of the pathology and crime-scene photographs we were then shown. No matter how much we had tried to prepare ourselves, there was no way any human being could remain emotionless while viewing graphic evidence of what had been done to a loved one. I fought very hard to retain control but was consumed by an all-pervading fear that I would vomit in front of the prosecution team.

Some family members had to make their apologies and hurriedly rush from the room. A few did become ill from the shocking images they had just viewed. They were the most upsetting images I had ever seen in my life – and, as far as I knew, they would have the same impact on the jury that they had on us. I wasn't wrong. The prosecutors kindly decided it was a good time to take a break – and we were left alone with our tears, heartache and images that would haunt our dreams.

I struggle to recall any time in life where there was such a collective sense of pain among everyone around me – up until that moment, I don't think any of us had realised the enormity of the horror that had been visited on our brother. Those colour photographs depicted in remorseless detail how Jason's skull was smashed after being struck again and again by a brick and a baseball bat. The only way I can describe what it was like was to say that viewing those photographs was akin to an assault on my senses. They were beyond anything I had ever experienced before – they were like something you only expected to see in a war zone.

My abiding feeling was one of terror. I was scared, to the very core of my being, at the thought that Tom and Molly might just manage to get away with what they had done. I had done everything I could; my family had put everything into supporting the North Carolina authorities. I knew the Davidson County prosecutors and police had worked day and night to prepare the case. But it all rested now on what 12 ordinary citizens thought had happened. What scared me most was that it might all boil down to a single juror who only had to take a contrary position to the other 11 and find Molly and Tom not guilty for their own reasons.

Over the course of the next week we acclimatised to North Carolina as best we could. The southern US state was settling into the blazing heat of high summer. Sometimes it got so hot at lunchtime all you could do was run for the shade or air-conditioning. Every morning I chatted over Skype with Dean, Adam, Jack and Sarah – it was the one part of my day that kept me sane. It was also a welcome relief not to have to think about the trial, which was due to open the following Monday, 17 July.

A further boost came from the kindness of Jason's colleagues and friends. They insisted they wanted to do something for us, just to get us out of the hotel for a day. There is a place in Davidson-Rowan County called High Rock Lake. Its stunning setting is matched by its reputation as the best fishing lake in North Carolina. Jason's friends had organised two motorboats and loaded them with food and ice-cold drinks.

The boats cruised across the lake for the day as everyone did their best to help us take our minds off the trial proceedings. The stunning setting, the wonderful company, the easy conversations and the glorious sunshine were like a tonic for our battered psyches. That day was like a reprieve from the horrors of the trial and I will never, ever forget the kindness shown to Dave and me.

From Friday 14 July, the media coverage began to step up a gear. Details of the impending trial featured in all the Irish newspapers. The North Carolina press were also detailing the trial to come. And we were being bombarded almost daily with requests for interviews from all major US TV stations, including ABC, CBS, NBC and Fox. We politely declined them all – the last thing in the world we wanted was to say anything that might cause last-minute problems for the Davidson County prosecution team. I emphatically told every reporter who contacted us that we would be making no comment until after the verdict.

On the opening day of the trial, Lexington was a sweltering 105 degrees. That morning we walked en masse and supported by District Attorney's Office assistant Karen Coe into the breeze-block Davidson County Superior Court past a phalanx of US and Irish media, including reporters, photographers and TV crews. There must have been close to 20 there. A few Irish reporters, some familiar to us, nodded and smiled as we passed by in what we took as a gesture of solidarity.

Everyone entered the court complex via a metal detector, with the families, witnesses, legal teams and jury panel members given priority. Once through, I preferred to go inside the courtroom and get settled for the events about to unfold. Dave, myself and our family and friends took up seats on the right-hand side of the public gallery in the vast confines of Courtroom C. Each morning ahead, we would meet in the District Attorney's Office to be briefed on what was to be presented that day.

If they emptied the courtroom of seats and the portraits of historic judges that lined the walls, the room could easily pass as a basketball court, it was so large. I watched as members of the Martens and Earnest families took up positions to the front of the left-hand side of the public gallery.

Tom Martens was wearing a smart suit, crisp white shirt and tie. Molly had adopted what I called her 'nanny outfit' – a simple single-colour dress, plain cardigan and low-heeled shoes. Her long blonde hair was tied back in a ponytail with a ribbon. I had rarely seen Molly dress that simply when she was with Jason so I suspected it was her idea of how she thought the court should see her.

I tried not to glance in their direction but couldn't help myself. As I did, Tom and Molly turned in their seats and stared over at me. I was frozen and couldn't look away fast enough.

Both stared at me and, almost in unison, they smiled and then immediately turned away. I was furious with myself because I had wanted to simply ignore them. It felt as if they had just won the first psychological battle of the proceedings.

Over the next few hours, I noticed that members of the Martens family kept glancing over at me. I tried to keep my focus away but it was impossible to ignore their looks. Eventually, Dave noticed what was happening and realised how the glances were beginning to unsettle me. He swapped places with me so that he was now directly between me and any looks that Tom, Molly or others might direct at me.

Minutes after we entered the court, we heard the noise of large numbers of people filling the bench seats behind us. I realised that this was the jury panel from which 12 jurors and two alternates would be selected. The media were then allowed into Courtroom C, seated in the back row until some of the potential jurors would be dismissed and they could move forward.

To speed matters up, the District Attorney's Office had prepared special questionnaires that each potential juror now needed to fill out. Each questionnaire was 16 pages long and dealt with everything from a person's experience of crime, the law and the police, to their family history and even their military service. Each jury panel member was also asked, in detail, about what they had heard or read about the case, particularly in terms of the media coverage around the time of Jason's death.

'You will try to find the truth and reach a verdict or verdicts in this case. You alone will determine the truth,' Judge David Lee explained to the packed room. He reminded the jury panel that all questions had to be answered – and had to be answered honestly and with the maximum detail required. Judge Lee also stressed that all potential jurors had to be aged 18 or over, must be English-speaking citizens of both North Carolina and Davidson County and must not be disqualified from serving on a jury through any prior convictions.

For the next hour, the sound of pens scratching on paper echoed throughout the hushed confines of Courtroom C. But the media already had their story for the day. Tom and Molly were now only facing a second degree murder charge – the North Carolina authorities had decided to drop the voluntary manslaughter charge, which meant Molly and Tom wouldn't have a lesser charge to fall back on with the jury. We understood that this was a tactical decision but weren't going to explain that to any of the reporters.

I knew the reporters would also shortly have a second story. Lawyers acting on our behalf had issued civil proceedings against Molly and Tom Martens, as well as Sharon Martens, for the wrongful death of Jason. We were determined that Molly should not benefit from Jason's estate at Jack and Sarah's expense, and the statute of limitations was due to expire on 2 August, two years after Jason's death. We had been assured this civil action would not interfere with the criminal proceedings already ongoing. But we also knew it was an important move for many reasons – not least that it gave Molly and Tom something else to think about and two sets of legal teams to organise and pay for. Coincidentally, from the day the wrongful death lawsuit papers were served, neither of them ever stared or smiled over at me in the courtroom again.

The 143 members of the jury panel were split into three groups of 50, 50 and 43. The selection process would begin with the first group of 50 and then continue to the next as they ran out of potential jurors. The first two groups had to stay in the courthouse while the third group was sent home to be called back if necessary.

I had been warned that jury selection is a very intensive and painstaking process in the US. Prosecutors believe that by carefully questioning jury panel members the selected jurors would ultimately be much less likely to cause issues that could result in trials collapsing or forcing retrials. In Ireland, so one of the Irish journalists told me, a jury would usually be selected in a matter of an hour, two hours if it was a very complex case. In Lexington, I suddenly realised on Tuesday afternoon that we would be lucky to have a jury selected and sworn by the start of the following week.

My unquenched thirst for justice for Jason meant I was too involved in the trial process to take a detached view of the jury selection process. Now, with the benefit of hindsight, I realise it was a fascinating glimpse into the heart and soul of America. The ordinary working people of that jury panel, who were just like me, helped us understand so many things about the US that, up until then, had mystified me. For instance, the deep and abiding admiration they held for the US military and anyone who had served in uniform. Not to mention the respect they held for the police. And how proud they were of their own community and living in North Carolina. But there were also darker insights. I was genuinely shocked by how many people admitted they or their families had been the victims of violent crime. One potential juror said he had a relative who had killed someone. The man had been convicted of murder and sentenced to death in North Carolina. He was currently in prison on death row. The prospective juror proudly told the court he supported the death penalty. The sentence on his relative, he added, had made him 'feel good'.

Another man had a cousin who had beaten his partner to death with a tyre iron because she had thrown their baby out of the window of a speeding car, killing the infant instantly. There was a horrified silence around the courtroom as people digested the horror of the story that had just been told. I started crying at how cruel the world can be. The man then added, almost as an afterthought, that he felt the killing of the wife had been 'justified' because of what she had done to the baby.

Another woman broke down and wept as she told how her older sister, while just a teen, had been brutally attacked and raped by an older man living in the area.

There were less violent experiences of crime as well – houses being burgled, goods being stolen and various road traffic matters. Sitting there in North Carolina, I realised that the fears and emotions were precisely the same on both sides of the Atlantic when it came to being a victim of crime. It didn't matter whether it was Lexington, North Carolina or Limerick, Ireland – crime left precisely the same scars.

If a jury panel member confirmed they had served in the US military they were immediately thanked by the court for their service to the United States. The admiration was palpable. One man revealed that he had served with the 101st Airborne Division during the vicious Khe Sanh battles in Vietnam. Another elderly man, who was so nervous his entire body was trembling, said he had never fully recovered from his Vietnam experiences and told the court there was no way he could serve on a murder trial jury. His nerves, he stressed, just wouldn't be able for it.

Others were discharged after they admitted they had worked for Jason's firm, MPS, or after they displayed an inordinately close interest in the case. One elderly woman, who looked as if she had stepped off the set of *The Waltons*, told the court she hadn't heard much about the case in the newspapers or on TV. But she was later questioned by Mr Martin as to whether she had told other jury panel members, as they waited for proceedings to get underway, that 'Miss Molly' had changed her appearance, looked nothing like she did in the newspapers or on TV. The woman was quietly discharged.

Prospective jurors were warned that they would have to examine graphic images of the bedroom where Jason died. They were told that viewing such graphic images might make them feel unwell – something our family could all too readily attest to. The defence echoed this warning. Mr Freedman told the jury the photos might be distressing. 'There are going to be gory pictures – there is no getting around that. There was a lot of blood in that bedroom on 2 August. There was blood on the walls, there was blood on the floor, in the hallway and in the bathroom. It is not going to be easy – some people might get queasy,' he said.

The defence, during their cross-examination of jury panel members, went to great pains to stress that neither Molly nor Tom was charged with first degree murder which, of course, carried the death penalty in North Carolina. 'Mr Martens was not indicted with first degree murder. It [premeditation] is not an issue in this case. The State is not alleging premeditation. He is charged with second degree murder which is a killing with malice,' Mr Freedman said.

Both Mr Freedman and Mr Holton also went to great lengths to stress that the burden of proof rested entirely with the prosecution – neither Tom nor Molly had to prove their innocence. They were innocent as it stood. Mr Holton made a point of arguing that they didn't have to offer any evidence at all if it suited. Both lawyers also emphasised that there was no requirement on either the father or daughter to offer sworn evidence in their own defence. If they declined to offer sworn evidence that could not be held against them by any jury member. I still didn't know if Tom and Molly would take the stand. My gut instinct was that Tom would testify but I couldn't imagine any circumstances where Molly would.

Just when I thought we were making progress, most of the 12 jury panel members that I thought would make it were discharged. No reasons were offered for the discharges. But it meant the entire process had to basically start again. We would be lucky if the case got to its opening by the seventh or eighth day.

There were moments of private humour. I couldn't help but smile when Mr Martin asked the first prospective juror if he had any problem with Irish people. 'Mr Corbett was a resident of the Meadowlands but he was a citizen of the Republic of Ireland. Do any of you have any bias towards Ireland or Irish people? Do you have any bias towards Irish folks?' the Assistant District Attorney asked. The look of horror on the man's face spoke volumes. I smiled when I thought that while we might be in the heart of the south, in a state that had voted for Donald Trump for president and hundreds of miles from the traditional Irish centres of New

York, Chicago, Boston and San Francisco, but Ireland was still a country that the majority of people appeared to have fond feelings towards.

By Thursday morning, 20 July, seven jurors had been provisionally agreed, five women and two men. As it transpired, one of these – a lawyer – would subsequently also be discharged. But, with two alternative jurors also required, it meant we still had another seven jurors to go. We reached ten prospective jurors on Friday. By Monday, everyone was astonished when the trial reached 12 prospective jurors with just the two alternates yet to be selected. It would ultimately take another day and half of questioning before both the prosecution and defence settled on one man and one woman as alternates. Incredibly, the process had seen the third and final jury panel group of 43 people reached.

The two alternates would sit through every minute of the trial, take notes alongside the other 12 jurors and view every single piece of evidence. But, when it came time for a verdict to be delivered after closing arguments, if the original 12 jurors were in place and ready to deliberate, the two alternates would be thanked and simply sent home.

The jury to be sworn in for the trial comprised nine women and three men. They had been confirmed on Monday, 24 July. With the two alternates in place the following day, the trial was now ready to open on Tuesday afternoon.

9

Shocking Evidence

The trial formally opened on Tuesday, 25 July when the fourteenth and final alternate juror was agreed by the prosecution and defence teams after 11 days of work. By 11 a.m., Judge Lee was able to instruct the trial jury of nine women and three men and hand the case over to the prosecution for their opening. That was when the first surprise had come. The media had been speculating that veteran Davidson County Assistant District Attorney Greg Brown would deliver the prosecution opening. But we knew it would be delivered by Alan Martin, another Assistant District Attorney. Fellow Assistant District Attorney Ina Stanton, the final member of the three-strong prosecution team, would focus on cross-examination and specific legal issues arising.

Mr Martin, like Mr Brown and Ms Stanton, had already impressed us with his legal skills, passion for the case and kindness towards us. His opening statement didn't disappoint and I firmly believe that, from 11 a.m. that searing-hot July morning, the net of justice finally began to close on Molly and Tom Martens.

For the first time, people heard just how violent Jason's death had been. It also emerged that traces of a powerful sleep drug, Trazodone, prescribed for Molly on 30 July, just three days before Jason's death, were found in his system. My brother did not suffer from the sleep issues for which the drug was prescribed and, sitting in the public gallery, I felt it was yet further proof that what had happened to Jason was no accident and was not a spur-of-the-moment attack.

Mr Martin said that, despite their 2011 marriage, Molly had remained only a stepmother to Jason's two children by his late first wife – and her husband was considering moving back to Ireland. He said that while Jason was discovered in the bedroom naked and blood-spattered with a crushed skull, there wasn't a single visible mark on either his wife or his father-in-law when police and paramedics arrived. This was despite their claim that they had acted only in self-defence that night.

'Thomas Martens – [had] no injuries, no bruises, no swelling, no cuts and no blood appeared to come from him,' Mr Martin said. 'Molly Martens Corbett – [had] no bruises, no swelling, no cuts and no blood appeared to come from her,' he said.

But, as Mr Martin went on to explain, Jason's injuries were a completely different story. 'His skull was badly crushed,' he said. When a Davidson County sheriff arrived at the scene early that morning, a paramedic warned him: 'It is bad.' When the paramedic tried to help Jason – who was lying naked and blood-covered on his bedroom floor – he attempted to move his head and found the back of his skull to be 'squishy'.

'There was nothing that could be done,' Mr Martin said. 'Jason Corbett left that room on a board and his head was badly crushed.' During the subsequent post mortem examination, a pathologist moved his scalp and 'pieces of his skull fell out onto the table'. Pieces of his shattered skull had also been driven into his brain. 'It was like a hard-boiled egg that had been dropped on the counter,' Mr Martin said.

The damage was so severe that a pathologist couldn't even determine the precise number of blows he had sustained. 'It was not two, it was not four, it was not six and it was not eight. It was at least ten times [he was struck].'

The only mark on Molly at the scene was a little redness on her neck akin to 'a sunburn'. Mr Martin said that, at the scene, Molly was also asked repeatedly to stop rubbing her neck. 'That was how they walked out of that room – but Jason Corbett left it on a board.'

Both Tom and Molly Martens refused emergency medical treatment at the scene. Jason's blood was found all over the bedroom floor and walls, as well as in the hallway off the bedroom and bathroom. Mr Martin told the jury that expert medical, forensic, pathology and pharmacology evidence would be introduced at the trial. Blood spatters indicated that Mr Corbett was subjected to a sustained series of blows, with blood-spray patterns indicating that he was, at one point, near the ground when his head was struck. 'The State will [try to address] why? Why didn't they stop?' Mr Martin asked.

David Freedman, for Tom Martens, in his opening remarks said the father of four and retired FBI agent heard noises coming from an upstairs bedroom of his daughter's home early that 2 August morning. The noises sounded like a disturbance and, on the spur of the moment, he grabbed a metal baseball bat that he had brought as a present for Jack. On going to investigate from his basement bedroom, he said he saw Jason holding his daughter by the throat.

'Jason's hand was around Molly's throat – his little girl had her husband's hand around her throat.' Mr Freedman said that Tom instructed Jason to immediately release Molly. '[But Jason said] "I'm sorry – I shouldn't be doing this,"' he said. However, he claimed that Jason then put his entire arm around his wife's throat.

'"I am going to kill her – I am going to kill her,"' Mr Freedman said the Irishman warned his father-in-law. At this point, he said Tom used the baseball bat to defend himself and his daughter.

Mr Freedman pointed out that Jason was much bigger than either Tom or Molly Martens. Both the father and daughter feared for their lives at the time and he argued that Tom acted as any father would in the circumstances – to defend his daughter and then himself.

Walter Holton, defence lawyer for Molly, said that a strand of the Tennessee woman's hair was later found in Jason's dead hand. But this was not preserved by forensic experts or analysed at the scene. Mr Holton attached major importance to this fact, though I struggled to understand precisely what it meant. He also said police statements indicated that Molly was in severe shock at the scene.

As the opening arguments ended and the court began to hear from the first witness, I couldn't help but be amazed. That was it? That was the explanation for what had been done to my brother? Without a single scrap of supporting evidence, Tom and Molly were prepared to trash Jason's name and reputation. I seethed as I realised that this trial wasn't just going to be about getting justice for Jason – it was also going to be about defending his good name.

The prosecution's first witness was Karen Capps, the female emergency dispatch operator who had received a 911 call from Tom Martens at the Panther Creek Court scene. The two defence teams had objected to supplementary prosecution submissions as to how the female 911 operator had perceived Tom's demeanour during the call. During such submissions, the jury were asked to go into their deliberation room and the legal issues were thrashed out by the judge, the prosecution and the defence teams. One thing I learned was that, while in Ireland such legal argument had to be carefully ignored by the media, here in the US it was perfectly legitimate for reporters to detail precisely what was being argued over.

In submissions to Judge Lee, the prosecution claimed that the operator would say the former FBI agent was 'surprisingly calm' and 'was not out of breath'. The operator would claim that this was not normally how callers in such circumstances appear, people tending to be 'very upset' or 'excited'. It fitted exactly with my belief of what had happened that night and that Jason was far beyond human help when that 911 call was made.

In legal argument, Ms Capps also confirmed aspects of the call. 'He [Tom Martens] was calm – surprisingly calm. He stayed calm throughout the call,' she said. 'He said he hit him [Jason] in the head with a ball bat.' The dispatcher said that information automatically made the call an issue for both paramedics and the Davidson County Sheriff's Department.

Ms Capps said undertaking CPR for any lengthy period is an exhausting process. 'CPR is very exhausting – it is very hard physically,' she explained. Those on a 911 call that requires CPR are asked to do two chest compressions per second. The dispatcher instructed Tom to check Jason's airways, to place him on his back and to begin CPR until paramedics arrived.

Ms Capps said she noted that Tom did not at any time during the lengthy call appear out of breath or gasping despite the fact that he had been asked to do 400 chest compressions, an exhausting task even for a fit, younger man. Molly had been asked to do 200 compressions to relieve her father. 'I noticed he was not out of breath. He did not sound like most people sound. He wasn't panting or gasping or out of breath. There was a lot of communication back and forth but he was not out of breath.'

Ms Capps said Molly later came on the phone. 'She was very tearful – a little excited I guess would be a good word.' At one point, Molly was shouting out the CPR count. 'She counted like she was yelling – like she wanted to make sure I heard she was counting.'

In direct evidence, Ms Capps, a 16-year veteran of the Davidson County Emergency Call Centre, confirmed she took the 911 call from Tom Martens at 3.02 a.m. on 2 August. The entire 911 call was played to the jury and Molly dramatically began weeping, wiping her eyes and nose with a tissue.

There was silence in the courtroom as the recording was played.

I felt sick as I heard Tom and Molly talking about my brother's prone and bleeding body. One of the remarks that I'll never forget was passed by Tom who, when asked by the dispatcher if he was sufficiently rested to take over CPR efforts on Jason from his daughter, coolly replied: 'I guess I have to be.' Seconds later he told the 911 operator: 'I'm not seeing any signs of life here.' When police officers finally arrived his only concern was for Molly: 'I need to get my daughter out of there.'

When the call ended, I felt as if I had been hit by a train. These were the first recorded words spoken after Jason's death, with my brother lying dead in a pool of blood on the bedroom floor at the feet of Molly and Tom as they dialled 911. There was no discernible anguish or heartache in their voices. To me, it sounded as if Tom Martens was dialling up to order a pizza or get his car serviced. I had desperately been listening for remorse, pity or upset in their voices on that recording. I found none.

There was silence in the courtroom as people stared at each other and wondered about what they had just heard. But I felt like jumping to my feet and shouting that Tom and Molly had engaged in the most vile of acts, pretending to help my brother to the emergency services when in fact they were putting on a cruel act to try to escape responsibility for what they had just done. The questions I had broke my heart. Was Jason still alive while they engaged in this charade? Did they callously watch him die? Was he aware of the awful act playing out beside him? But I had to retain my composure, though there were times I felt I had a volcano inside me just waiting to erupt.

Judge Lee directed a short break before resuming with the second witness, Katie Wingate-Scott of KPC Health Centre. A qualified nurse, Ms Wingate-Scott confirmed that both Jason and Molly were clients of the KPC complex in North Carolina. She confirmed that Molly was prescribed Trazodone in 50mg doses on 30 July – three days before her husband's death. The prescription was given after Molly complained that she could not sleep due to a congenital circulatory problem with her left foot. Molly was listed on KPC's records as a homemaker who had had a history of sleep issues.

Trazodone is a powerful sedative normally used in cases where people experience serious sleep problems. The drug was originally developed for the treatment of depression but was found to be far more effective as a therapy for sleep problems. The drug was never prescribed for Jason, despite traces of it being found in his system by pathology tests.

Ms Wingate-Scott confirmed she had treated both Jason and Molly during her time with KPC. Jason had attended the clinic since 2012, a few months after he had moved his family permanently to North Carolina.

She said that one medical note detailed that Jason was complaining of high stress levels, anxiety, malaise, fatigue and occasional feelings of being overwhelmed. He had been referred to a heart specialist and the appointment was arranged for 5 August – three days after his death. I turned to look at Dave and he understood my glance – no wonder Jason was feeling stressed and anxious. He was a pawn in a cruel game being played by Molly. The tragedy was he didn't understand that until it was too late.

The next witness was James Hiatt, a pharmacist working with CVS, one of the biggest pharmacy chains in the US. He confirmed that the prescription for Trazodone given to Molly by Ms Wingate-Scott was filled on 30 July and issued in 50mg tablet form.

Wednesday, 26 July 2017

This was the single day of the trial – with the obvious exception of the verdict – that I had dreaded most. In all my preparations for the trial it was the pathology evidence I was most concerned about. I had no idea how any of our family was going to be able to sit through evidence that was both gruesome and heartbreaking. But I also knew we had to do it for Jason.

Nothing could ever have prepared me for the awfulness of it. It was like being trapped in a horror movie and unable to close your eyes to protect yourself.

When the photographs of Jason were displayed to the jury in Courtroom C I felt frozen. I knew what they contained. But not even that knowledge could have prepared me for a fresh sight of photographs which, in a clinical, surgical manner, set out in gory detail just how Jason had died. They graphically illustrated the horrific injuries to his head which, because they were now in poster-size enlargements, seemed even more gruesome.

Deep down, I knew that the photographs were a vital part of showing the jury that this wasn't a case of self-defence. How on earth could Jason have suffered injuries this terrible, this shocking after having attacked two people who walked away without a scratch, a bruise or a mark? It simply wasn't possible. But that didn't make them any easier to view. So why did I stay? Why didn't I slip out of the courtroom?

The answer is simple – I wanted the jury to recoil from those images and then see our reaction to what had been done to a kind, generous and caring man by the people who were supposed to love him. I wanted the jury to see what I now saw when I looked at those awful images – what they were capable of under the veneer of a pretty dress and a sharp suit.

My gnawing fear was that I'd faint or get sick. I desperately didn't want any distractions for the jury. I wanted them to focus entirely on what the prosecution were saying and gauge whether these types of shocking injuries were consistent with people acting in self-defence who walked away without so much as a scratch on them.

A total of 12 photographs were introduced to illustrate the injuries suffered by Jason – and were displayed to the jury as giant cardboard copies. Everyone in the courtroom could see what Jason had suffered. In one photograph, Jason's scalp was effectively 'drooping [off] with gravity'. Judge Lee warned the jury that the photographs involved were 'very graphic.' All the photographs were taken during the post mortem examination conducted by Dr Nelson in a Davidson County hospital on 3 August.

Then I heard the sound. At first I thought I'd imagined it. Surely not? Then it dawned on me as I saw the bailiffs running to get tissues that one of the jury members was getting sick. The sound of her retching – and her desperate attempts to regain control of herself – echoed throughout the hushed courtroom. No one seemed quite sure what to do about the photographs of Jason lying dead, his head smashed open and his grievous wounds visible to all. Should they be taken down, at least temporarily?

Eventually, the female juror was helped from the courtroom and into the jury assembly room. She managed to compose herself and, after a drink of water and a 10-minute break, was able to reassure Judge Lee that she was able to continue. I couldn't help but wonder whether, given the awful images and evidence to come, the trial could now last far longer than even the most pessimistic experts had indicated. This was only the second day of evidence and already we were having to take unexpected breaks. It had taken seven days to select a jury and some were speculating that the trial could last into the middle or even end of August.

North Carolina Chief Medical Examiner's Office associate pathologist Dr Craig Nelson was younger than I had expected him to be. He was in his late thirties and spoke in a clipped voice and he was authoritative, detailed in his evidence and absolutely certain about his conclusions.

He confirmed that Jason's skull was badly shattered and the damage was so severe that he could not determine at a post mortem examination precisely how many times he had been struck. Jason sustained at least 12 blows. But Dr Nelson acknowledged that it could easily have been more.

Complex injuries were sustained to both the left and right side of his skull. The blows were sufficiently violent to drive fragments of skull into his brain – and, when he touched Jason's scalp during the post mortem examination, parts of his skull fell out onto the surgical table.

The blows were also concentrated around specific areas of the back of his skull. This resulted in the skull being not just fractured but effectively fragmented.

I glanced around me and realised that every single member of my family was as frozen by the evidence as I was. We all knew Jason had suffered a horrific death. We had even viewed the pathology photos before the trial to prepare ourselves for the horror of it. But hearing it described like this – in such analytical tones – made it almost surreal.

Jason's nose was also broken, there was swelling to the orbit of one of his eyes and there were injuries to his torso and his legs and arms. Dr Nelson said it was clear that Jason had suffered blunt force trauma blows to the head rather than sharp force blows.

'It [post mortem examination photo] shows detachment of scalp from the skull and the connecting tissues,' he explained. 'It illustrates the depth and underscores that this was a laceration and therefore a blunt force trauma injury rather than a sharp force injury.'

Dr Nelson noted that at least one of the injuries to Jason's skull was sustained after he was already dead. 'It [one wound] has the appearance of a post mortem injury. There was very little bleeding suggesting it was post mortem, it was after death.' Dr Nelson said that toxicology tests showed the presence of ethanol (alcohol) but at a relatively low level. The blood test also confirmed the presence of the sedative Trazodone but in a below-therapeutic dose. Dr Nelson added that Jason was six foot tall and weighed around 260lb. His time of death was confirmed as 3.24 a.m. but he said it was not possible to determine precisely when my brother's great heart had stopped beating.

If we thought the trauma of the day would end with Dr Nelson's evidence we were sadly mistaken. We still had two more witnesses to hear from and while one, Carolina Clinical Health Services official Russell Patterson, would be relatively brief, the second, Corporal Clayton Dagenhardt of Davidson County Sheriff's Department, would deliver evidence that was extremely difficult for us to listen to.

Mr Patterson was a pharmacology expert whose evidence focused on the Trazodone found in Jason's system. *I* knew why the sedative was there. But for the prosecution, proving why traces of it were found in my brother's blood was an entirely different matter.

Mr Patterson explained that the traces found in Jason's system were at sub-therapeutic-dose levels. In what was quite complex evidence, it emerged that there could be multiple reasons for why the dose was below therapeutic levels, ranging from the amount ingested to the time lapse since the dose was administered.

Cpl Dagenhardt's evidence was far less complex but much more traumatic. He was the first police officer to arrive at the scene – and he was the one who, as he entered Panther Creek Court at 3.16 a.m., was warned by a paramedic that 'It's bad in there – real bad. Horrible scene.'

Cpl Dagenhardt, a 14-year veteran who said he had attended more than 200 scenes where blood had been spilled, confirmed the grim sight that greeted him inside the house. 'There was blood on the floor – fairly large amounts that already seemed to be congealed,' he said. 'There was blood on the bed, blood in the hall and blood in the bathroom. I saw some [blood] on the floor – puddles and on the walls. It was starting to dry.'

Cpl Dagenhardt explained that fresh blood that comes from the body is 'runny'. But he said some of the blood he saw that night appeared to be congealed like 'Jell-O' or jelly – the clear inference being that Jason's blood had been spilled some time earlier. He also confirmed that Jason was naked and lying on the floor in a pool of blood with visible injuries to his face and head. There were also large amounts of blood on his head and chest.

With his colleague, Cpl Rusty Ramsay, Cpl Dagenhardt asked Tom and Molly to leave the house to allow the officers to do their job and to help preserve the scene. The police officer spotted a blood-stained brick and bat near a wooden dresser in Jason's bedroom. There were puddles of blood across the floor.

The two police officers decided the best option was to ask Sharon Martens, who was in a basement bedroom, to look after Jack and Sarah while they attended to other matters. Cpl Ramsay was also determined that the two children sleeping upstairs should not see their father's blood. So, on waking Jack and Sarah in their bedrooms, the officers carried both children downstairs, insisting the youngsters push their faces into the crooks of the officers' necks, both men walking carefully down the stairs so the youngsters wouldn't see the true horror of what had happened. It was a kindness and professionalism for which I will be eternally grateful to them.

They knocked on Sharon Martens's bedroom door. '[She was] calm,' he said. 'She asked if everything was OK.' The children were then left in her care.

Outside the property, Tom Martens – who was dressed in a red shirt and shorts – asked if he could use the bathroom. 'I said I couldn't allow him back into the residence,' Cpl Dagenhardt explained. The doors of two police cars were then opened and the former FBI agent urinated in the shelter provided between them. Cpl Dagenhardt said Tom was calm and cooperative throughout. However, he said Tom briefly became upset in a police car as he was being driven to a station for questioning.

'He became agitated and asked where we were going and were we even in the same county.' Bizarrely, Cpl Dagenhardt said the agitation began when he declined to fully wind up a window in the patrol car as requested by Tom.

10

Left to Die

By Thursday, 27 July, I was praying for the weekend and some relief from the trauma of the murder trial. I knew it would be tough sitting through the evidence but my mind kept spiralling back to the early hours of 2 August in that master bedroom. I just couldn't help but think about what Jason must have gone through.

Did he attempt to run for his life? How was he unable to escape? Maybe he was asleep when the first blow was struck? Had Molly hit him and then, knowing Jason was badly injured, called to her father for help? Was Jason so badly injured by the time he managed to rouse himself that it was already too late? Where was Sharon Martens? The evidence to come would raise further suspicions that this was precisely what happened.

The next witnesses were all paramedics who had arrived at Panther Creek Court to battle to save Jason's life without knowing it was already too late. Two Davidson County emergency medical services officials, David Bent and Amanda Hackworth, told the trial they were taken aback by how cold Jason's body appeared to be when they arrived.

When they arrived, Jason's body was lying naked in the master bedroom in a pool of blood. It was cramped and, with no light on, it was difficult for the paramedics to see precisely what they were doing. So the decision was made to remove Jason on a stretcher board into a waiting ambulance and undertake their life-saving work there.

'He's cool – how long has he been down?' Ms Hackworth asked after she noted the coolness of the body as she reached across and brushed his torso with her bare forearm while tending to him in the ambulance.

'It was fairly alarming,' she said. 'I asked Sergeant [Barry] Alphin …
I said: how long did they say they waited before they called 911? He said
[they said] they called the minute he went down. I felt the patient was
cool – his torso was cool.' Ms Hackworth also noted that there was dried
blood on Jason's body, raising further question marks over the timeline
offered by Molly and Tom.

Fellow paramedic David Bent said he also noted the coolness of
the body. 'I also determined that he felt cool to me as well,' he said. 'It
was also pointed out to me by Amanda Hackworth that when she was
attempting to gather leads to hook on the patient, she pointed out, she
reached over – the skin portion of her arm touched the patient and [she]
said he felt cool. It was a very important determination.'

Mr Bent said that the coolness of Jason's body, combined with the total
lack of electrical signals from the heart and the severe trauma sustained
to the back of the head, was used in deciding to stop life-saving measures
at around 3.24 a.m. 'There was no electrical activity. There was [severe]
trauma to the head.'

Paramedic Sergeant Barry Alphin confirmed that at no time did
ambulance staff get any heart rhythm from Jason. Sergeant Alphin, in
trying to move Jason's head, was shocked when his hand and fingers
slipped inside the back of the shattered skull. Jason was so covered in
blood the paramedics initially didn't know precisely how severe the
injuries he had sustained were. When this comment was passed, I felt an
involuntary shudder run through me. It was as if someone had reached
out and squeezed my heart. My brother had been beaten to such a pulp
that the back of his head was basically left gaping open.

Mr Bent said he later saw Molly lying on her side on the ground
outside the property. He went over and examined her using a pen-light. 'I
observed a redness on the left side of her neck. There was a light redness.
[But] there was no significant injury [to her]. [There was] no abnormality
to her eye.' But Molly claimed she had been attacked. 'She stated that she
had been choked.'

However, she refused all requests from the paramedic to go to a local hospital for medical assessment and possible treatment. Mr Bent pointed out that Molly then signed a special medical refusal form. '[It means] We have assessed them and they made a decision not to go to hospital.'

Former Davidson County police officer David Dillard was tasked at the scene with staying by Molly at his patrol car. He spent around 90 minutes with her as the emergency services attended to the scene. 'She was making crying noises but I did not see any visible tears,' he explained. 'She was also rubbing her neck in a scrubbing motion – she would do it and then stop, do it and then stop. She was upset. I heard crying noises but I did not see any visible tears.'

Jason's neighbour David Fritzsche was next to offer evidence. I'd always liked Dave – he was the kind of neighbour you always prayed you'd have and I knew Jason thought the world of him and his wife, Michele. He lived next door to Jason and Molly with his wife, son and daughter. An accountant by profession, he worked in High Point and shortly after Jason and Molly moved into Panther Creek Court in 2011 the families became firm friends.

'It was a pretty social neighbourhood,' he told the trial. 'There was a familiar relationship between our families. We would engage in social activities, usually in the neighbourhood.' As well as their children often playing together, the families would attend barbecues together and Jason also joined a football team that Dave played with.

On 1 August, he explained, both Jason and he were cutting their respective lawns. But whereas the Fritzsche family had about one-third of an acre of lawn, Jason had two-thirds of an acre because of his bigger site. When Dave finished his lawn, like the good neighbour he was, he crossed over onto Jason's property to help him finish.

I started my mower and I followed behind him [Jason] to help him complete his lawn sooner. Afterwards, we had a few cold beers in the driveway. My wife Michele came out [to join them] and also Molly

166

[around 3.30 p.m.]. They sat with us. We would have one cold beer from my garage and have one cold beer from his. We didn't break up for a while until 8 p.m. or so. We had maybe six or eight beers. It was typical – [we were] very calm, relaxing after mowing the lawn and enjoying a cold beer. But I did not observe any sign of impairment [with Jason].

Dave said that around 8.30 p.m. Tom and Sharon Martens arrived. He had met them a couple of times before. '[Jason] went to the rear of the car to help them unload their belongings.' He explained that he didn't notice anything out of the ordinary. I knew from Jack and Sarah that Jason had no knowledge that Tom and Sharon were due to visit. In fact, we later learned that Molly had said to Jason, shortly before Tom and Sharon arrived, 'What would you do if my parents arrived?'

The families said goodbye and the Fritzsches headed out for Saturday night dinner. At 3.30 a.m., Dave got up to go to the bathroom and spotted the police and ambulances parked outside the Corbett home. 'I felt at the time – and I still feel – there wasn't anything to be done by me going out there.'

At 5.30 a.m., there was a knock on his front door and Molly, accompanied by a Davidson County police officer, asked could she use the Fritzsches' bathroom. She used the bathroom twice over the next 90 minutes. 'She was upset,' he explained. '[But] I did not notice any injury.'

A barrage of forensic evidence then began with the keynote testimony of Lt Frank Young, a veteran crime-scene analyst. I had known from the outset that the trial would likely hinge on three things – the pathologist's report, the crime-scene analysis and the testimony of a blood-spatter expert who had been contracted by Davidson County District Attorney's Office to examine the crime-scene photos.

As Lt Young took the stand, the second of the trial developments I had been dreading occurred – the baseball bat and concrete brick that had taken Jason's life were produced in evidence. Lt Young took the stand

and, shortly after being sworn, produced two nondescript brown paper evidence bags. I felt myself holding my breath as he opened first one and then the other to display the weapons used against Jason. Instinctively, my husband put a comforting arm around me.

The black-coloured Louisville Slugger baseball bat with red lettering was 28 inches in length, made of aluminium and designed for Little League or juvenile play. The garden paving brick, roughly the size of a large book, still had visible stains on it. It was clearly heavy and represented a ferocious weapon if used against someone's head.

'[I found the bat] in the master bedroom of the residence – the bat was standing in front of the dresser. It is a Louisville Slugger aluminium baseball bat,' Lt Young explained. He said the only difference to the bat from when he found it at Panther Creek Court two years ago was the current presence of grey volcanic ash traces that had been used by forensic examiners to lift fingerprint samples.

He also displayed the garden paving brick he had seized at the scene to the jury. It was the brick I found the most difficult to look at.

Whatever hope Jason had of surviving a blow from the baseball bat, there appeared to me to be no chance of anyone recovering from a full-strength blow from that heavy brick. Again I prayed the jury would ask themselves the obvious question: what was a brick like that doing in the bedroom that night?

'The cement paver appears to be stained with blood,' Lt Young added. 'I also recovered a strand of hair from the cement paver.' Such was the violence of the blows sustained by my brother that his detached scalp and hair were found in both the master bedroom and hallway. It was like something from a horror movie. Clumps of his scalp were found on the floor. His blood was found on the floor, walls, bed, bedclothes, bathroom and even utility equipment. Jason's blood was found on both the bat and brick while his hair was discovered embedded in the paving stone. When the brick was lifted off the carpet by forensic experts, the outline in blood of the concrete paver was left on the floor carpet.

Lt Young confirmed that a blood pattern expert had examined the Panther Creek scene – and photographs of the markings singled out by the expert were shown to the jury. Lt Young had crucially taken photographic and video evidence at Panther Creek Court, having been called to the scene by Davidson County Sheriff's Department early that morning. I didn't realise it at the time but the painstaking and methodical manner in which Lt Young had recorded the scene would prove absolutely crucial in the trial.

Lt Young photographed and noted that substantial quantities of blood were on the bedroom skirting board and on an electrical socket located around 30cm off the carpet. He said that blood was also found on a vacuum cleaner in the corner of the bedroom. He examined the vacuum and noticed that the blood-drip patterns on the machine indicated that it had been moved by someone at the scene. 'It was as if it was laid down and moved back up,' he explained. I wondered whether it hinted that someone had tried to alter or change the scene.

The forensic expert also noted a number of indentations on the walls. These weren't explained in any detail at this point in the trial but I knew they were the marks where the bat had impacted the walls either after striking Jason's skull or while being drawn back to inflict another blow. A plastic switch plate, located just off the ground, was also found to be blood-spattered and cracked.

But Lt Young wasn't just asked to record the crime scene – he also had to detail Molly and Tom's physical condition.

When he arrived at the property, Molly was already seated in a marked patrol car. Lt Young said he asked her for permission to photograph her to note any injuries she might have at the scene. She did not object.

Lt Young said he noted no injuries on the young woman's neck or throat at the scene after she emerged from the car to be photographed. She was wearing sandals, a blue-patterned pyjama suit, which had a sleeveless top and baggy trousers, and had on a fur-type coat for warmth as she stood outside in the early morning cool.

'There was initial consent to be allowed to take photographs,' Lt Young said. 'Ms [Martens] Corbett continually pulled and tugged on her neck with her hand. I asked her to stop doing that. After several requests, she did [stop].' The police officer said he photographed Molly's neck from all angles but said he spotted no visible injuries. 'None that I noted,' he stressed. But Lt Young said he did observe blood smears and blood spatter on Molly's face and hair. I knew this was Jason's blood and not hers.

An overhead projector was used to display the crime-scene photographs to the jury. Much as I wanted to look away, I felt I had to view the images. In my mind, I felt it was important that the jury should not just view the images but see that we were looking at them too. Our revulsion at what was done to Jason needed to be recognised.

The trial didn't sit on Friday due to a previous court scheduling commitment for Judge Lee. It meant we effectively had a long weekend.

But I would much rather have kept ploughing through the evidence.

Courts novice that I was, I was afraid the three days off might jeopardise the momentum of the prosecution case or, worse still, that the jury might forget key elements of the evidence already offered. I needn't have worried.

When the trial resumed on Monday and Lt Young concluded his evidence, North Carolina State Crime Laboratory (NCSCL) fingerprint expert Adrianne Reeve told the trial that no identifying fingerprints were found on the blood-soaked Louisville Slugger baseball bat found at the scene. Ms Reeve said fingerprint-type ridges were found in a dark-red dried substance believed to have been blood. 'There were no identifying latent [hidden] print on Item 1 [baseball bat]. [I] saw some ridge detail – but there was not sufficient quantity or quality of it available.'

Another NCSCL expert offered evidence on hair samples found at the scene. Melanie Carson explained that hairs recovered were, under analysis, consistent with the hair samples taken from Jason's scalp.

Five of the hairs found on the brick were grey and required mitochondrial root DNA testing rather than simple microscopic analysis. The other hairs could not be definitively identified, though one strand had both similarities and differences to Molly's hair sample given to Davidson County Sheriff's Department. That single hair strand could not deliver any conclusive analysis.

Ms Carson said that hair-like material recovered from the end cap of the baseball bat could not deliver a conclusive analysis for identification purposes though one strand could have come from Jason.

The next witness was NCSCL genetics expert Wendell Ivory. He confirmed that his tests for DNA proved positive on both the Louisville Slugger Little League baseball bat and the garden paving brick. He said he performed tests on the baseball bat and the paving brick as well as items of clothing supplied to him including pyjamas, a red polo shirt and a pair of boxer shorts.

'There was generalised staining of the bat. There were multiple indicators present of blood on the bat,' Mr Ivory explained. He said the DNA tests on the items matched the DNA sample received from Jason.

He pointed out that the match was a 1 in 1.99 trillion chance compared to the North Carolina DNA Database for the Caucasian population. The brick found in the blood-spattered bedroom yielded a total of 25 hairs for forensic inspection.

The blitz of forensic evidence was now interrupted by testimony from a co-worker of Tom's. It confirmed my long-held suspicions of exactly how Molly's father had felt about not only his son-in-law but also his Irish in-laws. JoAnn Lowry worked alongside Tom at the US Department of Energy facility at Oakridge in Tennessee. Both worked in a security unit that specialised in counter-intelligence at the federal agency.

She was asked by the prosecution to indicate how she knew Tom Martens and if he was in court. She pointed to Tom and said, 'Tom is over here to my right – he has nice beautiful grey hair and he is wearing a dark suit, dark tie and white shirt.' Several people in court smiled at the compliment. But, as I glanced over at Tom, I realised he was staring grim-faced and unsmiling at his former co-worker. I was lost in admiration for how Ms Lowry calmly gazed back at him.

Ms Lowry was questioned by Assistant District Attorney Alan Martin about any dealings she had with Tom about Jason and his Irish family.

She explained that it was 'common knowledge' in the unit that Tom intensely disliked Jason and also had little love of me and my Limerick family. She said the depths of Tom's feelings were made apparent in one conversation.

We have a room where we do our classified work and the computers are right next to each other. So I went in to work and Tom was sitting by me. I said: 'So, Tom, how did your weekend go?' He said, 'Fine.' He said: 'The children were home [for the weekend]. You know, you are always glad to see them come but you are always glad to see them leave.' And he said: 'That son-in-law – I hate him.'

Tom's comments came just four weeks before Jason's death.

Ms Lowry further pointed out that Tom's dislike and disdain for Jason and our family dated back even further. She said that when Molly was about to get married to Jason, Tom had passed disparaging remarks about us. 'Jason and his friends – they were going to be at the wedding and were at the house. He was not very fond of Jason and his rowdy friends. They were very rowdy in the home. Rude. It was general and open [in the office] of his dislike for Jason.'

Then the trial moved into evidence that I knew would be absolutely crucial to delivering the verdict we wanted. I had understood in the days before the hearing opened that the evidence of Florida-based forensic scientist Dr Stuart James was going to be absolutely central to our hopes of a conviction. His expertise would help to unravel precisely what had happened in the master bedroom that night. I also hoped his testimony would demolish Molly and Tom's flimsy claims that they were only defending themselves.

Dr James was a man in his sixties with a professorial air about him. He ranked as arguably one of the foremost experts in his field anywhere in the world. He had written a book on blood-spatter study that many now considered to be one of the key reference works for forensic analysis. Dr James had worked since 1971 in around 40 US states, but such was his reputation that he had been recruited to work overseas too – he had even lectured on blood-spatter analysis in Australia. He had also testified in more than 200 trials as an expert forensic witness.

He was hired by the Davidson County prosecution team to help explain the extensive blood patterns found inside the Panther Creek Court property and to study blood spatters found on the red polo shirt and white patterned boxer shorts worn by Tom that night. He also studied Molly's blue-patterned pyjama suit. Dr James worked on two reports for Davidson County District Attorney's Office – one focused on the clothing and the other attempted to explain the meaning of the blood-spray patterns in the bedroom, hall and bathroom of the property.

Moments after Dr James took the witness stand, Molly's and Tom's clothing was produced. Each garment was carefully pinned to giant display boards and brought close to the jury for careful examination.

Dr James focused immediately on blood stains found on Jason's bed. 'The patterned stains [are] up on the bedding here and the saturation stain is down on the skirting. There's an impact incident that took place there. That may well be where the bloodshed first occurred. I concluded in this instance that a bloodshed event occurred closer to the south side of the bed to produce impact spatters on the underside of the quilt.' In essence, Dr James had said he believed the first blow may have been suffered by Jason while he lay in bed.

Dr James then dealt with Tom's clothing. He said blood spatters on the inside lower hem of the patterned boxer shorts were different in direction from those on the front. The analysis included examining the fabric in minute detail with a Celestron microscope. The depth of penetration of the blood into the fabric would determine whether it was a spatter or soak transfer.

He said the blood spatters inside the lower hem were different from the spatters on the outside of the underwear. 'The source [of the blood] has to be [from] below. The blood droplets had to travel upwards. They have to be – on the inside of the hem, it is not a soak-through stain,' he explained. I instantly understood that this meant Tom was standing directly over Jason when his head was violently struck. Such a position, I believed, does not support a self-defence argument. Dr James said he considered the blood spatters on the boxer shorts to be generally part of 'one pattern'. But he acknowledged that it was likely, in his opinion, that the spatters on the front and inside hem of the boxer shorts were from two different blows to Jason's head.

Dr James also examined the blood-spray patterns on the walls of the bedroom. He explained how some were created by blood flying off the baseball bat after it had struck Jason's head. Some walls had large blood-spray patterns, several from an impact-type transfer. I knew this was most likely Jason's head hitting the wall after he had been struck and was falling to the ground. Staring at the photos of the bloodied bedroom, I realised that most of the blood-spray patterns were at lower heights, as if Jason was struck either falling to the ground or while he was trying to get up.

'These patterns are consistent with impacts to the head of Mr Corbett as he was descending to the floor with his head impacting the south wall in the areas of impact. Some of the spatters can be [attributed] to his head impacting the wall itself as well as the object striking him. You can see the ray of spatters – a large amount of blood with downward flow patterns.' The impact spatters went from five feet over the ground to a height of just five inches.

Such was the quantity of blood in the property that Dr James had to break his analysis into 15 separate areas. Blood wasn't just found on the walls and the carpet. It was found in Jason's bed, on the mattress, the blinds, the bedroom dresser, the skirting boards, electrical sockets, a lamp shade and the vacuum. There was even a blood smear mark on the face of Tom's watch.

When it came to the brick and the baseball bat, Dr James was even more blunt. 'There was blood on about every particular surface of that [brick] object. In my opinion it is consistent with more than one impact because of the distribution of blood on all edges. The presence of blood on all surfaces of the brick is not consistent with a single impact.' As I sat there I realised that meant that the brick was basically soaked in Jason's blood, hair and tissue. The realisation made my stomach churn. Jason had been repeatedly hit with the brick and yet Tom said he did not see the paver? I knew in my heart that Molly had brought the brick into the bedroom for a reason. I was convinced that the first blow Jason had suffered to the head, most likely as he slept, was from the brick wielded by Molly.

But it would get worse. Dr James analysed Molly's and Tom's clothing. He found some of the garments were soaked not just in Jason's blood but even with his tissue. 'My conclusions are these impact spatters are consistent with the wearer of these boxer shorts [being] in proximity to the victim Jason Corbett when blows were struck to his head. The head being the source of the blood in this particular case.'

Dr James said that the blood-spatter pattern on the boxer shorts meant the wearer was standing directly over Jason when he was hit. 'The source of the impact spatters is most likely the head of Jason Corbett while it was close to the floor of the bedroom.'

Dr James's cross-examination by Mr Byrd and Mr Holton, for the defence, basically took the form of the lawyers trying to pick holes in his conclusions. They pointed out that he hadn't actually examined the scene itself at the time. They also argued about the fact that not all of the blood spatters had been analysed for DNA. But Dr James insisted this wasn't necessary as the photographic record of the scene compiled by Lt Young was 'excellent'.

When pressed about his conclusions, Dr James was staunch in defence of his findings. 'The whole reconstruction of this case we are trying to reconstruct a very dynamic event where there was a lot of movement from one area to another. I gave my best opinion based upon the available data which I felt was sufficient to draw my conclusions.'

11

A Tribute to Jason

I had been away from the four children almost two weeks when Greg Brown communicated that Judge Lee had prior commitments in his calendar for Friday, 28 July and the following Wednesday, 2 August, which was the second anniversary of Jason's death. There would be no trial hearings on those dates. It was simply too much and I was slowly starting to become overwhelmed by the horror of the trial coupled with missing the children so much.

I was beside myself with worry each day. Every new development I viewed as a potential threat to a conviction. Now, on top of this, I faced spending from Thursday evening to Monday morning in North Carolina, away from home and with nothing to do but wait. I briefly considered flying home to Ireland from Charlotte just to see Jack, Sarah, Adam and Dean. But I would have no sooner arrived home than I would have had to leave again.

Also, realistically, we just couldn't afford the airfare. I felt completely trapped. I recognised I was under tremendous stress and this was a reaction to it. But knowing that and being able to do something about it were two different things. I wept and could not be consoled for hours. I wanted this moving forward so I could get home to our children. The waiting was a crippling strain on us all. But I also knew that being here in North Carolina for the murder trial was the last thing I could do for Jason and I wasn't giving up. I had Dave by my side and he gave me so much strength to carry on – I would be lost without him.

Throughout the days I would get little clips from Dean, Adam, Nuala or David's sister. They ranged from Jack diving into the ocean to all of them out for a walk. The clip that made us all laugh was where Dean had bought a new vacuum cleaner. It automatically went around the floor on its own. So there were our four children, aged 26 to 11 years, sitting quietly on the couch sending me a feed of a robot vacuum while they watched in fascination. It made me feel they were doing OK. To be honest, they were so busy and spoiled that they had little time to sit and ponder. Mostly they were away from TV and shops and they were all as prepared as Dean and our extended family could have them.

It was particularly hard not having my mobile phone on in court in case one of them needed to talk to me, especially due to the time difference. I spent many nights calling one of the kids at 2 a.m. and then talking through the night. Sometimes the media released information on Twitter or other social media platforms and that's how everyone back home got news. There was simply no way we could compete with that. It must have been so very difficult for them.

Having lost a day of the hearing the previous Friday, we had a second pause in the trial proceedings on Wednesday, 2 August, Jason's second anniversary. I genuinely don't know how we got as far this point. I guess you never know until you go through it. Until then, you don't realise you have the strength to face what life has coming down the tracks.

In hindsight it was a relief to have that day away from the court because having to hear gruesome details of Jason's killing on the second anniversary of his death would have been too much to bear for all of us. I wanted to remember Jason for the person he was on this day – not the manner of his death.

First thing that anniversary morning we spoke to the children. They had been to the Castlemungret graveyard the previous day. It is difficult looking at Mags' and Jason's beautiful smiling picture, full of life in each other's embrace, on a cold marble headstone. More often than not you are standing there on a rainy Irish day and recalling the moments when you heard the awful news and nothing but sadness surrounds you.

We showered, dressed and had breakfast in Archdale, all the while thinking how our lives had changed so irrevocably two years beforehand. Karen had made each one of us little green ribbons to underline our Irishness on this special day.

Jason's former MPS colleague Melanie Crook had informed us that his former workmates wanted to do something to mark the anniversary. It was decided a special memorial ceremony would be organised and we would be invited to come along. The ceremony would take the form of a balloon release from the MPS plant off Lexington Parkway. A few words would be said about Jason and then we would be invited inside the company plant to chat with Jason's former workmates and have some light refreshments. It was all kept low key, which we appreciated

In a gesture we found quite moving, the balloons to be released were in the green, white and orange of the Irish tricolour. At 12 noon, in the omnipresent heat, the balloons were released into the azure blue of a North Carolina sky, with the entire MPS workforce gathered for the event. The balloon release was metres from where a tree had been planted in Jason's memory. Beside the tree was a simple plaque that read: 'In dedication to a great leader and friend – Jason Corbett – August 2015 – Conas atá tú?' The plaque was framed by two Irish shamrocks. I was so glad to see it, as it reminded me that, no matter how difficult it must have been for Jason, there were people in his life who cared for him and expressed that. It gave my family hope and comfort. But we couldn't look at the memorial without tears misting our eyes.

It was always going to be an emotional day for us but I think a lot of pent-up frustration and revulsion from the trial was now released. We had attended a private Mass and the MPS ceremony seemed to represent an emotional tipping point for many of us. As I looked around, I realised that most of us were fighting to control our emotions as we walked inside the

Lexington plant. I remember thinking of our many shared conversations at 7:30 a.m. US time as Jason drove to work while the TomTom GPS directed him in the background. I would always joke about how he still needed it years on, but his sense of direction was terrible. I felt I was retracing his daily life, the details and the way his employees spoke of their morning routine with him, how he had hired them, befriended them … it gave colour to his life for me. It was another scorching hot day and, for a few of us, the tears running down our faces mixed with sweat from the intense heat.

We had wanted the MPS memorial ceremony to be low key for publicity reasons. The last thing we wanted were US TV crews there to broadcast the event. Two Irish journalists and a photographer had attended on the strict understanding that they would leave us alone and be sensitive with their coverage. They all kept their word impeccably. It was quite moving for us to see the photographer fighting back tears of his own as he stood with his colleague. There was a decency in the reaction of the Irish journalists that we were very grateful for that day.

Jason had so many friends in the Meadowlands community and we had significant support from them over the years. We kept in regular contact with them and sent pictures and video clips from Jack and Sarah. On the night of his anniversary, more than 20 of the neighbours gathered in a friend's house in Meadowlands along with all of us from Ireland. They all brought food, shared stories of good times and made us feel so very welcome. We all had written our own private notes to Jason that, at the end of the evening, we each burned in the fire pit in the summer darkness. Jason was remembered with fond memories and smiles as we made a toast to him.

The Meadowlands and Panther Creek Court community now stage a 'Big Kick' to honour Jason. This tradition started when Jason was alive and still continues on the day of the NFL Super Bowl final. Prior to the start of the game, friends gather behind Tony Turner's house and kick and punt a football. The distances are totalled and the contestant with the longest tally gets his name added to the ball bearing Jason's name. Tony recalled that, while Jason was a rugby fan, he wasn't the best with the oval ball. 'Every year, Jason was determined to win the Big Kick or at least improve upon the previous year. Respectfully said, he sucked, never coming close to winning, but good naturedly he endured a lot of ribbing.'

The emotion of the anniversary was just a brief respite from the judicial battles about to resume and we fell into bed exhausted that night. I knew I would be called to give evidence for the prosecution and I was determined not just to do honour to Jason's memory but also to do my part to help convict his killers. Each morning we would meet with members of the prosecution team in the District Attorney's Office. We would get a rundown of witnesses who were expected, though things would change as the prosecution found necessary.

As the trial resumed evidence on Thursday, 3 August, I discovered that the prosecution had just three witnesses left to call, including myself. That morning was the second day that I expected to give evidence. I had a terrible night tossing and turning; nightmares were a constant presence. I showered and got dressed, put on my blue jacket, had a little cry and then put on my make-up carefully, as I did each day to try to cover the visible effects the trial was having on me. I looked myself in the mirror and told myself: 'You can do this.' In fact, Sarah had a little saying: 'Let's do this.' We all adopted this before court. I carried in my hand the necklace of hearts made for me by Sarah. I also had an angel in my pocket each day, given to me by Jason's friend, Claire Delap, that was inscribed: 'I will never leave you.' They gave me great comfort.

The first witness that day was Lieutenant Detective Wanda Thompson, the investigation supervisor. None of the other investigating officers would be called to give evidence. Before she could take the stand there was substantial legal argument over what evidence she could offer. There was also a legal issue about material in relation to a Maine-based insurance company that had a policy on Jason's life. I knew this was the

Unum policy that was reported on in the media from civil proceedings. Dave and I were aware Jason had set this policy up with 25 per cent each to Jack and Sarah and 50 per cent to Molly. He had decided this in 2011, as he told me Molly wanted to be included. At the time she'd argued about why the kids should be named as it wasn't necessary. Later, Jason told me he did not agree and wanted the children included. Jason signed all his policies and I have each copy. But no matter how we try, we cannot get a signed copy of the 2014 policy when it was inexplicably changed. We were told it was changed online. The change gave 100 per cent to Molly in the event of Jason's death. I know that was a decision he would never have made knowingly and it still puzzles us.

The defence complained about the delayed receipt of documentation relating to police communications with the insurance firm. They demanded that any of the issues related to it could not now be introduced before the jury. It was finally agreed between the prosecution and defence that this evidence would not be entered.

I also discovered, not to my surprise, that Tom Martens would offer evidence in his own defence. There was never a moment when I thought that he wouldn't take the stand. I had heard that his attorney David Freedman said he had the best witness he could ask for.

I always believed that Tom would feel he would have to convince the jury that his story, implausible as it was, was the truth of what happened that night. I also understood that he was arrogant enough to believe that being a retired FBI agent would help paper over the gaping holes in his tale.

But what I was surprised by was the legal procedure he had to go through with Judge Lee to stress that he fully understood the implications of doing this and that, if convicted, he potentially faced a sentence of life imprisonment. Tom replied 'Yes, your honour' to each of the questions put to him, including the warning that his testimony might actually help to incriminate him. It did and, while I cannot go into all the detail as there are still legal issues pending, it was helpful.

Lt Det. Thompson then took the stand and confirmed that she was a 22-year veteran of the Davidson County Sheriff's Department. For the past five years she had led the criminal investigations division. She was a formidable woman. In evidence that I found disconcertingly brief, she confirmed that Molly had been asked to make a statement on 2 August about the circumstances in which Jason had died.

'She voluntarily gave a written statement,' Lt Det. Thompson said. The statement was given at 7 a.m. – almost four hours after Jason was pronounced dead. I had watched the interview, where she admitted hitting Jason over the head with a brick, yet this was not used at the trial. I believe they could not do so as she was not giving evidence. We all sat there knowing through this whole legal smokescreen created by the defence that she had admitted hitting Jason with the brick. Molly's written statement given to the police was then entered into the exhibits list. But it was not read out to the court – rather it was handed to the jury. The policewoman confirmed that when Molly wrote out her statement, the room was covered by both audio and visual recording systems. In brief cross-examination by the defence, Lt Det. Thompson confirmed: 'She [Molly] agreed to everything I asked.' That concluded her evidence.

I didn't know much about Irish prosecutions but I knew that evidence from Gardaí usually formed the centrepiece of the state's case. The evidence offered by the supervising police officer in Jason's death was among the briefest of the trial so far and I wondered what that meant. Neither of the two police officers who spearheaded the investigation, Detectives Brandon Smith and Michael Hurd, was called to offer evidence.

I was the next witness. David squeezed my hand and opened the swing gate for me to enter. Mr Freedman and the Martens family were to my left with the defence and jury to my right. I faced the jury, put my hand on the bible, looked directly at them and swore to tell the truth. I then stepped into the witness box.

As I took the stand I felt as if my heart would jump out of my mouth with nerves but I was determined to do what I needed to for the prosecution. I was also determined to show Molly and Tom that I hadn't been deterred in the least by the vindictive mind games and provocation they had engaged in over the previous two years.

I looked down at my amazing family and friends and drew so much comfort from them. I knew they were silently sending me strength to get through this ordeal. I imagined that I had Jason and some of my favourite people next to me. Initially, I was to be questioned by Mr Martin. However, he had left on a family emergency the previous day so Ms Stanton took up his role.

Almost immediately I was flooded with memories as they showed me a smiling picture of Jason taken by his friend at a golf outing. He was beaming with happiness and I confirmed it was him. I tried to keep my voice clear and stop it from breaking or faltering. I was looking at this picture of happiness while still in my sightline were images of the sickening brutality he had suffered.

It fell to me to explain the circumstances of how Mags died and why Jason needed to hire an au pair. I wanted the jury to know how much my brother had loved Mags – and how he had fought so hard to save her that awful night in November 2006. I explained about the asthma attack and how Jason had desperately performed CPR by the roadside as he waited for the ambulance to arrive.

I then outlined how he met Molly, how they had married and then moved to the US. I explained that we had stayed in close contact and would visit with Jason, while he also reciprocated with visits to us in Limerick.

The defence wanted me to say little and the voir dire, or preliminary examination process, rules further limited my responses. I explained how I knew Jason was planning to leave the US and resettle in Ireland. Jason was homesick and I knew he wanted to make the move back to Limerick before Jack started secondary school. All of this gave Molly motive because Jason didn't plan to return Jack and Sarah to North Carolina. I had planned to tell the jury about Jason's exit plan that he had relayed to several of his friends and me – how he had planned to get the children home first and then return to deal with his affairs. At that point he had communicated to us that he was concerned how Molly would react when he told her he was going home with or without her.

Mr Freedman challenged me over Jason's travel plans but I pointed out I was aware that, while he hadn't gotten to book the flights, he had researched tickets with various carriers to come home on the morning he was killed. I had spent weeks tracking the screenshot and information with the service provider about Jason's travel plans. I had even found an online diary reminder where Jason had left a memo to himself not to forget to book the flights. I am convinced he was going to fly home on 2 August, with the previous Friday night's humiliation by Molly the final straw.

But the defence kept repeating that no flights had been booked and that Jack and Sarah were scheduled to return to school in North Carolina. The lawyers needed to be very clever with their words. Molly had registered Jack and Sarah for school – but it was in a different area and over 180 kilometres away. It was near her brother Bobby's house. But if that information was introduced, the obvious question arose – why was Molly moving Jack and Sarah over 180 kilometres away from the home she shared with Jason? They were due to begin school the day after they were removed from her.

They were never going back to Meadowlands or their school, Wallburg.

In fact, we had also uncovered that Molly and her mother had viewed several houses in July, before Jason's murder. She had also told the children that they were going to have their names changed and they would never see us again.

Giving evidence, I made a point of glancing over every so often in Molly and Tom's direction. I wanted to look directly into their eyes and for them to understand that I hadn't for one second believed their lies or been intimidated by their PR campaign. Tom, arrogant as ever, stared right back at me without a hint of remorse or regret on his impassive face. Molly, however, seemed to become agitated by my looking in her direction and she fidgeted and looked away. Her attorneys were clearly aware of her reaction to me at the pre-trial hearing when I called her 'Molly Martens' and she objected, insisting on being called 'Molly Martens Corbett'. Judging by the seating arrangements in the Lexington court, I felt efforts were being made to shield her from my sightline. I also realised beyond doubt that there was no way the defence legal team were ever going to put her on the witness stand – there was simply too great a risk of Molly losing control and showing the jury who she really was.

The prosecution case concluded with MPS executive Melanie Crook. She offered evidence about how Molly had arrived at the Lexington plant on 4 August, just 48 hours after Jason's death, to claim her husband's possessions. I found the speed with which Molly wanted Jason's things returned nothing short of extraordinary. Jason was still in the morgue but she was worried about getting his work things? I felt it just didn't make sense. Why would a widow go to her husband's workplace just days after his death? I wondered whether it was because Molly wanted to locate and destroy his will. Then again, they had also contacted the insurance companies by that time, as I had been provided with the letter and information pertaining to their requests. But no one commented on this during the evidence. Ms Crook, not being aware of the circumstances in which Jason had died, had hugged Molly to offer her condolences in the MPS plant lobby. Melanie explained:

They came to collect the personal belongings from Jason's office. I did give her a hug. I saw all around her neck area. Molly had a jeans and a T-shirt on. It had a boat neck and short sleeves. Her hair was [tied] up. I saw no injuries [to her]. I did not observe any scrapes, scratches, bruises or swellings [on her neck].

Jason's belongings had been put into a box for Molly and this was taken off the premises by her once the items had been signed for.

As soon as the prosecution case ended, the defence legal teams sought a dismissal. The state case had closed on the twelfth day of the trial after hearing from a total of 21 witnesses. Both Mr Freedman and Mr Holton formally asked for the dismissal on the basis that, they claimed, nothing had disproved their argument of self-defence.

This was vehemently opposed by Mr Brown for the prosecution.

'I would contend there is no evidence to show malice – and no criminal offence,' Mr Freedman argued.

Mr Martens was acting in self-defence and getting anything else before the jury would be speculation at this point. The State, even by their own admission, [indicate] it would go towards excessive force and nothing else. The State doesn't have a theory in this case – the State's whole theory is to disprove the defence case. But the State has to provide credible evidence of malice.

Mr Holton argued it was clearly a case of self-defence:

The evidence is clear and clean and it is 100 per cent self-defence. The evidence is so overwhelming there is nothing but self-defence in the State case.

There is nothing to contradict that Mr Corbett was the aggressor.

There needs to be some physical hard evidence as regards who started this confrontation. All of the evidence is that he [Mr Corbett] was the aggressor with murderous or felonious intent.

It is an issue of self-defence. Everything they put forward is consistent with what Mr Martens and Ms Martens Corbett said. This was an altercation, the evidence was overwhelming that Mr Corbett started it, the evidence is overwhelming that this was self-defence for these two defendants.

However, Mr Brown argued that precisely the opposite was the case. 'The physical evidence in this case overwhelmingly and absolutely goes against that this was self-defence for Thomas Martens and Molly Martens Corbett.' The Assistant District Attorney argued that the shocking injuries sustained by Jason, the mass of forensic evidence, the total lack of injuries to the two defendants and other circumstantial evidence totally countered the claims of Mr Martens and Ms Martens Corbett about precisely what happened that night.

Judge Lee clearly wasn't impressed by the defence arguments. He ruled that, having carefully weighed the legal arguments involved and the mass of evidence heard so far, there were 'substantial' grounds to deny the motion for dismissal. He confirmed that the jury would be asked to deliberate on a verdict.

I heaved a sigh of relief. There was only one hurdle left to clear before we had justice for Jason. The jury had to see what I had realised from the very start – that Molly and Tom had murdered my brother with brutality, cruelty and malice. It was, as Mr Martin would later claim, 'heinous, atrocious and cruel'.

12

A Turning Point

I stared in the hotel bedroom mirror and cast a critical eye over my outfit. I wanted it to be absolutely perfect. My suit was red – a strong, unmissable and eye-catching shade of red. I had brought it from Ireland especially for this day. Because when Tom Martens took the stand and stared at the court while swearing to tell the truth, the whole truth and nothing but the truth, I wanted his eye to be inexorably drawn towards me. I wanted him to see me. But most of all I wanted him to understand from the look on my face and the conviction in my eyes that I knew the truth of what had happened on 2 August, no matter what he said. If it gave him pause for thought, all the better.

If I'm honest, I felt the entire trial hinged on this day. The forensic evidence was critical but I suspected Tom believed that his performance on the witness stand – and I knew it would be a performance – would be vital if the defence were to successfully sway any jurors. What made me nervous was that he only needed to sway one juror to avoid a conviction and deny us the justice we had waited two years for.

This Friday, 4 August would be the thirteenth day of the trial. I hoped it wouldn't be an unlucky omen. While the hearing had once been painstakingly slow, the fast pace of proceedings had now taken everyone – ourselves, the public and even the media – by surprise. The speed with which the prosecution closed and the defence opened meant there was little likelihood of the trial dragging on into mid-August. Privately, Davidson County District Attorney's Office staff had indicated that we would most likely have a verdict by 11 August if the jury didn't have a hold-out juror.

I took up my usual seat in court, Dave by my side, and squeezed his hand in a bid to control my nerves. We both knew that this day could well decide the entire trial. After Tom concluded his evidence, the cross-examination would be handled by Mr Brown for the prosecution.

That questioning would, I felt, prove a defining moment of the prosecution case. My opinion was that Tom's cross-examination was every bit as important as the closing arguments to the jury so beloved of all US trial lawyers. The holes in Tom's story simply had to be identified and highlighted for the jury.

I closed my eyes and said a silent prayer that Tom would do what I hoped he would – allow his arrogance to be displayed for all to see. My brother was from a proud working-class background. It shone through in everything he did. I knew that many in Davidson County, including, I suspected, most of the jurors, were from the same blue-collar background and shared our values of hard work, community pride, devotion to family and loyalty to community. Tom was intensely proud of his education, his wealth and his career. There was nothing wrong in that. In fact, I consider those values to be commendable. But Tom allied those values to a manner of looking down on others he considered inferior to him, such as Jason and my family – not to mention those who didn't have his level of education. I hoped and prayed the jury would see the real Tom on display.

Before he could take the stand, there was one holdover issue from the pre-trial hearing. Judge Lee had to make a ruling on Tom's determination to have his statement about Michael Fitzpatrick entered into evidence. It was clear what the strategy was – muddy the waters as much as possible over the circumstances of Mags's death and hope that some jurors would look at Jason in a different light.

Tom's statement was as follows. '[Mr Martens was] approached by Michael Fitzpatrick (since deceased), the father of Jason Corbett's first wife ... he believed that Jason had caused the death of his daughter Margaret.' The defence team insisted they were not suggesting that this was actually what had happened in November 2006. But they said it was relevant to Tom's state of mind on 2 August 2015 when Jason was killed.

The legal point being made was that if Tom had a genuine concern over the safety of his daughter that night, his actions might not have resulted from malice – a key component required for a second degree murder conviction.

But the hints of arrogance shone through even in this statement. Tom referred to the late Michael Fitzpatrick as 'uneducated'. He said he found it difficult, at times, to understand what he was saying. But he also said he was 'shocked' by what Jason's father-in-law had told him.

Ms Stanton, for the prosecution, vehemently objected to the statement being put before the jury. She argued that it was both highly prejudicial and inflammatory. The Assistant District Attorney also pointed out that Mr Fitzpatrick, before his death in Limerick, had made a sworn statement to an Irish solicitor denying that he had ever made such a remark to Tom. I also knew that Mags's mother, Marian Fitzpatrick, and her sister, Catherine, had given detailed interviews in which they underlined the 'loving and caring relationship' between Mags and Jason, something the defence were clearly trying to bring into question.

Judge Lee rejected the defence submission for the statement to be allowed. He said the statement had been objected to as both 'self-serving' and 'prejudicial'. 'I have determined that the apparent value of this statement is outweighed by the prejudicial value and the potential to mislead the jurors.' I closed my eyes, looked to the ceiling and said a quiet prayer of thanks. It was a small victory but verdicts could hinge on such matters.

A short time later, there was an expectant hush in the courtroom as Tom took the stand. I noticed that there was an increase in the number of people in the public gallery. Tom was immaculately dressed in a dark suit, white shirt and tie. I stared intently at him and noted no sign of nervousness or hesitation. When he took the bible in his hand to swear his oath, he stared directly at the jury and replied 'I do' in a strong, loud voice with his confidence clearly apparent.

His testimony was led by Mr Freedman, who began by asking Tom questions about his background, education and career. A graduate of Emory University and a qualified lawyer, Tom said he was 67, was married to Sharon and had four children, Bobby, Molly, Stewart and Connor. He had served for 31 years with the FBI before being subjected to mandatory age-related retirement. It was clear he was very proud of his FBI service. I also detected a sense that Tom wasn't happy about his retirement but nothing else was said about it.

Molly had written in her 2006 diary that her father was added to the list of the depressed. 'He retires [from the FBI] in two days and after 30 years it seems somewhat anticlimactic like no one really cares.' Molly wrote that her mother thought such behaviour was selfish and was worried about having her husband around the house all the time.

He explained that he then went to work for the US Department of Energy at their Oak Ridge facility in Tennessee, not far from his home in Knoxville. Tom, given his FBI background, was assigned duty in a unit dedicated to counter-intelligence work.

'It is basically spy versus spy,' he said, staring at the jury. 'Every country in the world has an intelligence apparatus and we are a very attractive target. Most [government agencies] have a counter-intelligence apparatus [in support].' Tom proudly confirmed to his lawyer that he also boasted the highest possible level of security clearance in the Oak Ridge complex.

Mr Freedman immediately asked Tom about his Oak Ridge duties and any dealings he had with Ms Lowry, whose evidence for the prosecution I had found so fascinating. Tom confirmed he had daily dealings with her and they mostly chatted, during breaks, about their families and leisure pursuits. In a single word, Tom then answered my prayers. He used the word 'specificity' in denying that he had any recollection of Ms Lowry's testimony that he said he had hated Jason. He used the word three times in his testimony. It might seem a small thing but I immediately sensed he was only using the phrase, so rare that I had never heard anyone else utter it, just to impress the jurors with his education. It was the first glimpse of the arrogance that would ultimately shine through like a beacon in Tom's testimony when he talked about his late son-in-law. He made absolutely no effort whatsoever to hide his disdain for Jason.

'He was not my favourite person. I did not like him. I am sure I said disparaging things about him,' Tom calmly confirmed. He said Jason and his friends had done 'a lot of drinking' at his home during the pre-wedding party he hosted. He also said there was a lot of smoking and 'foul language. It was a general behaviour that was inconsistent with what I think is polite,' he explained. That is not what happened that day. But, apparently, Tom considered it enough to explain away his dislike for Jason and his Irish siblings and friends.

The questioning then focused on the events of 1–2 August. Tom said he had had dinner plans in Tennessee with his wife, Sharon, and some friends.

However, when one couple cancelled, he claimed they decided to visit their daughter, son-in-law and grandchildren. It was an almost five-hour drive to Panther Creek Court. The one thing I knew about Tom was that he was not a spontaneous type of man. He had decided to bring a cut-down tennis racket and a Louisville Slugger baseball bat, both previously used by his sons, as a present for Jack and Sarah. When they arrived around 8.30 p.m., Tom told the court that he found Jason intoxicated. 'He was sitting in a lawn chair with his neighbour. I saw him drinking a beer.' Tom said Jason got up, walked over to his car and said 'welcome' to his father- and mother-in-law. 'Jason was obviously drunk at that time.'

Tom was open about his feelings for Jason. 'Our relationship was at that point like it had been for some time. We made nice with each other. We were superficially friendly. I am sure he knew I had some feelings about …' Tom said, before pausing.

He told the trial he had a small glass of wine before Molly ordered takeaway pizza for herself, Jason, Sharon, Jack and Sarah. His wife, he said, had brought fresh mint from Tennessee and that was used to make a mojito cocktail. Sitting watching Tom, I wondered whether that was how Molly's sedative entered Jason's system that evening – via a spiked mojito. After chatting, he said, he felt tired and went to bed in the basement bedroom. Tom said there was no disagreement or cross words spoken before he went to bed.

'I was awakened from a sound sleep and I didn't know what time it was. I heard thumping like loud footfalls [from upstairs]. Then I heard a scream and loud voices. There was some obvious disturbance going on above me in the house. I got out of bed. It sounded like a matter of urgency,' he told the trial.

Tom said he grabbed the baseball bat, which was lying on the floor by his luggage, and went upstairs to investigate what was going on. When questioned about why he armed himself, he replied: 'It seemed like a good idea. I was going up to something confusing and I would rather have the baseball bat in my hand than not. [But] I did not call 911.'

He said he determined that the noises were coming from Molly and Jason's master bedroom. He opened the door and said he was shocked by what he saw inside. 'In front of me, I would say about seven to eight feet from me, Jason had his hands around Molly's neck. I closed the door – I don't know why. I said: "Let her go." He said: "I am going to kill her."' Tom said he repeatedly told Jason to let Molly go but received the same reply.

'He said he was going to kill Molly. I actually felt he was going to kill me. They were facing each other. I said: "Let her go." He said: "I am going to kill her." I told him again, several times, to let her go. He was really angry and I was really scared.'

Tom then did what I expected – he shed the tears you would naturally expect from any father who had seen his daughter threatened. With his voice quavering with emotion, he explained that Jason shifted position so that he was behind Molly, holding her by the neck in the crook of his arm. Tom said Jason then began to edge towards the bathroom. But, in explaining that, his emotional upset vanished like fog on a summer morning.

I was afraid he would get into the bathroom and close the door and that would be the end of that. I would not have been able to save her. So I took a step and hit him in the head with the baseball bat. It seemed like the most effective place to hit him. I did not want to hit Molly. [But] his head was taller than hers. I know I hit him that time. But it didn't have any effect – except to further enrage him.

Tom said he struck Jason again to try and free his daughter. He claimed Jason moved into the hallway. 'Molly was in a very tight choke-hold. She was no longer wiggling. I don't know how effective these hits [with the baseball bat] were. I tried. I was determined that he was not going to close that bathroom door between me and her.'

At one point, Tom said, Jason suddenly lunged at him, grabbed the baseball bat from him and sent him flying across the bedroom, landing painfully on his knees on the bedroom carpet. Then, unbelievably, Tom explained how he, a 67-year-old retiree, jumped up from the carpet, charged across the bedroom, was not hit by the baseball bat in the process and managed to tear it away from my nearly six-foot-tall brother who weighed 260lb.

I don't know how many times I hit him in the head. I was scared. That's what I remember. I am shook up. Molly was screaming [at Jason]: 'Don't hit my dad.' Things looked pretty bleak. He had the bat. She [Molly] is trapped. If I get out of the bedroom he is going to kill Molly. He is bigger, stronger and younger than me. I felt both our lives were in danger. I just did the best I could. But I am shook up.

Tom then said that Jason, after multiple blows to the head, finally fell to the ground.

I am trying to hit him with anything I can. I win. He loses his grip [on the bat]. I don't want him to take the bat from me and kill me. I hit him until he goes down. I hit him until I thought that he could not kill me. He said he was going to kill Molly. I am shaken. I felt that both our lives were in danger. He goes down.

I step away. I did the best I could. I started thinking a little more clearly. I tried to take a few deep breaths. Molly is in bad shape. I told her to find a phone. I told Molly we need to call 911.

Tom recalled the details of the 911 call and then stepping out onto the porch when he saw the lights of the Davidson County police cruiser and ambulance pulling up outside. When the first members of the emergency services arrived, he was wearing his boxer shorts and a red polo shirt. He said he was asked to stay outside while Jason was attended to.

Mr Brown handled the cross-examination. The veteran prosecutor was more than ready for the challenge. What only a few of us understood was that it was also his swan song. After this trial, Mr Brown was set to retire.

I listened intently as he, in my humble opinion, tore apart Tom's story of self-defence and the sequence of events he claimed had happened that night. Despite the concrete paving brick being soaked in Jason's blood, hair and tissue, Tom stubbornly stuck to his story that he had no recollection of it being used to strike his son-in-law. He most certainly couldn't recall it being in Molly's hand even though she had admitted as much in a police statement.

He had also effectively said the same thing to his employers. But, according to Tom in the Lexington courtroom, the brick might as well not have been in Jason's bedroom that night.

Even more bizarrely, he said his wife, Sharon, had never left the basement bedroom despite the violent mêlée upstairs in which her son-in-law was beaten to death. Tom said he never called downstairs to his wife, he didn't hear Molly shout down the stairs to her and neither the father nor daughter asked her to ring 911 and alert the police. Even after the incident was over and Jason was lying dead on the bedroom floor, Sharon never came upstairs. 'I did not tell my wife to call 911,' he said.

Tom admitted that, despite his claim that Jason had sent him flying across the bedroom during the struggle, landing on the carpet on his knees, he was found to be uninjured when examined by paramedics. In the photographs taken by Lt Young, there were no marks or abrasions on his knees.

Tom also said 'I don't remember' when pressed about how many times Molly had rung him and his wife as they drove from Tennessee to North Carolina for the unplanned visit on 1 August. The prosecution revealed that multiple phone calls had been made – none of which was ever explained. I couldn't help but wonder whether Molly had learned of Jason's plan to return to Ireland with the children and rang her father to inform him.

I sat there and glanced over at the jury. They were intently watching Tom in the witness stand. I thought to myself that you can use big words, you can show off your education and offer elaborate constructs of what you claim happened during an incident but people have an innate curiosity and common sense. I found Tom's story simply incredible – it just didn't make sense on so many different levels. I looked at the jurors and hoped that they similarly found that the story jarred badly with how an ordinary person would have reacted in similar circumstances.

Mr Brown then focused again on Tom's relationship with Jason. Tom was as forthcoming with him as he had been with his own lawyer about how much he disliked my brother. He acknowledged that he did not consider his daughter to be in 'a good marriage' and had encouraged her to consult a lawyer and consider a divorce. 'I love my daughter. He did not match up to what I thought my daughter's standards should be.' Part of me wanted to scream in rage at him because of what I had learned about his daughter and her conniving behaviour towards Jason.

But Tom wasn't stopping. He said he also thought Jason was 'controlling' of Molly and he didn't like the way he told her what she should wear and how much she should spend. He also didn't like that Jason, he claimed, regularly checked Molly's computer records – all of which I knew was simply untrue. I desperately wanted to tell the jury that Molly had spent $90,000 in the nine months before Jason's death – most of it on clothing and personal items for herself. Her spending was so bad that Jason had repeatedly tried to get her to stick to a special household budget. I had also learned that Molly would often pay for meals on her credit card while out with friends, including myself, and then accept her friends' share of the bill in cash. Molly pocketed the cash and Jason was then left to pay for the entire meal when the credit card bill arrived. But I had to bite my tongue in frustration.

After repeated questioning from Mr Brown, Tom explained 'an issue of contention' arose because Jason did not allow Molly to formally adopt Jack and Sarah after their 2011 wedding. Tom made it clear he had raised the issue with his son-in-law. 'Jason represented to me that he was going to have Molly adopt the children. It became an issue when he did not follow through on that.'

I knew the adoption was an issue from the day of the wedding when Jason learned how Molly had lied both about knowing Mags and being Sarah's biological mother. Jason was adamant he would never sign adoption papers in favour of Molly. In fact, Tom once approached Jason when they were playing golf and said what a wonderful birthday gift it would be for Molly if he would only sign the adoption papers. Tom offered to pay for the legal fees so that the adoption papers could be gift-wrapped and given to his daughter as a present. Jason quietly told Tom if he ever mentioned the adoption again, it would be the last time they ever played golf together.

Tom acknowledged that Jason had provided all the funds for the luxury

€350,000 ($390,000) Panther Creek Court home he shared with Molly, which was entirely mortgage-free. He acknowledged that my brother had also paid him €45,000 ($49,000) towards their 2011 wedding costs at Bleak House. 'Sure,' he smiled. When asked about accepting the wedding payment, Tom simply said: 'Who wouldn't?' Mr Brown also pointed out that Jason had given Molly €75,000 ($82,000) to furnish their new North Carolina home.

Davidson County isn't like the Hamptons in New York or Beverly Hills in California. This isn't a particularly wealthy place. Would a person who readily agreed to fund a wedding, home and furnishings for his wife be that controlling or mean-spirited? It didn't make sense.

Mr Brown pressed Tom further on his feelings towards Jason. He asked him about his colleague Jonathan Underwood, who recalled Tom explaining his reasons for not going on a combined family holiday to Washington with Jason as 'If I was going on vacation, why would I want to go on vacation with that asshole?' But Tom insisted he had no recollection of having made that statement. He also denied ever saying he 'hated' his son-in-law. 'I try to avoid the use of the word "hate" – it is an ugly word. I tried to get along with him – and he tried to get along with me. [I was] superficially friendly with him.'

Tom also acknowledged that he had never had any knowledge of Jason being physically abusive towards Molly. 'I never observed physical violence on my own part to August 2.' He also confirmed that as part of an internal inquiry conducted by Oak Ridge staff after Jason's death, he told one investigator: 'I will say this, I never saw him physically abuse her.'

But he was blunt about wanting his daughter to end the relationship with Jason. 'I had a talk with her – I suggested to her that [it] did not look to me like a good marriage. She should consider a divorce. I love my daughter.'

Tom confirmed that, during his time in the FBI, he did receive training in the use of lethal and non-lethal force. He also confirmed he had been based in Miami with the FBI at a time when it was extremely violent because of the activities of Cuban drug gangs. The inference clearly was that, had there been any confrontation on 2 August as he claimed, he had both the experience and training to have handled it with far less deadly consequences.

Tom also admitted he told investigating Davidson County detectives it was 'a great time to be young in Miami' in the 1970s and said doors would be kicked in as part of criminal raids. 'I liked all my work with the FBI,' he said. Tom also said he told police that, during his time with the FBI, he had grabbed a young agent during an operation and told him: 'Make sure I don't do anything stupid.' But he denied that he had any problems maintaining control.

As the cross-examination reached its conclusion, Mr Brown was blunt in his questioning. He asked whether Tom, with his daughter, had murdered an unarmed, naked man lying face down, helpless and blood-covered on the floor of his own bedroom. 'That is not the truth,' Tom shot back.

I am trying to take responsibility for what I did. I am trying to tell you as truthfully as I can what I did. I made the decision to hit him on the back of the head with the baseball bat to end the threat to my daughter. I was aware of nothing at that point except my survival. He goes down, he goes down face down against the wall. I hit him until I considered the threat to be over. I hit him until he went down, that's all I know.

But, in a telling admission, Tom said that while both he and his daughter had knowledge of CPR neither performed it on Jason until directly instructed to do so by the 911 operator. The cross-examination concluded with Tom confirming that Molly was the beneficiary of a $650,000 insurance policy on Jason's life. With the value of Jason's home,

Molly now stood to inherit over $1 million from Jason's death. It didn't matter that she wasn't named in the will – she was the main beneficiary under US law.

The defence then called their second witness, William 'Bill' Cole. A fit, grey-haired man in his sixties, Mr Cole was a resident of Knoxville in Tennessee and worked for the Department of Homeland Security. He was also a former Marine Corps officer and a long-standing acquaintance of Tom's.

He told the trial, in exceptionally brief evidence, that he thought Tom was a decent, honest and hard-working person. 'I think he is an honourable person – a person of integrity, truthful and reliable. Tom is a calm and deliberate person. I have never seen him get angry or do anything impulsive.'

When Mr Cole concluded his evidence, there was just one further issue before the prosecution and defence teams began their closing arguments. The defence wanted the North Carolina statements made by Jack and Sarah in August 2015 to be allowed into evidence. It was clear that those statements were now critical to the defence. I knew instinctively that Molly wouldn't shy away from inflicting hurt and pain on Jack and Sarah if she thought there was even a remote chance such evidence would help her. The Molly I knew was nothing if not self-serving.

Judge Lee explained that he had carefully considered the issue since the pre-trial hearing. He had studied relevant case law and was now ruling that the statements would not be allowed in the trial. The judge noted that the North Carolina and Irish statements were, in parts, effectively contradictory – and that the children were now taking issue with some of the things said before they left for Ireland. 'There was some evidence of recanting by both children,' he explained. I knew the children had said a lot more than recanting their earlier statements. On that basis, none of the statements would be allowed to be entered in evidence before the jury. I tried to hide my smile. This was, I was sure, a huge victory for the prosecution.

With that, the defence case was over. Molly was not going to be called to offer evidence – though I never expected that she would take the stand. We had suspected the defence would call their own expert to try to undermine the forensic evidence offered by the prosecution but even this didn't happen. Despite my having examined all possible developments at the trial ad nauseam, I was still shocked that the defence case was so short.

We had the weekend to brace ourselves for the trial conclusion. Judge Lee would consult with the prosecution and defence teams over his charge statement to the jury. Then we would hear a total of four closing arguments. Normally, the prosecution would offer just a single closing speech but, because there were two separate defence closing statements, the state would be allowed a second speech.

The closing arguments would be delivered by Mr Brown and Mr Martin for the prosecution, Mr Freedman for Tom and Mr Holton for Molly. Over the course of Monday and Tuesday, 7 and 8 August, the four speeches would prove every bit as dramatic as I expected. I had been told that closing arguments in Irish trials were rather long-winded. Sometimes, it was hard to stay focused given the repetition of everything from the trial. But that most certainly wasn't the case here. There was a sense almost of the theatrical in how both the prosecution and the defence tried to get their messages across to the 12 jurors.

Jurors visibly jumped in shock as Mr Martin repeatedly struck a table with the metal baseball bat to underline the type of force used to kill Jason. I almost jumped out of my own seat with the crash as the metal struck the heavy wooden table. With the help of Mr Brown and a female assistant, he also recreated in the courtroom how Jason lay prone on the bedroom floor as smashing blows fell repeatedly on his unprotected skull.

'They literally beat the skin off of his skull with that bat and that brick,' Mr Martin said. 'They, acting in concert, her and him, literally crushed his skull. They turned his skull into something that resembled a bad Humpty Dumpty cartoon. They beat him after the threat was over –

after he went down. They hit him after he was dead. It takes a lot of force to crush a skull.'

With each point he made, Mr Martin crashed the bat down onto the table. I thought at one point the table might splinter under the huge force of the blows. The smashing sound echoed throughout the courtroom. I noticed that people around me seemed almost too shocked to breathe. At one point, I even saw a Davidson County police officer, complete with 9mm sidearm, wince at the sound. But it was genius on the part of the Assistant District Attorney. The sheer violence of the blows brought home to everyone in the courtroom the type of force that was used on Jason. To strike anyone over the head with even a single blow like that would be lethal. To strike someone lying bleeding and helpless on the ground such a blow was nothing short of evil.

'They didn't just split his skull or rip the flesh off the bone. They crushed his skull. It takes "I hate you" force,' Mr Martin continued. He explained that such was the horrific damage to Jason's skull that a pathologist thought the injuries were akin to someone involved in a bad car crash or a fall from a height.

'This is what they did to Jason,' he said as he reminded the jury of the post mortem photographs. I fought the urge to look away or faint.

Then Mr Martin held up the photographs of Tom and Molly taken by Lt Young. 'This is what Jason did to them – nothing.'

He urged the jury to carefully consider the forensic evidence as to the violence of the attack on Jason. In particular, he urged them to remember that the evidence indicated my brother had been beaten while lying helpless on the ground.

Mr Martin also asked the jury to consider how someone the size and weight of my brother could be engaged in a life-or-death struggle for several minutes, as claimed by Tom and Molly, and yet not leave a single mark on either of them. Critically, he also pointed out that, when photographed after the incident at the scene, Molly was wearing a delicate bracelet that had not been damaged, bent or marked in any way, despite the ordeal she claimed she had just gone through.

Mr Martin spoke bluntly, his voice booming across the courtroom:

You know what malice sounds like? I want to divorce him – but I want his kids. He is beneath me and I am above him. He is not good enough for my daughter. I don't like him and his rowdy Irish friends who cuss too much, drink and smoke outside my house. He is less than and I am greater than. I hate him. That's what malice sounds like. Murder, to cover up an assault by either one of these two people, is malice.

He asked the jury to consider whether Tom was doing everything he could to shield Molly. While Tom had a detailed recollection of almost every single blow he said he'd struck Jason, he had said nothing about Molly striking her husband. 'He is going to make sure every word out of his mouth protects or preserves Molly. The enemy [here] is not the Russians, the Chinese or the North Koreans. If you smash someone's skull and you are trying to get away with it, the enemy is justice.' I felt it was a telling comment and wondered whether it struck home with the jurors the way it struck home with me.

Mr Martin was relentless in focusing on the holes in Tom's story, particularly in relation to the brick in the bedroom. 'How is that possible? Tom's testimony has a void in it – and it is that Molly didn't do anything.' He also asked how it was possible for Tom's wife, Sharon, to remain in a downstairs bedroom totally oblivious to the fatal incident unfolding overhead. 'It is like she [Sharon] vanished from the face of the Earth in Tom Martens's testimony. Why? Because three people keeping the story straight is darn near impossible. It is not consistent [with the evidence]. It is simply not credible.'

Mr Brown, for his part, asked the jury to focus not just on the forensic evidence about what happened but also to consider what the paramedics at the scene had said. They noted that Jason's body was cold to the touch.

He argued that this had a very specific meaning.

'All the evidence conclusively shows that excessive force was used [to cause] the heinous, atrocious and cruel death of Jason Corbett. [They were also] staging for their story,' he said. 'He was bludgeoned to death by Thomas Martens and Molly Martens Corbett with a metal baseball bat and a concrete brick.'

The State would suggest to you that Mr Martens was calm and not even out of breath after a battle for his life and that of his daughter.

Jason was left to die before 911 was ever called so as to allow the FBI agent and lawyer [Mr Martens] to develop the story he was going to tell and match wits with you and determine the outcome of this criminal prosecution. Where was Jason's body when he was being beaten with a bat and a brick given the blood stains in the bedroom and the bathroom?

The saturation of the brick – blood on the front, the back, the bottom, the right side and the left side. Not only did it have blood – it also had hair and tissue. There was not one drop of blood on his [Mr Martens's] hands. They said they called 911 'the minute he went down'. But that is not supported by the evidence. It is not self-defence – this is second degree murder.

Why didn't he stop when Jason was on the ground? Why did he continue to bludgeon him? Why didn't they stop? Malice? Yes. Hatred? Yes.

Excessive? Yes. The evidence is that Jason was retreating ... he was naked in his marital bedroom and unarmed. His children were asleep in the house.

Mr Brown said that injuries to Jason's hand and arm indicated he may have desperately tried to defend himself. Both Mr Brown and Mr Martin concluded their arguments by asking the jury to convict Tom and Molly of second degree murder.

The defence, for their part, focused on a devoted father acting to protect his beloved daughter. Mr Freedman insisted Tom had no inkling of what was about to unfold on 2 August. 'Tom Martens went to bed in a dream and awoke to a nightmare that night,' he said.

> Mr Martens has been trained in every firearm known to mankind. If he went with any inclination [of violence] he would have brought something more than a Little League baseball bat. What do we know about Tom and what he did for the previous 40 years? He spent the previous 40 years defending this country.
>
> I remember when being in law enforcement was a good thing. We have spent the last few days disparaging the FBI. He has served us, he has protected us – that is what Tom Martens knows how to do. So what do you think he was going to do, knowing his daughter and his grandchildren were up there? He was going to protect when he grabbed that baseball bat. All the evidence has shown that is all Tom Martens thinks about – raising a family, raising children and protecting.

Mr Holton repeated pretty much the same story. But he also insisted that Molly had nothing to gain from her husband's death. I sat in amazement as he made this claim, given that it had already been made clear that Molly wanted Jason's children – and also stood to inherit more than $1 million in cash and property. Had we not fought such a vigorous legal battle, she would have got both.

'She was not in the will. It was not about the children. They are gone home – they are in Ireland. She now lives with her parents. She has no assets. This is a tragedy and a bad situation. But this was self-defence,' he said. Mr Holton also laid great emphasis on the fact that the hair found in Jason's hand at the scene was not preserved and tested. He also suggested that Molly wasn't properly examined at the scene for petechial haemorrhages, a tell-tale sign of attempted strangulation. Again, I sat amazed. Had he forgotten that it was Molly who refused to go to hospital for assessment?

I knew both defence arguments were all about muddying the waters. It was the job of defence lawyers to create doubt where, in my opinion, there was absolutely none. I gazed over to the nine women and three men of the jury. Were they as convinced as me about what had happened that night? Did they see the holes in Tom and Molly's stories as clearly as I did? Or was some semblance of pity now clouding their vision?

Judge Lee then formally addressed the jury after his charge speech had been presented to the defence for review. At 3.22 p.m. on Tuesday, the jury were sent out to consider their verdict. I had done everything in my power to secure justice for Jason. Now, the outcome was beyond my control. It was firmly in the hands of 12 ordinary North Carolinians.

13

Justice for Jason

I wasn't in the courtroom when the jury shocked everyone by indicating that they had reached a verdict. Dave and I had stepped outside the air-conditioned confines of the court building to stand in the sun. But we, with our family and friends, were careful not to move too far away from Courtroom C in case there were any developments. We were even afraid to walk the 100 metres or so to the Black Chicken coffee house, the closest café to the courthouse. I was a bag of nerves and couldn't help second-guessing when the jury would be ready with a verdict.

As usual, we had gone to the District Attorney's Office for our morning briefing. There, just metres away, was Molly, sitting propped up on the ground munching food and staring at me. I refused to be baited and simply ignored her.

Suddenly, one of the court bailiffs raced up to us and urgently whispered that a verdict was imminent. We were needed back in the courtroom immediately. The final knock on the jury room door came just after 11.25 a.m. – almost exactly a week since we had shed rivers of tears at the MPS plant in Lexington for the ceremony to mark Jason's second anniversary. What shocked us most was that all the speculation had been over whether the jury might reach a verdict by Friday evening or how long the trial might drag on into the following week.

The nine women and three men had resumed their deliberations at 9.35 a.m. that Wednesday, 9 August having already considered a verdict for one hour and 45 minutes on Tuesday after closing arguments. Their first query on Wednesday morning was for extra writing material. At 10.50 a.m., they had summoned a bailiff to ask Judge Lee if it was possible for them to take a 15-minute coffee break, as they were weary from deliberations. I had sighed, as I felt this indicated a verdict would most likely take place next week.

Just 20 minutes later came the knock on the door that signalled that a verdict had been reached. One Irish journalist who was present in court said the bailiff's back went ramrod straight on hearing the news. 'Judge, there is a verdict,' he told the court staff present.

The news spread like wildfire. We raced back into the court and took our normal positions in the right-hand section of the public gallery.

By now lawyers, journalists, trial observers and dozens of locals began to flood back into the courtroom. I was trying desperately to control my emotions because everything we had all worked for over the past two years boiled down to this moment. My mind went into overdrive – was it good that the jury were back so soon? Surely not, I thought; this can only be negative from our point of view.

Outside the courthouse, US TV crews, including outside broadcast teams from NBC, ABC, CBS, Spectrum and WXII, scrambled to prepare for an item they knew would dominate the headlines on both sides of the Atlantic. In the seats behind us were dozens of journalists from Irish and American newspapers as well as radio and TV stations.

I also noticed that the number of police officers seemed to have doubled or even trebled. Courtroom C always had two or three armed bailiffs and Davidson County Sheriff's Department officers in attendance at all times since 17 July. But now there were ten officers, male and female, with sidearms clearly visible in holsters. They carefully spread out across the front and side of the court.

When Judge Lee entered the courtroom, I looked down at my hands and realised I couldn't stop them shaking. I fought to control my emotions because everything since 2 August 2015 depended on these next few moments. They would reveal whether or not we would receive justice for Jason.

Judge Lee warned that anyone who breached strict standards of court behaviour would be held in contempt. The penalty for such behaviour could involve up to 30 days in a Lexington jail and a $500 fine. After staring around the court to make sure everyone understood his message, he turned to the bailiff and indicated that the jury should be brought back out and the verdict delivered.

The jury filed out of their deliberation room and, as they settled back into their seats, I realised just how hushed the giant courtroom had become. I squeezed Dave's hand and was almost afraid to breathe. I felt sick at the awful thought that Tom and Molly could walk free – how on earth could we live normal lives knowing they had not been held accountable for what was done to Jason?

The jury foreman, Tom Aamland, quietly indicated to Judge Lee that they had reached verdicts in respect of both Thomas and Molly Martens. He confirmed that both verdicts had been by unanimous vote of the 12-member jury. With that, he handed two issue papers to the court clerk, who brought them over to Judge Lee.

Tom and Molly were now standing with their legal teams by their sides. I glanced over at them and both seemed emotionless. Those next few seconds seemed like an eternity as we waited for the verdicts to be revealed. I said a silent prayer for Jason and waited for our agony to be put at an end.

There was total silence in the courtroom as the court registrar took the written verdict forms from the jury chairperson and returned to the bench in front of Judge Lee. The judge turned to the jury chairperson and asked, 'Have you reached unanimous verdicts in respect of each defendant?' The jury chairperson nodded solemnly and said, 'Yes.' The two defence legal teams stood up, along with Tom and Molly. Judge Lee asked for the verdicts to be read out and the registrar immediately confirmed that: 'Molly Martens Corbett [was] guilty of second degree murder.' There was a gasp in the courtroom, which was quickly suppressed as the registrar continued: 'Tom Martens [was] guilty of second degree murder.'

I felt like a balloon had burst inside me and I was swamped with a feeling of relief. But I couldn't stop the tears that welled up in my eyes. Around me, my family and friends were fighting and failing to hold back similar tears. None of us uttered a sound. I was so proud of the dignity we all displayed in that moment – it was something the Irish media would comment on in the days that followed.

Around us, discreet handshakes and hugs were exchanged. One supporter leaned forward and whispered to me, risking the judge's wrath, 'Justice for Jason.' Tears streamed down my face as it dawned on me that everything we had fought, prayed and worked for over two long years had finally been delivered. I felt such an outpouring of gratitude to the jury and the people of North Carolina.

It was a different story on the other side of the courtroom. The visible shock among members of the Martens and Earnest families quickly gave way to tears and sobs of anguish. Molly collapsed into wails of distress that echoed around the courtroom. She briefly covered her face with her hands. Tom cast a quick look over his shoulder at his wife, Sharon, who was seated several rows behind him.

She was crying softly, her brother, Michael Earnest, beside her with his arm wrapped around her. But Tom never lost his composure.

It was then I realised why the police officers and bailiffs had placed themselves so strategically around the courtroom. They slowly gathered around the father and daughter, ready to take them into custody. Two police officers were now standing directly behind Tom. After 40 years in law enforcement with the FBI and other federal agencies, he knew what was coming next. Without a word, he stood, pushed his chair back and held both hands out behind him so they could be handcuffed.

A female officer, her firearm strapped to her side, walked over to Molly and indicated that she too should stand. Molly was weeping uncontrollably and was being comforted by her lawyer, Cheryl Andrews.

As she stood, Molly turned and stared directly at her mother, brother, aunt and uncle in the public gallery behind her. 'I'm really sorry, Mom – I wish he'd just killed me.' It was typical of her. She had just been convicted of murdering her husband and yet, in her final minutes of freedom, was still intent on assassinating my brother's character.

I wasn't surprised that she was still playing her mind games. At this stage, maybe she even believed her own lies? But I didn't care what she said. She was nothing to me. Molly no longer evoked any feeling in me. We had gone to North Carolina looking for justice and, God bless them, the people of Davidson County had delivered justice for us.

Assistant District Attorneys Greg Brown and Alan Martin confirmed to Judge Lee that the prosecution were ready to proceed to sentencing immediately. After the length of the jury selection process, I was now astounded at the speed with which the US justice system got into gear.

The defence lawyers sought extra time. Both Mr Freedman and Mr Holton asked for an adjournment for their clients before sentencing.

But Mr Martin suggested that a 15-minute adjournment should be sufficient. Judge Lee agreed and directed that both father and daughter be taken into custody. Tom and Molly were led out of the court to allow for sentencing submissions to be prepared. As they left, Judge Lee adjourned the court for 15 minutes and, like a dam breaking, our pent-up emotions ran free.

Just metres from me, Sharon Martens was weeping uncontrollably. At one point, she had to be supported by her brother. Her sister-in-law, Mona, was also trying to console her while, beside them, Molly's younger brother Connor was a picture of anguish. Connor's upset became so great at one point that he had to lean forward and bury his face in his lap in a bid to stifle his sobs. Eventually, I noted that Sharon was given permission to go and speak to her husband.

I took no pleasure in the grief of the Martens family. We had gone through our own grief – far worse, in fact – and we wouldn't be Christian to wish that pain on any other human being. Justice was now being served and Tom and Molly would face the consequences of their actions. But at that moment I had other things to concern me than the Martens family. I now had to brace myself to fulfil the concluding part of my final promise to my brother.

Before Judge Lee dealt with sentencing, we had been given the opportunity to deliver victim impact statements. I would deliver two – one on behalf of the entire Corbett family and the second on behalf of my elderly mother, Rita. She was insistent she wanted her voice heard in the North Carolina courtroom and for people to understand what had been taken from her. Both she and my father had been unable to travel to Lexington, and part of me was glad they were spared the ordeal of this day. The third victim impact statement would be delivered by Alan Martin on behalf of Jack (13). It was in its original format as written by Jack, scribbled changes included.

We had had to prepare for all eventualities when we flew to North Carolina that July, and sorting out victim impact statements in case of a conviction was one of the things that had to be organised. I had also prepared material in case of a hung jury and, God forbid, in case Tom and Molly had been found not guilty. Believe it or not, I had three separate statements with me in court on 9 August – one in case Molly and Tom were acquitted, one in case of a manslaughter conviction and one in case of a murder verdict.

As I had worked on the statements in our Limerick home in the build-up to the trial, Jack and Sarah had been curious about what we were doing. I explained, as gently as I could, what those statements were for. I was flabbergasted a short time later when Jack quietly asked if he could write one.

I wasn't so sure it was great idea for him to do so, being fearful it might upset him and prove a setback to his recovery after all the trauma of August 2015. But having trained as a foster parent myself, I knew the importance of a child being listened to. A counsellor put it succinctly when he said: 'Jack has a voice and he wants it to be heard – do you think he deserves to have it listened to?' So Jack wrote out his statement and we were proud to bring it to Davidson County for him.

Before Tom and Molly were brought back into the courtroom, Mr Martin indicated to Judge Lee the prosecution position on sentencing. Neither Tom nor Molly had any previous convictions, which meant the sentence fell into a specific category that was lower than the maximum sentence of life imprisonment. Unlike in Ireland, where a life sentence is between 14 and 16 years, life in North Carolina meant that you were released when you stopped breathing or you were so medically incapacitated you weren't far off stopping breathing.

Mr Martin said the Davidson County District Attorney's Office was now proposing sentences for the father and daughter of between 20 and 25 years. With a start, I realised that the term was outlined in months rather than years, 240 to 300 months, so everyone in the court was doing quick mental maths to confirm the proposed prison terms involved.

Mr Martin then delivered a sentencing submission that was every bit as powerful as his closing argument. 'There is no joy, no triumph, no pride – there is just grief, grief and more grief,' he said.

'Jason Corbett did not have to die. What is left before the court is a truly senseless murder. It was brutal, it was vicious, it took time, it was heinous and it was atrocious. It was cruel for Jason to die at the hands of these people with his children just upstairs.' With that, I was asked to address the court. I knew how important the words I was about to utter were so I fought to control my emotions and the nervous shaking in my hands and feet. I wanted Jason to be proud of me.

My name is Tracey Lynch and I am a sister of Jason Corbett. I have been asked to read this statement to the court to tell you what type of person Jason was. I want you to understand the impact his murder has had on his family and on his mother. I want you to understand how the actions of Molly Martens and her father have impacted on Sarah and Jack, Jason's children.

Jason was my baby brother – we were so proud of him. He was charismatic, kind, fun, loving, generous and thoughtful. He was a very uplifting and amiable person. He had gone through hard times when his first wife, Mags, died but he kept himself going for Jack and Sarah.

He loved his children and was devoted to them.

Jason worked very hard to provide for them and make sure they had everything they needed. They also knew he loved them. He doted on them. He did all he could to make them happy. He was a healthy, happy man. Then that changed for all of us. August 2 will be imprinted on all our minds for all the wrong reasons – the day my brother was killed and my niece and nephew were made orphans.

My parents lost their child and we lost the most wonderful brother and friend. Our day-to-day lives were lived under constant pressure and worry. This was on top of grieving for our loss. On top of the custody [battle]. On top of the guardianship. All because Molly and Tom Martens murdered my brother.

We will never come to terms with Jason's horrific death. He was beaten and battered thousands of miles from his family in his own home. No photographs or evidence will depict for you what we endure every day and how we suffer because of the vision of how Jason died in pain. Was he in pain? Did he cry? How long did he lay there before his last breath?

Our hearts will never heal from the sadness we feel. Although we are broken, the love and support we have gives us the determination and the strength to carry on. We have tried to find the words as a family to tell you how Jason's murder has impacted on our lives but there really are no adequate words to describe the pain, anger and despair that we have felt from his murder.

Jason's murder took everything from his children. It took their innocence and security. It made them orphans. It fundamentally changed the course of their lives. They sometimes have trouble finding joy in simple pleasures of life. Being happy doesn't seem right anymore. They are now painfully aware that there is violence and evil in this world. That they cannot trust because adults break that trust.

I speak for all my siblings when I say that sometimes the feeling of despair becomes so overwhelming, so oppressive that it literally takes my breath away. I never know what sound or sight is going to trigger in my mind a memory. And while the memories of Jason are so precious, with them comes the realisation that he is gone and the visualisation of his battered body – each time the realisation hits my heart and it is devastating.

We sat here and listened to how he died. Those memories will never leave us as a family. Jason was the baby, my mother Rita's youngest child. Their baby did not deserve to be so cruelly taken from them.

They did not deserve to have to live the rest of their lives with this pain and without their child.

I paused briefly to compose myself before I delivered the statement my mother, Rita, had prepared. I was fighting a losing battle to stay calm – I desperately tried not to think of my mother, fiercely loyal and loving, sitting heartbroken in our Janesboro home, waiting in vain for her baby son to return home. That image would cost me the fragile hold I had over my emotions so I pushed it to one side.

In a voice I fought to make as strong as I could, I read out what my mother had written.

Jason was my pride and joy. He was kind, generous and sensitive. He wanted to see the people around him happy and he contributed to this with his love for life, devotion and kindness.

He was very caring to his family and friends. He was a devoted father to his children. The day I was told Jason was dead was the worst day of my life. It was 6.10 p.m. on a Sunday evening. My son,

Wayne, had received a brief 30 second call from Sharon Martens, Molly's mother, to say Jason is dead.

An ocean divided us but we tried everything, every way to contact Molly. We tried desperately to ring Sharon and Molly back. To this day I have never heard from Molly Martens or any of her family since the day of Jason's murder. Not one word, call or letter to acknowledge that I was his mother, that he was dead – nothing. No call at the time to allow me to speak with my grandchildren. No contact. A hastily arranged funeral without communicating with his family in Ireland.

It seemed she wished to wipe our existence out along with Jason's from Jack and Sarah's life. My life will never be the same but I tried and am trying every day to carry on the best I can. It was very hard because I had to watch Molly and Tom Martens carry on as if nothing had happened – as if they had the right to kill my child, my lovely son, Jason.

My family and I were and continue to suffer a level of emotional pain that words will never cover. I miss Jason so much and see him in front of me every day. Every night when I go to bed and close my eyes all I can see is his battered and bruised body lying on the floor. When I come down my stairs each morning, I open my front door looking out remembering Jason coming in saying 'Rita, we are home' and my heart breaks all over again knowing I will never see him. Sometimes I don't know what to do – shout, roar or go mad but I cannot and will stay strong for my family.

They are so good and I am so blessed to have them all. Tracey and David are now parents to Jack and Sarah along with their other children, Adam and Dean. They are doing their very best for the children and helping us to cope with the trial – it is so hard to keep going but we all find strength in each other. Our lives will go on.

Jason died suffering in such a way. I could never forget what was done to him. It was inhuman and barbaric. Instead of Jason's warm embrace I now look at a cold marble headstone in a graveyard. My heart is still broken and I will never recover. It is up to the court to decide Molly and Tom Martens's sentence and although there will never be justice for Jason, I beg of the court, for Jason's sake, for his family and for myself, to give Molly and Tom Martens the same leniency they have my son.

I had one final statement to make before my court ordeal was over. I wanted everyone in the court to understand the debt they now owed to my brother.

Many people spoke inside and outside this court about what a decent man Jason was. The sentence you pass will be the last thing that anyone can do for Jason in this horrific case. All we are asking for is justice for Jason, for his family, for his friends and especially for Jack and Sarah.'

I walked back to the public gallery and thought everyone in the court would see my entire body shaking with emotion. Dave discreetly held my hand and offered a squeeze of reassurance. I was so relieved to have my family around me at that moment. But, just seconds later, everyone was gripped by an emotion of a different kind as Jack's words, movingly read out by Mr Martin, echoed around the courtroom. Alan Martin is as fine a human being as he is a prosecutor and I started weeping as the emotion of the occasion even got to him. His voice quavered as he read out a child's explanation of what was inflicted on him and his sister through the murder of his father.

My dad's death has been life-changing for me and my family. My dad was there for me in every aspect of my life. My dad was always cheering me on in sport, school and just regular life. I don't have that from him anymore. I always hoped after that night that he could see me score a try in rugby or score a goal or just see me succeed in life.

He can't see that anymore. He won't be there for me if I get married or have kids. He won't be there for me or help me when I'm down or had a rough day. He will miss everything I do in life, the good and the bad, and he won't be there to give advice. I will never be able to give him a hug or a present or a Father's Day card. He won't see me grow from a kid to a teenager and into my adult life.

It changed my way of thinking on life. I can never go to the movies and pass a ball without feeling bad cause that's what me and my dad did. I just want to make my dad and my family proud. I don't know if I should call David 'Dad' because I don't want my dad to feel offended or feel like he was replaced.

This has affected my little sister a lot as well. She knows her daddy won't be there to walk her down the aisle. She will never have a father–daughter dance and Sarah and my dad had been planning [one] for ages. My family and I are not seen as we were before my dad was killed. We are now seen as the family of the Irish man named Jason Corbett who was murdered by Molly Martens in his home in North Carolina trying to make a new start, a new life for himself and his family.

That was taken away from him by a murderer named Molly Martens who is so many bad things. One of the things that she is not a part of and never will be is the Corbett family. She has put this burden on our family and it won't be lifted until she is put away. That's where she belongs.

My dad will not be forgotten. He will be remembered by his good life, how he made everyone feel good about themselves, how he was there for you if you needed him, how he always focused on the positive, how he was the best dad ever and the best friend, brother and son ever. Molly Martens will not be forgotten as well – she will always be remembered as the woman who killed her husband for no reason. She will be remembered as a murderer.

Jack's hard-hitting letter concluded with a public statement that our children, Dean and Adam, had been like brothers to himself and his little sister since the tragedy. Somewhere in Heaven, I know my brother was looking down on Jack and Sarah and his heart was bursting with pride.

Mr Martin finished Jack's letter and the court echoed to a muffled sob and wail from Molly. I knew Jack's words would shake her from whatever fantasy world she had buried herself in – there was absolutely no hiding place from the impact of the words of a child you had orphaned by your actions. This pain, this grief was the direct consequence of her selfishness and her cruel, violent behaviour.

I glanced briefly at Molly and then deliberately looked away. Justice had been done for Jason and, as far as I was concerned, Molly and Tom Martens would no longer have any hold over or involvement in our lives.

Their futures would be very different from ours. And that is precisely how I wanted it.

As I turned away from the Martens, I looked over at the jury and realised, with a start, that Jack's letter had left many of them in tears. Five of the 12 jurors were openly weeping. It was a simple gesture of such compassion. Until that very moment I hadn't fully understood how difficult it was for those 12 brave souls. The trial had been gut-wrenchingly difficult for Jason's family. But it had clearly been very trying for the jurors too. No one wants to sit in judgement of others. None of us with a conscience approaches a trial like this lightly. But those 12 jurors reinforced still further my admiration for North Carolina citizens and, in particular, residents of Davidson County.

With the prosecution submissions concluded, Judge Lee quietly asked if the defence teams had anything they wanted to place before the court before sentences were imposed. Mr Freedman said that, as Tom Martens had already addressed the court, he would have nothing further to say.

However, he said he would call a single character witness.

Michael Earnest, brother-in-law to Tom and uncle to Molly, was called to the stand. Mr Earnest said that his brother-in-law was 'one of the finest people I have ever met. He has been the most terrific husband to my sister. She could have gone the entire world over and not found a better husband than Tom Martens.'

Tom Martens stood as Judge Lee, in a brief sentencing summary, imposed a sentence of between 20 and 25 years as proposed by the prosecution.

The duration of the sentence will ultimately be decided by the North Carolina parole board. But I knew that, in the US, he would now serve a minimum of 20 years behind bars for what he had done before he could think about release.

Judge Lee now asked whether Molly had anything to say before sentencing.

I didn't expect her to say anything but, having learned just how much she liked being the centre of attention, I shouldn't have been surprised that she grasped a final opportunity to be the focus of the court. Molly consulted with her lawyers, Walter Holton and Cheryl Andrews, before getting somewhat unsteadily to her feet.

Eyes already reddening from crying, she spoke to the judge before half-turning to the packed courtroom in a dramatic gesture. 'I did not murder Jason – my father did not murder Jason,' she sobbed. Molly said the events of 2 August 2015 were no different from other occasions in her life but for the fact her father had been present in the house that night. I felt a mixture of anger and disgust that, standing on the precipice of a 20-year prison sentence, her final words to the court should be yet another slur on Jason's reputation. There was no remorse, no regret, no explanation and no apology – not even to the two children she professed to love but whom she had orphaned. But, from now, there was also no platform for Molly and her lies – her future would be spent in a North Carolina prison cell. Molly, just like her father seconds earlier, stood as Judge Lee imposed a sentence of between 20 and 25 years, as proposed by the prosecution for her second degree murder conviction. Once again, to our surprise, the sentence was delivered in terms of months (240 to 300) rather than years.

With that, Molly and Tom were led out of the courtroom in handcuffs. I took a few minutes to draw breath and compose myself. The past hour had been like a high-octane emotion-charged roller-coaster. I felt drained – exhausted and weary from it all. I squeezed Dave's hand and, with a single look, we both understood that all we wanted to do now was go home to Limerick to be with Dean, Adam, Jack and Sarah.

My mind switched back to the immediate challenges facing us. We knew we had a horde of reporters and TV crews waiting for us outside the courthouse. I had prepared a statement and felt it was important to say a public 'thank you' to the many people, both in Ireland and the US, who had supported us over the past two years. But every single member of our family was now focusing on how quickly we could organise flights back to Ireland.

We spent about 45 minutes in the courts complex thanking the Davidson County police, District Attorneys and court staff for their kindness, co-operation and professionalism since 2015. Without them, we would never have gotten justice for Jason – and I wanted to thank every single one of them.

Once that was done, I braced myself for the 30-metre walk outside, through the metal detector at the main entrance one final time, and directly into the media storm that was waiting for us. But nothing could detract from the fact that, after 17 days of court proceedings, 23 trial witnesses and two sentencing witnesses, it was all over. I had fulfilled my promise to my little brother. We had gotten justice for Jason.

14

Emotionally Exhausted

We walked out of the Davidson County courtroom and into a media scrum.

Everywhere I looked there seemed to be TV cameras, stills photographers or reporters holding up iPhones for social media postings. Out of the corner of my eye, I spotted that a few of the jurors had also waited by the walkway that led to the court's side entrance.

Nothing can prepare you for what it is like. You are the sole focus of what seems like a media hurricane – you are totally surrounded by cameras and microphones with questions being shouted at you from all directions.

I recognised many of the reporters present, having become familiar with them over the past four weeks of the trial. The overwhelming majority were friendly and very respectful towards us. But there were also a number of new faces, many from some of the top TV crime shows in the US. I had a brief statement prepared because there were a number of people and organisations I wanted to thank and I was terrified I'd be so nervous I might omit some. I said:

We trusted the jury to understand that on 2 August 2015 my niece and nephew were made orphans in a brutal and merciless killing. My parents lost their child and we all lost the most wonderful brother and friend. Jason was unarmed, he was struck while he was lying down in the middle of the night, two people battered him until he was dead. Then, they battered him again.

223

When we sat there and listened to the evidence we found [what happened] to be so unbelievable. Who keeps a brick on their nightstand? We worried that the jury might not find the two accused guilty. But they did and we thank them for it. I can promise the jury that we will now fulfil our duty to help create a good future for Jason's two children whom he loved so dearly.

I can also promise you that our family is going to stick up for Jason's memory – that this was a good man. Jason was a loving man and he was a great father. You can be sure that Jason Corbett's family will make sure he is remembered for what he was and not for how he died. We would again like to extend our thanks to the people of North Carolina and our supporters in Limerick.

A few reporters shouted additional questions but Dave, Paul and the others were prepared and we moved in a phalanx away from the cameras and microphones. We walked quickly towards our parked cars so we could head back to our Archdale hotel. I wanted to make some phone calls home to brief my parents, Dean and Adam on what had just happened. I was desperate to talk to Jack and Sarah too. We also had the small matter of trying to organise flights so we could get back to Ireland as quickly as possible.

I had been flooded with requests for interviews from TV shows in the US and Ireland. But I felt I had said everything I wanted to at that point. I also suspected that one channel, ABC, had more material than the others, including pre-trial interviews conducted with Tom and Molly. We had been asked to participate in the programme but I had been very wary. I felt an interview given by us could lend legitimacy to any outrageous claims made on the programme by Molly and Tom. The interviews were later broadcast as part of the *20:20* programme – and I was proved correct to have been wary.

The one thing I was glad to miss was the scene of Tom and Molly being led in handcuffs from Davidson County courthouse and into a waiting prison van. Speaking truthfully, I hope I never see them again in my lifetime. I can never forgive them for robbing us of Jason and then attempting to destroy his good name in an attempt to evade justice.

Don't get me wrong – I had no sympathy for them. They got the justice they so richly deserved. But I took no pleasure in it. In fact, I would have considered such gloating to be beneath us and, above all, something that Jason would not have wanted. All I knew was that Jason was no longer in our lives. No matter how many years Molly and Tom would serve behind bars, it wouldn't bring Jason back.

Later I learned that two hours after the sentencing hearing Tom and Molly were led away to begin their prison sentences. Both had changed out of their own clothing and were required to wear prison-issue garments. Both were also handcuffed and manacled to chains around their waists as they were led to the waiting prison-transfer van.

The photographs of them being led to the prison van dominated the US and Irish newspapers the following morning, though it would be several days before I had a chance to glance over the coverage. Molly kept her head bowed during the short walk to the prison van. She wore a dark cardigan, a blue denim smock-style dress with black, low-cut shoes. Once again, her long hair was in a ponytail.

In the days after the verdict and sentencing, I was told the father and daughter had remained silent in the prison van that brought them to their respective prisons. There was apparently no conversation about the dramatic events that had just taken place or about the appeal their lawyers had signalled. When they parted company on arrival at the first prison, I was told they did not even say 'goodbye' to each other.

Molly was sent to the North Carolina Correctional Institute for Women outside Raleigh for processing. She was later given the inmate number 1551729 and would undergo the normal medical and psychological tests required for all inmates.

Tom was taken to Central Prison, which was also just outside Raleigh. It was nicknamed 'CP' and was home to some of the most notorious offenders in North Carolina, including many convicted of gangland murders. Almost every evening of our stay in North Carolina had been marked by TV news reports of fatal shootings in Raleigh, Durham, Greensboro and even Winston-Salem. Those convicted of such killings were sent to CP. Tom received the inmate number 1553797. Like Molly, he underwent routine screening, though I understood he would be under special observation and protection measures given that he was a former FBI officer. In September, Tom would be moved from CP to Alexander Correctional Institute, a thousand-bed prison built outside Taylorsville that boasted special units for security-risk prisoners and inmates with chronic medical and mental health issues.

Before I had even left the courthouse, I knew that Tom and Molly would appeal the convictions. After all, they had absolutely nothing to lose. What I didn't realise was that one of their avenues of appeal would hinge, at least in part, on juror interviews given from almost the same spot outside Davidson Courthouse from which I had just spoken.

In Ireland, jurors are a central but anonymous part of the judicial system. But in the US, once a trial is over, interviews with jurors are relatively commonplace. In Lexington, US TV crews conducted a series of interviews with some of the jurors who had just convicted Tom and Molly.

Jury foreman Tom Aamland was one of those who gave interviews outside the courthouse. Along with two other jurors, he was also interviewed for ABC's *20:20* programme, which ran a two-part special on the trial later that week. He said the jurors fully accepted what the prosecution claimed happened that night. 'I believe we reached the correct decision. I think it was clear that the level of force used here was totally excessive. It might have started out as self-defence ... but it became something else [murder]. There are no winners in this case. Everybody loses to some degree. No one should take any joy in this verdict.' Like ourselves, he also noted how Tom did not have any clear memory of the brick in the bedroom that night or when it was used during the attack on Jason.

When it was broadcast some 48 hours later, the *20:20* programme left me relieved that I had decided not to participate in it. In fact, the material broadcast from Tom and Molly was nothing short of disgraceful. It was certainly hurtful. Two convicted murderers were essentially given a platform to slander my brother. Molly was allowed to level wild allegations about Jason – and no one from the programme bothered to ask her why, if she felt so strongly about these issues, she hadn't taken the witness stand and introduced them in evidence under oath.

The ABC programme featured two interviews given by Tom and Molly before the murder trial had even opened. It also featured material from the defence legal teams, the Davidson County District Attorney's Office and three jurors, Tom Aamland, Nancy Perez and Miriam Figueroa.

The ABC show also saw Mr Holton defend the decision not to put Molly on the witness stand. 'Why? What burden of proof do we have? That's not the way the system works, it's not up to us to prove innocence,' he said.

In her ABC interview, the only remorse Molly displayed for the events of 1–2 August was for their impact on her father. 'It makes me feel like, you know, I've ruined his life. That I've impacted my whole family. And it's not a good feeling.'

Molly admitted she felt 'horrible' that her father was prosecuted for murder after a lifetime of service to the US. She insisted neither of them had murdered Jason – and tearfully replayed the self-defence argument while adding a few outrageous details she hadn't bothered to give as evidence herself during the trial, claiming Jason had abused her and she was afraid of him. Another bizarre offering was that some science of the future might help exonerate her.

Watching the programme I felt physically ill. This issue, that Jason was allegedly abusive and that she lived in fear of him, was apparently incredibly important to Molly and yet she had never had it entered as evidence during the trial? There wasn't one passing reference to it during the four-week hearing. With her entire future at stake, Molly had never offered this explanation to the jury. But she felt perfectly relaxed about throwing it out during a TV programme? It made absolutely no sense. I couldn't believe that any TV show would allow her to make such accusations unchallenged, let alone when she hadn't uttered one word about them during her own murder trial. The fact that her interview was pre-recorded made it even more disturbing. In my opinion, it was scandalous.

The only thing I remember from Tom's contribution to the programme was his smug self-confidence. Looking at him being interviewed on the ABC show, I was convinced he actually believed he was going to walk free after the upcoming trial. 'I feel righteous – when you get involved in a fight, you either lose or you win. It is what it is,' he told the interviewer.

But my upset at the ABC programme was more than offset by the confirmation that we would fly home on Friday and get to see Dean, Adam, Jack and Sarah after five long weeks. We were laden down with presents for them all. But most of all we were flying home with justice – the most precious gift of all.

First, we had some essential things to do. On Thursday Dave and I had an appointment with our lawyers but first we travelled to Lexington to say thank you to the Davidson County District Attorney's Office staff and the Davidson County police department led by Sheriff David Grice. There were two separate meetings and both were very emotional.

Over the past two years, we had grown very close to some of the people in both departments. We had put our trust in them and they had not only delivered for us but had also done so in a manner that had combined professionalism with compassion. I don't think my family will ever be able to repay the debt of gratitude we owe to Mr Frank and Sheriff Grice and their respective teams.

Sheriff Grice had little gift bags for the children that included a Davidson County Sheriff's Department star-shaped badge. It became one of Jack's most prized possessions and, to this day, it has pride of place on his bedside locker.

Alan Martin gave us a card embossed with a clover leaf. It had been given to him by the family of a North Carolina murder victim after he had successfully prosecuted the killer. The grateful family said they hoped the token would bring him luck in future prosecutions. The card had been on his desk every single day of the Davidson County trial. He wanted us to have it in the hope it would bring us good luck and happiness in our future lives back in Ireland.

The trial and its stresses took their toll. I fell ill just 48 hours after we arrived back, with my GP warning that I was drained from the exertions of the previous months. I wasn't the only one. In the weeks afterwards I heard about others, including members of the media, who were so exhausted from the North Carolina trial that they also fell victim to various illnesses. With Dave, I decided we needed time alone with Adam, Jack and Sarah. I was afraid the maelstrom of media attention would follow us to Ireland so I wanted to get them away until things died down a little.

We arrived back in Ireland on Saturday morning and, on Sunday, went for a walk with the children in Curraghchase Woods. Our phones never stopped ringing and we had repeated callers to our home. The case seemed to dominate every TV bulletin, radio station and newspaper front page. I turned to Dave and asked if there was no escape. There and then, we decided the best thing was to head overseas for a break to escape the attention. The children couldn't go outside to play, couldn't walk to the shop and couldn't turn on the TV or radio.

So we went to Portugal for a one-week beach holiday. Part of me wanted nothing more than to stay in our Limerick home and unwind with our friends and family. But going to Portugal had the advantage of taking us out of the spotlight and giving us some priceless time alone with each other to chat, reflect and, if necessary, even console each other. In Portugal, we were blissfully anonymous. I had missed the children so badly and needed some quality time with them and Dave. It was such a shocking and traumatic time for us that our twenty-third wedding anniversary came and went without either Dave or myself realising it.

The media weren't ready to leave us alone. Being in North Carolina had, in many ways, been like living in a bubble. Even though I had regular contact with friends and family in Limerick and they constantly told me about the extensive coverage the trial was getting at Ireland, I was completely unprepared for the avalanche of queries that awaited us. I work as the chief executive of Tait House Community Enterprises in Limerick, a not-for-profit organisation that employs 130 people across eight enterprises. My staff had been bombarded with calls from the media. It seemed as if every single person in Ireland had been following the trial's progress on a daily basis and now had a million questions they wanted us to answer.

I was swamped with requests for interviews, statements and photographs. Every single Irish TV station wanted us to take part in special programmes about the trial or to participate in chat-show discussions. As far back as 2016, I had received book offers from various publishers eager to help us tell our story. But my priority was to spend time with Jack and Sarah. To shield them as best I could.

I hoped that, over time, the publicity surrounding Jason, Molly, Tom and the trial would ease and that we would slip out of the headlines.

In that regard I was badly wrong.

We issued a brief statement in response to a lot of the claims coming in support of Molly and Tom from the US. I felt it was important to place the focus where it belonged – on the trial verdict:

It does not matter what the Martenses said or say, at this point. We all know what happened. That Jason was beaten around his head when in bed. That they continued to beat him after he died. Jason's children, Jack and Sarah, had to be sheltered by police from seeing what the Martenses had done to their father. It does not matter what the Martenses say now. They are convicted killers and liars. When we heard the verdicts, our first thoughts went to Jack and Sarah. Their daddy was now vindicated. We rang them to tell them the news. Our first priority after the trial and sentencing was to get home to them as quickly as possible. We were never as anxious to get on a flight as we were on Thursday last. We wanted to talk to Jack and Sarah and our own children and just hug them and hold them tight. We are grateful to the people of Limerick for the fundraising they did to help us get Jack and Sarah home and to help us clear Jason's reputation.

We thank them for the thousands of acts of kindness to us, to our parents and other family members. We are grateful for the Masses, the cards, the prayers and everything else they did for us. It really means so much that your own people are backing you during a horrible time.

Our statement ended with a plea for privacy as we said we wouldn't be doing any further media interviews.

Days after we had returned to Ireland, I became aware of a special Internet funding campaign in aid of Tom and Molly. It was founded by Mona Earnest and the page had the goal of raising $300,000 (€250,000) towards the legal costs of their appeal. What was appalling was how the appeal was introduced and the unforgivable way in which Jason was again described. It was difficult for us – we wanted to react, to express our disgust at what had been posted on the Internet about someone unable to defend themselves. But we also knew that if we reacted it would simply give the fundraising appeal the oxygen of publicity it craved. So we seethed and stayed silent.

But dozens of ordinary people, both from Ireland and the US, went online to express their outrage at the remarks in the appeal introduction. A short time later, it was changed. The appeal itself proved a major disappointment – at least it terms of fundraising. That was despite Mona Earnest even posting a social media appeal directly to former US President Barack Obama.

The desperation of Tom and Molly's supporters to win public sympathy for them sometimes left us shaking our heads in amazement.

Connor Martens posted an update on the funding page to highlight what he described as the terrible treatment his sister was enduring in prison in North Carolina. Complete with a fresh photo of Molly at a family wedding a short time before her trial commenced, Connor claimed her hair had been cut against her will in prison, had been dyed and that Molly was being reprimanded when she tried to keep fit and active during recreation breaks in prison. Within days, the North Carolina prison system had confirmed that Molly's hair had not been cut against her will or been dyed. Prison officials also vehemently rejected any suggestion of mistreatment or that Molly's personal hygiene requests were being ignored. Fresh photos of the father and daughter released by the prisons showed that Tom now had a grey beard. Molly's hair was still blonde though I wondered, studying her facial expression, whether the events of the trial and her incarceration were now taking a mental toll on her. She seemed to have aged dramatically.

It was no surprise to us that Tom and Molly were challenging their convictions to the North Carolina Court of Appeals. But what was a surprise was that, in a series of legal submissions, Tom and Molly's legal teams were seeking that Judge Lee quash the Davidson County Superior Court convictions on the basis of alleged juror misconduct.

Davidson County District Attorney's Office vehemently opposed the defence challenge and made a series of detailed submissions to Judge Lee on how the jurors had acted appropriately and that there were no grounds for overturning the verdicts and convictions. Judge Lee set 8 September as the closing date for all legal submissions about the challenge and then took almost three months to carefully consider the position.

We received an early Christmas present on 1 December 2017 when Judge Lee formally confirmed that he was rejecting the defence submissions and refusing to overturn the verdicts and convictions. It was a huge relief because I felt that, of the two challenges lodged by Tom and Molly, the one at Davidson County Superior Court level was the more serious.

Molly and Tom now had a single avenue of appeal left open to them. Their challenge to the North Carolina Court of Appeal will likely be heard in mid to late 2018 and will be based entirely on legal aspects surrounding their trial. It will not hear new evidence unless that evidence shows that material presented at the trial was false or misleading. If the court fails to overturn the conviction, Molly and Tom then have the right to lodge an appeal with the North Carolina Supreme Court, the state's highest court. This court will represent Molly and Tom's last port of call in their challenge to their convictions and sentences.

Any hopes we had that the case would fade from the headlines were proving to be in vain. Molly's name and photograph always seemed to be appearing somewhere. There always seemed to be a development in the case, a fresh twist on something or a new revelation on social media.

I realised that if a newspaper published a story about Molly or Tom, others would either follow it up or go looking for their own 'exclusives'. The North Carolina trial even made it into Ireland's major headlines of 2017 for the year in review.

There was press coverage of Molly's transfer from the Raleigh prison to another facility, just south of Lexington. Molly was now expected to serve the bulk of her sentence at the Southern Correctional Institution in Troy, North Carolina, on the outskirts of the Uwharrie National Forest. It was only a short drive from where Jason had worked for MPS. Less than three months after she'd arrived there, Molly was cited for a breach of prison rules.

Incredibly, Molly chose the exact anniversary of Mags's death, 21 November, to go on what the North Carolina Department of Public Safety (NCDPS) referred to as 'unauthorised leave' at Southern Correctional Institution. Molly either left a supervised area without the permission of prison guards or did not report to a supervised area as required. It was a very serious matter. Within two weeks of the incident occurring, NCDPS had revised Molly's scheduled release date.

NCDPS files indicated that while Tom has a scheduled release date of 3 August 2037 – a minimum 20-year prison sentence – Molly now had a scheduled release date of 28 July 2041, almost four years longer than initially indicated. The North Carolina parole board will ultimately decide her release date. But Molly has maintained her inexplicable behaviour – despite being convicted of Jason's murder she has insisted on being referred to by the NCDPS by her married name of Corbett.

If Molly and Tom's appeal against their conviction and sentence fails, he will be 87 years old before being released. Molly will be 53 years old before she can qualify to be granted maximum parole. If her sentence is confirmed as being lengthened because of her prison infraction, she will be 57 when she next sees the cobalt-blue skies outside a North Carolina prison. But at least she will eventually have a life to resume – something that Jason was robbed of.

The never-ending publicity is the reason you are now holding this book in your hand. All I wanted – all my family wanted – was for the dust to settle and for us all to be allowed to grieve and get on with our lives. But there was always another story about Molly, another request for a TV or radio interview or even a suggestion that someone was thinking of writing a book about the trial. It was relentless and inescapable. It slowly dawned on me that there was no line in the sand, no cut-off point when the publicity would stop. Worse still, there seemed no end to the feeding frenzy on social media about what had really happened to Jason. The armchair detectives were having a field day and debating the evidence on open Internet forums. My concern was that Jason was being lost in all of this. No one had focused on who he was: the wonderful son, brother, father and husband who paid with his life for loving too much, trusting too much and trying so hard to help the woman he loved but who was too warped or selfish to be rescued from her demons.

I realised that if I didn't tell Jason's story, someone else would – and the real Jason, the 'gentle giant' we all loved so deeply, would be lost in the telling. How could anyone outside our family paint an accurate picture of the person Jason was? Could someone who didn't know Jason describe what he was like? I didn't want to have to write this book, but in the end, I felt I had to. Jason deserved to be given a voice, for people to understand who he was, what he stood for and how deeply he loved Mags, Jack, Sarah and, tragically, even Molly.

Jason would not have wanted the lies to go unchallenged – that I knew for certain. He would have wanted people to know the truth. His good name was precious to him throughout his life. That good name is now even more precious to me after his death. Jason also would have wanted all the proceeds from this book to go to the children and that was the condition on which the book was undertaken.

Each morning, in the split second before I open my eyes, I pray that this has all been a bad dream, a nightmare that the bright sunshine of morning will banish to the darkness. Then, as my mind comes into focus, I realise that it isn't a nightmare – it is the reality of the daily life we now have to cope with. This has been Jason's journey.

But how I wish, from the deepest recesses of my heart, that his journey had a different, happier ending.

15

Back in Mags's Arms

It is a quiet, peaceful place.

Castlemungret Cemetery is located about 7 kilometres south-west of Limerick, just where the urban sprawl of the city begins to slowly turn into the rich, rolling farmland so typical of Ireland. It is less than a five-minute drive from my home. Just across the road is Mungret St Paul's GAA sports pitch and, on occasions, the excited shouts and cheers of youngsters can echo across the graveyard.

The cemetery is located just off a spur of the busy N20 Limerick to Cork Road, with the equally busy N69 Limerick–Foynes road just a short distance to the north-west. The Shannon estuary village of Foynes was, of course, where the flying boats that started the transatlantic service from Ireland to the United States operated from back in the 1930s and 1940s.

The cemetery, which only opened in 2001, is on the right as you approach from Limerick heading towards the sleepy village of Mungret.

It is located behind a stone wall with spaces for maybe 15 parked cars on the roadside. The noise of traffic is barely audible as you walk into its depths, with an ESB sub-station located to the rear of the cemetery. There is woodland to the left and open fields sweeping away to the right. In the darkness of an early February evening you can see the lights of Limerick city illuminating the horizon.

The only sounds here are bird song, cows bellowing in the rich dairy pastures or the faint echo of a tractor working in a field. Children have placed wind chimes on the saplings that line the rear wall and they tinkle gently in the breeze. In a reflection of modern multicultural Ireland, the left rear section of the cemetery contains an area for Islamic graves.

As I carefully park my car, I realise that I'm alone at the graveyard with not another vehicle in sight. That suits me perfectly, particularly on this day. I pause before opening the car door and think about how many times my brother must have sat in this very place, pretending to read the paper and eat his lunch while all the while thinking of his beloved resting less than 50 metres away.

It is a short walk from the car. From the entrance gate I head automatically into the left section, about three-quarters of the way down the cemetery. Jason's grave is four rows from the left boundary wall, about six metres from the footpath. I don't even have to concentrate as I walk – my feet know the way from countless previous visits. A few seconds later, I'm standing by the headstone. It is a beautifully polished brown-hued marble with rippled hints of pink that Jason himself picked out for Mags.

The inscriptions on the headstone are simple and in gold lettering.

The dedication to Mags reads: 'A wonderful wife and mommy.' On the top left is a wedding photo of both Jason and Mags, chosen by Jack and Sarah, in which they look so young, totally in love and blissfully unaware of the unfairness that life held in store for them. The photo is placed directly above a stylised cross entwined with a rose bush.

The headstone carries two heartfelt tributes. The first reads: 'Suffer little children to come unto me – erected by her loving husband Jason, son Jack and daughter Sarah.' Directly underneath is the second inscription: 'There's got to be a reason and we have to understand, God made us and at any time he'll reach down for our hand, there might not be a warning, we won't know where or when, the only thing I'm certain of, we will meet again.'

Carefully placed on the left plinth of the headstone are two little keepsakes – one is a simple piece of stone etched with the word 'Remember'. The second is a tiny figurine of a winged fairy. Directly in front of the headstone are flowers, candle-holders and some solar lights.

The plot is immaculately kept, thanks to almost daily visits from Jason and Mags's family, friends, neighbours and work colleagues. There isn't so much as a blade of grass out of place. Because of the day that it is, what would have been Jason's forty-second birthday, there are fresh flowers. Before the day is over, I expect there to be lots more flowers and memorial tokens. Jason's family and friends, just like Mags's family and friends, have not forgotten.

I visit regularly with the children but I'm also grateful that I have such moments alone here. Sometimes the memory of what we all had and then lost can be too much to bear. I'm not ashamed of people seeing me cry. But being able to grieve and weep privately is something I much prefer.

The hardest visits here were at the beginning. There were times when I felt like sinking to my knees and screaming in rage to the heavens at the unfairness of it all. First Mags and then Jason. The world robbed of two such wonderful, kind-hearted and loving people. But, worst of all, two little children, on whom their parents doted, being robbed of the love, protection and affection that Jason and Mags would have showered on them for all the years of their lives.

Over time, the pain and rage eased and I settled into an aching sense of loss. I miss my brother – I miss his laughter, I miss his smile and, as one of my friend's children once quipped, I miss his bear hugs that no matter how bad your day was made you feel like all was suddenly right with the world. I miss the phone calls asking me how my day was or what plans I had with Dave for the weekend. It is the little things that bother me most.

I read somewhere that grief is the price we pay for love, but memory is what allows us to carry the burden of such loss. For Jason's fortieth birthday, we all gathered – Jason's friends and the Corbett, Fitzpatrick and Lynch families – at Spanish Point in Clare. It was probably his favourite place on this awe-inspiring planet. That evening we lit a bonfire near the beach, all came together and watched the flames swirl into the sky as we swapped stories about Jason. Later, we scribbled messages of remembrance that we attached to Chinese lanterns and released to be swept out over the dark Atlantic beyond the shoreline. It was such a special evening and played a big part in our grieving process. Such moments also gave me the strength to face the legal battles that lay ahead.

I have evolved a mechanism for coping with the sense of loss. When I start to dwell on the sadness of losing first Mags and then Jason, I make a mental note reminding myself that, in a way, I still have both of them in my life. I smile when I think about Jack and Sarah – their courage, their loyalty, their good humour and, above all, the love that they have showered on all of us on a daily basis. They reflect the very best of their amazing parents.

I see Jason and Mags in both of them every single day – it could be a look, a smile, a roguish burst of laughter or simply a hug offered in thanks for a small kindness. I know, with every fibre of my being, that Jason and Mags would be so very proud of those two children and the fine young adults they are about to become. But that very thought brings its own sadness and a realisation of not just what we have lost but also what was stolen from Jack and Sarah.

Here in this cemetery I never think of Molly and Tom. It is as if they no longer exist in our lives – as if any thoughts about them should be carefully left at the cemetery gate. In the days after 9 August 2017, I came to this graveside and tearfully told my brother I had kept all my promises. I placed my hand on the cold marble and swore once again that I would look after his and Mags's children with the same love and devotion as I care for my own Dean and Adam.

Yet there are still times when I find myself heartbroken to stand here and remember all that has happened. I also struggle to grasp just what it must have been like for Jason to come here having lost Mags – to stand by the grave, to read her the newspaper and to talk to a silent headstone about the events of his day. For Jason, this was a place of profound heartbreak – but it was also the place where he felt closest to his lost love.

I smile briefly to myself as I realise that Jason eventually found himself back in the only place on this earth he ever wanted to be – in the arms of his beloved Mags. I know I'm being selfish when I wish Jason hadn't been brought to rest here until decades later as a very old man. But how can I begrudge my brother a resting place beside his soulmate, his one true love and the woman who fulfilled his dreams from the moment he set eyes on her?

Jason's journey brought him to the only destination he ever wanted – back to Mags.